LIBRARY OF NEW TESTAMENT STUDIES
333

Formerly the Journal for the Study of the New Testament Supplement series

Editor
Mark Goodacre

MATTHEW
AND HIS CHRISTIAN
CONTEMPORARIES

Edited by

DAVID C. SIM
BORIS REPSCHINSKI

t&t clark

Published by T&T Clark International
A Continuum imprint
The Tower Building, 11 York Road, London SE1 7NX
80 Maiden Lane, Suite 704, New York, NY 10038

www.tandtclark.com

British Library Cataloguing-in-Publication Data
A catalogue record for this book is available from the British Library

ISBN-13: 9780567044532
ISBN-10: 056704453X

Typeset by Free Range Book Design & Production Ltd
Printed on acid-free paper in Great Britain by Biddles Ltd, King's Lynn, Norfolk

CONTENTS

ACKNOWLEDGEMENTS

The editors would like to take this opportunity to express their gratitude to a number of people and institutions without whose assistance this volume would never have seen the light of day. First of all, we would like to thank our international team of contributors who shared our vision about Matthew and who have helped us to turn an abstract idea into an exciting reality. Thanks are also due to the excellent and helpful staff at Continuum who readily embraced this volume when it was proposed, and who have shown considerable understanding when it was necessary to make some unavoidable and significant changes. We appreciate as well their patience when the final manuscript was delayed. We would single out Becca Vaughan-Williams and Haaris Naqvi for special mention.

Much of the collaboration for this volume was made possible by a prolonged visit to the Melbourne campus of Australian Catholic University by Boris Repschinski. Boris was awarded an Honorary Distinguished Visiting Research Fellowship by the university to work with David Sim on this volume, and we were able to collaborate on this project during February and March of 2006. We wish to express our sincere appreciation to Australian Catholic University for the provision of this Fellowship, and we trust that its foresight and beneficence are well repaid in the publication of this volume. Thanks are due as well to Leopold Franzens University for granting Boris this period of leave, and to the Jesuit community in Parkville, Melbourne, for its hospitality during his stay. As usual David would like to thank his wife Robyn and son Michael for all of their support throughout the process of writing and editing.

Finally, this volume is dedicated with much gratitude and affection to our respective Doctoral supervisors. Professor Thomas H. Tobin SJ of Loyola University, Chicago directed the dissertation of Boris Repschinski, while Professor Graham Stanton, now of Cambridge University but then at King's College London, supervised David Sim's thesis. We were both privileged to study under such fine scholars, and we offer this volume as a tribute to the major contributions each has made to our lives and careers.

Boris Repschinski SJ
David C. Sim

Daniel J. Harrington SJ is Professor of New Testament at Weston Jesuit School of Theology in Cambridge, MA. He is the editor of *New Testament Abstracts* and the *Sacra Pagina* series of New Testament commentaries. The author of many books and articles, he wrote the commentary on the Gospel of Matthew for that series. He is a past president of the Catholic Biblical Association of America.

Martin Hasitschka SJ is Professor of New Testament Studies at Leopold Franzens University, Innsbruck. He is the author of *Befreiung von Sünde nach dem Johannesevangelium: Eine bibeltheologische Untersuchung* (Tyrolia), *Das Licht der Welt: Ein Meditationsbuch zu den Bild-Worten des Johannes-Evangeliums* (Tyrolia) and a co-author of *The Call of the Disciple: The Bible on Following Christ* (Paulist Press).

John Painter is Professor of Theology at the Canberra campus of Charles Sturt University (Australia). He has published extensively in New Testament theology and history, and his many books include *The Quest for the Messiah: The History, Literature and Theology of the Johannine Community* (T&T Clark), *Mark's Gospel: Worlds in Conflict* (Routledge), *Just James: The Brother of Jesus in History and Tradition* (University of South Carolina Press) and *1, 2 and 3 John* (Liturgical Press).

Boris Repschinski SJ is Assistant Professor of New Testament Studies at Leopold Franzens University, Innsbruck. He is the author of *The Controversy Stories in the Gospel of Matthew: Their Redaction, Form and Relevance for the Relationship Between the Matthean Community and Formative Judaism* (Vandenhoeck & Ruprecht) and the editor of the *Zeitschrift für katholisches Theologie*.

David C. Sim teaches in the School of Theology and is a member of the Centre for Early Christian Studies, Australian Catholic University. He is the author of *Apocalyptic Eschatology in the Gospel of Matthew* (Cambridge University Press), *The Gospel of Matthew and Christian Judaism: The History and Social Setting of the Matthean Community* (T&T Clark) and a co-editor of *The Gospel of Matthew in Its Roman Imperial Context* (T&T Clark International).

Huub van de Sandt teaches New Testament studies at the University of Tilburg. He is a co-author of *The Didache: Its Jewish Sources and Its Place in Early Judaism and Early Christianity* (van Gorcum), the editor of *Matthew and the Didache: Two Documents from the Same Jewish-Christian Milieu?* (van Gorcum) and co-editor of *Matthew, James and the Didache: Three Related Documents in Their Jewish and Christian Contexts* (Brill).

Jesper Svartvik is a Senior Research Fellow at the Swedish Research Council. He teaches at the Centre for Theology and Religious Studies at Lund University and also at Paideia, the European Institute for Jewish Studies in Sweden. He is the author of *Mark and Mission: Mark 7:1-23 in its Narrative and Historical Contexts* (Almqvist & Wiksell) and the editor of *Svensk Teologisk Kvartalskrift* (*The Swedish Theological Quarterly Journal*).

Jürgen Zangenberg is Professor of New Testament Exegesis and Early Christian Literature at the University of Leiden, and Researcher in New Testament Exegesis at Tilburg University. He is a co-director of the Kinneret Regional Project in Galilee, and has published widely on early Christianity and the archaeology of the Holy Land. His recent books include *Jüdische und frühchristliche Bestattungskultur in Palästina: Studien zur Literatur und Archäologie* (Mohr Siebeck) and, as co-editor, *Religion, Ethnicity and Identity in Ancient Galilee* (Mohr Siebeck).

ABBREVIATIONS

AASF	Annales Academiae Scientiarum Fennicae
AB	Anchor Bible
ABR	*Australian Biblical Review*
ABRL	Anchor Bible Reference Library
AGJU	Arbeiten zur Geschichte des antiken Judentums und des Urchristentums
AnBib	Analecta Biblica
ANRW	*Aufstieg und Niedergang der römischen Welt*
ATDan	Acta Theologica Danica
BECNT	Baker Exegetical Commentary on the New Testament
BHT	Beiträge zur historischen Theologie
BNTC	Black's New Testament Commentaries
BVB	Beiträge zum Verstehen der Bibel
BZ	*Biblische Zeitschrift*
CBNTS	Coniectanea Biblica New Testament Series
CBQ	*Catholic Biblical Quarterly*
CBR	*Currents in Biblical Research*
CRINT	Compendia rerum iudaicarum ad Novum Testamentum
CSHJ	Chicago Studies in the History of Judaism
EKKNT	Evangelisch-katholischer Kommentar zum Neuen Testament
ESTNT	Exegetische Studien zur Theologie des Neuen Testaments
EvT	*Evangelische Theologie*
FJCD	Forschungen zum Jüdisch-Christlichen Dialog
FRLANT	Forschungen zur Religion und Literatur des Alten und Neuen Testaments
FzB	Forschungen zur Bibel
GNS	Good News Studies
HBT	*Horizons in Biblical Theology*
HeyJ	*Heythrop Journal*
HTR	*Harvard Theological Review*
HTS	*Hervormde Teologiese Studies*
ICC	International Critical Commentary
IRT	Issues in Religion and Theology
JBL	*Journal of Biblical Literature*

JEH	*Journal of Ecclesiastical History*
JGRCJ	*Journal of Greco-Roman Christianity and Judaism*
JSNT	*Journal for the Study of the New Testament*
JSNTSup	*Journal for the Study of the New Testament,* Supplement Series
JSOTSup	*Journal for the Study of the Old Testament,* Supplement Series
JTS	*Journal of Theological Studies*
KAV	Kommentar zu den Apostolischen Vätern
KEK	Kritisch-exegetischer Kommentar über das Neue Testament
LCL	Loeb Classical Library
LNTS	Library of New Testament Studies
NHC	Nag Hammadi Codex
NIGTC	New International Greek Testament Commentary
NovT	*Novum Testamentum*
NovTSup	*Novum Testamentum,* Supplements
NTM	New Testament Message
NTMon	New Testament Monographs
NTR	New Testament Readings
NTS	*New Testament Studies*
NTT	New Testament Theology
PPFBR	Publications of the Perry Foundation for Biblical Research
PRR	Princeton Readings in Religions
RSR	*Recherches de science religieuse*
SBEC	Studies in the Bible and Early Christianity
SBL	Society of Biblical Literature
SBLDS	Society of Biblical Literature Dissertation Series
SBLSS	Society of Biblical Literature Symposium Series
SBS	Stuttgarter Bibelstudien
SC	Sources chrétiennes
SCJR	*Studies in Jewish-Christian Relations*
SE	*Studia Evangelica*
SJT	*Scottish Journal of Theology*
SNTSMS	Society for New Testament Studies Monograph Series
SNTW	Studies of the New Testament and Its World
SP	Sacra Pagina
SPSH	Scholars Press Studies in the Humanities
SUNT	Studien zur Umwelt des Neuen Testaments
SVTP	Studia in Veteris Testamenti pseudepigrapha
TBS	The Biblical Seminar
TCHS	The Church Historical Society
THKNT	Theologischer Handkommentar zum Neuen Testament
TLZ	*Theologische Literaturzeitung*

TNTIC	The New Testament in Context
TSAJ	Texte und Studien zum antiken Judentum
VC	*Vigiliae christianae*
VCSup	*Vigiliae christianae*, Supplements
VF	*Verkündigung und Forschung*
WBC	Word Biblical Commentary
WMANT	Wissenschaftliche Monographien zum Alten und Neuen Testament
WUNT	Wissenschaftliche Untersuchungen zum Neuen Testament
ZAC	*Zeitschrift für antikes Christentum*
ZNW	*Zeitschrift für die neutestamentliche Wissenschaft*
ZTK	*Zeitschrift für Theologie und Kirche*

INTRODUCTION

DAVID C. SIM

It has long been acknowledged that the Gospel of Matthew is the most Jewish of the four canonical Gospels and arguably the most Jewish of all the New Testament documents. Even in the ancient Christian church, Matthew was viewed as a distinctively Jewish text because it was considered to have been written by a Jew for other Jewish followers of Jesus.[1] Since that time the thoroughgoing Jewishness of both the evangelist and his Gospel has not been seriously questioned, except for a period in the 1950s to the 1970s when a number of influential scholars proposed that the author was in fact a Gentile who represented a predominantly Gentile community.[2] This thesis, however, suffers from a number of serious difficulties,[3] and in the last three decades has almost completely disappeared from view.

In the light of the return to the consensus view that the evangelist was a Jewish Christian (or a Christian Jew) who wrote for a Jewish Christian (or Christian Jewish) readership, it perhaps comes as no surprise to learn that Matthaean scholarship in the last two decades or so has tended to focus attention on the Gospel's Jewish context. Of primary importance in this regard have been two related questions. The first of these concerns Matthew's sustained polemical attacks on the scribes and Pharisees. This theme is much more prominent in this Gospel than any of the others, and much of the relevant material is redactional rather than traditional. In

---

1. The earliest explicit attestation is Irenaeus, *Adv. Haer.*, 3.1.1, in the late second century. Similar views are expressed later by Origen in his *Commentary on Matthew* (cited in Eusebius, *H.E.* 6.25.3-4) and Eusebius himself (*H.E.* 3.24.6).

2. The first scholar to challenge the consensus and propose that Matthew was a Gentile writing for a Gentile church was K. W. Clark, 'The Gentile Bias in Matthew', *JBL* 66 (1947), pp. 165–72. His views gathered support in the following decades. For a list of scholars holding this particular thesis, see W. D. Davies and D. C. Allison, *A Critical and Exegetical Commentary on the Gospel according to Saint Matthew* (ICC; 3 vols; Edinburgh: T&T Clark, 1988, 1991, 1997), I, pp. 10–11.

3. See the critiques by Davies and Allison, *Matthew*, I, pp. 9–58; and G. N. Stanton, 'The Origin and Purpose of Matthew's Gospel: Matthean Scholarship from 1945 to 1980', in H. Temporini and W. Haase (eds), *ANRW*, II, 25, 3 (Berlin: de Gruyter, 1985), pp. 1889–1951 (1916–19).

order to explain this prominent Matthaean theme, it is now customary to argue that the Matthaean community was in serious conflict with other Jewish groups struggling for recognition and authority in the period immediately following the Jewish revolt of 66–70 CE. The scribes and Pharisees of the Gospel narrative refer to the leadership of what is conveniently referred to as Formative Judaism, a type of Judaism that grew out of the pre-70 Pharisaic movement and which eventually developed into Rabbinic Judaism.

The second area of scholarly interest, and perhaps the issue that has most dominated Matthaean studies in the last two decades, is the question of the relationship between the Gospel (and its community) and the religion of Judaism. Did Matthew's group, despite its allegiance to Jesus, still consider itself to be Jewish and therefore identify its religious tradition as a Christian form of Judaism? If so, then the dispute between Matthew's Christian Jewish community and Formative Judaism was a purely internal Jewish debate.[4] Alternatively, it might be the case that this conflict had resulted in a definitive break between the evangelist's group and its Jewish roots. If this is the case, then this community had separated from the religion of Judaism and the dispute with Formative Judaism could now be described as a conflict between the Christian Church (cf. Mt. 16.18; 18.17) and the Jewish synagogue (cf. 4.23; 9.35; 10.17; 12.9; 13.54).[5] No clear winner has emerged in this important debate, and it is reasonable to assume that it will continue to dominate Matthaean scholarship for some time to come.

It is clear from the above that the focus of recent scholarly attention has been the relationship between the evangelist and his Jewish contempo-

---

4.   So J. A. Overman, *Matthew's Gospel and Formative Judaism: The Social World of the Matthean Community* (Minneapolis: Fortress Press, 1990); A. J. Saldarini, *Matthew's Christian-Jewish Community* (CSHJ; Chicago: University of Chicago Press, 1994); D. C. Sim, *The Gospel of Matthew and Christian Judaism: The History and Social Setting of the Matthean Community* (SNTW; Edinburgh: T&T Clark, 1998), and B. Repschinski, *The Controversy Stories in the Gospel of Matthew: Their Redaction, Form and Relevance for the Relationship between the Matthean Community and Formative Judaism* (FRLANT, 189; Göttingen: Vandenhoeck & Ruprecht, 2000).

5.   For this view, see the following: G. N. Stanton, *A Gospel for a New People: Studies in Matthew* (Edinburgh: T&T Clark, 1992); J. K. Riches, *Conflicting Mythologies: Identity Formation in the Gospels of Mark and Matthew* (SNTW; Edinburgh: T&T Clark, 2000); D. R. A. Hare, 'How Jewish is the Gospel of Matthew?', *CBQ* 62 (2000), pp. 264–77; D. A. Hagner, 'Matthew: Apostate, Reformer, Revolutionary?', *NTS* 49 (2003), pp. 193–209; *idem.*, 'Matthew: Christian Judaism or Jewish Christianity?', in S. McKnight and G. R. Osborne (eds), *The Face of the New Testament: A Survey of Recent Research* (Grand Rapids: Baker Academic, 2004), pp. 263–82; P. Foster, *Community, Law and Mission in Matthew's Gospel* (WUNT, 2.177; Tübingen: Mohr Siebeck, 2004); A. O. Ewherido, *Matthew's Gospel and Judaism in the Late First Century C.E.: The Evidence from Matthew's Chapter on Parables (Matthew 13:1-52)* (SBL, 91; New York: Peter Lang, 2006), and U. Luz, *Matthew 1-7* (Hermeneia; Minneapolis: Fortress Press, rev. edn, 2007), pp. 52–5.

raries, especially the scribes and Pharisees who comprised the leadership of Formative Judaism. While the discussion has for the most part been general in character, it is possible to individualize it. U. Luz has recently devoted some attention to a comparison of Matthew and his Pharisaic Jewish contemporary, Johannan ben Zakkai, the purported initiator of the movement known as Formative Judaism. Luz acknowledges the problems of reconstructing 'the historical Johannan', but he notes that there are striking similarities between some aspects of the Gospel and some features that emerge in the later Rabbinic traditions about this influential Pharisee.[6] The examination of this theme by Luz, brief as it is, is instructive and informative, and is worthy of further and more detailed consideration.

But it also raises a further point. Have Matthaean scholars, in focusing on the evangelist's Jewish context and his relationship with his Jewish contemporaries, neglected other important contexts and relationships that may be equally worthy of consideration? The short answer is that we have. W. Carter has rightly reminded the field that we have seriously neglected the Roman imperial context of Matthew,[7] but there is no reason to stop at this point because an even more obvious failing can be identified. I am referring here to Matthew's Christian context, and particularly his relationship with his Christian contemporaries. Where does Matthew stand within the variety of expressions of the first-century Christian tradition? How would he have reacted to these other traditions? What can we learn by comparing the Gospel of Matthew with other early Christian texts, and by comparing Matthew the evangelist with other early Christian authors? In which ways would Matthew have agreed with these texts and authors, and on which issues would he have disagreed with them? Does Matthew's Gospel, which has the honour of being the first book in the New Testament, stand out as a distinctive text within the Christian canon and other early Christian literature?

Many scholars would claim that, while Matthew as a Christian text does share many affinities with other early Christian writings, it is none the less a distinctive Christian document in some ways. The very Jewish nature of the text, which draws us to make comparisons with contemporary Jewish traditions, is the very aspect of the Gospel that invites us to compare and contrast the evangelist with his Christian contemporaries. The most striking issue in this respect is the role of the Torah in the Gospel itself and, by extension, its function in the Matthaean community. The key text is

---

6. Luz, *Matthew 1-7*, pp. 55–6.
7. See especially W. Carter, *Matthew and Empire: Initial Explorations* (Harrisburg: Trinity Press International, 2001). Also of importance is his *Matthew and the Margins: A Sociopolitical and Religious Reading* (Maryknoll: Orbis, 2000). Cf. too the collection of essays in J. Riches and D. C. Sim (eds), *The Gospel of Matthew in Its Roman Imperial Context* (JSNTSup, 276; London: T&T Clark International, 2005).

of course Mt. 5.17-19, a triad of sayings near the beginning of the Sermon on the Mount where the Matthaean Jesus first speaks about the fundamental issue of the Law. These three sayings have been subjected to a variety of interpretations,[8] but they are best taken literally in which case their meaning is perfectly clear and unambiguous.[9] Jesus has not come to destroy or abolish the Law (or the prophets), and all of the Torah with no exception remains valid until the *parousia*. Therefore those who follow Jesus must obey the whole Law and teach others to do so. It is unacceptable to relax even one of the least commandments and/or to communicate such a view to others.

The positive affirmation in these verses about the whole Mosaic Law has no close parallel in the early Christian literature. Not even Jas 2.8-26, which refers to the 'royal Law' and stipulates that the whole Law must be kept (2.10), is really comparative. The reason for this is that the text does not make clear whether the Law includes all of the Torah's requirements or whether it refers to the love command alone (cf. 2.8). Paul, too, occasionally says some complimentary things about the Law. He denies that the Torah is itself sin (Rom. 7.7) or against the promises of God (Gal. 3.21), and he describes it as holy, just and good (Rom. 7.12). Paul can even say that those of faith uphold the Law (Rom. 3.31), though this position seems to be dependent upon reducing the Torah to the love command (cf. Rom. 13.8-10). But despite these general and perhaps rhetorical flourishes on the part of Paul, the reality is that he believed that the Torah, as normally understood and practised in his day, was rendered irrelevant by the Christ event. The Law is a written code that kills and is a dispensation of death and condemnation (2 Cor. 3.6-9). Its purpose was to serve as a custodian until faith came with Christ, and now that this has happened we are no longer bound by it (Gal. 3.23-25). In other words, Paul could never agree with Matthew that Jesus had not come to abolish the Torah, that all of the Torah with no exception remains valid until the *parousia*, and that those who follow Jesus must obey the whole Law and teach others to do so. By the same token, Matthew could never follow Paul by using the term 'my former life in Judaism' (Gal. 1.13-14) or by referring to his Jewish pedigree as dung (Phil. 3.4-8).

The very great distance between Matthew and Paul on the validity of all the various demands of the Mosaic Law in Christian existence is not unique. We find similar distance between this evangelist and other early Christian authors. Mark, for example, contends that Jesus declared all foods to be clean (Mk 7.19b), thereby dismissing in a single action the Jewish dietary and purity regulations. It comes as no surprise to learn that

---

8.   See the discussion in Davies and Allison, *Matthew*, I, pp. 481–502.

9.   In agreement with D. C. Allison, *The New Moses: A Matthean Typology* (Edinburgh: T&T Clark, 1993), p. 182.

Matthew omits this tradition when redacting his Markan source. The Gospel of John attests that the Law was given by Moses while grace and truth came by Jesus Christ (Jn 1.17), a contrast that Matthew would never have made. The Johannine narrator explains that the Jews wished to kill Jesus because he broke the sabbath commandment (5.18). The Matthaean Jesus, by contrasts, fulfils the Torah by providing works of mercy on the sabbath (Mt. 12.1-14). Ignatius of Antioch drew the conclusion that Judaism and Christianity were totally incompatible with one another (cf. *Mag.* 8.1; 10.1-3). Although Matthew does not directly address this issue, we can well imagine that he would have rejected it completely. And one can find comparable points of contrast between Matthew and other New Testament documents and other early Christian authors. The sole exception might be the epistle of James but, as noted above, this is still a matter of dispute. If Matthew is such a distinctive text within the early Christian literature, then this particular fact is worthy of further exploration.

Making the point that scholars have not focused particular attention on Matthew and his Christian contemporaries does not mean that this theme has been totally ignored by scholars. The question of Matthew's relationship to Paul was raised long ago by C. H. Dodd,[10] and later scholars have also devoted some attention to this issue,[11] but the fact remains that the comparison of these two early Christians by R. Mohrlang remains the only monograph devoted to this subject.[12] Current Matthaean scholarship shows little interest at all in this question, since it is usually argued that Matthew is independent of the Pauline tradition, or simply un-Pauline to use the current catchphrase.[13] This position, however, is difficult to justify. Even on the view that Matthew is completely uninfluenced by the Pauline tradition, and this is itself unlikely,[14] a comparison and

10. C. H. Dodd, 'Matthew and Paul', in C. H. Dodd, *New Testament Studies* (Manchester: Manchester University Press, 1953), pp. 53–66.

11. See the survey of the literature in D. C. Sim, 'Matthew's Anti-Paulinism: A Neglected Feature of Matthean Studies', *HTS* 58 (2002), pp. 767–83.

12. R. Mohrlang, *Matthew and Paul: A Comparison of Ethical Perspectives* (SNTSMS, 48; Cambridge: Cambridge University Press, 1984).

13. Stanton, *Gospel for a New People*, p. 314.

14. Some scholars have argued that Matthew was influenced by the Pauline tradition and was even aware of some Pauline epistles. See M. D. Goulder, *Midrash and Lection in Matthew* (London: SPCK, 1974), pp. 153–70; T. L. Brodie, *The Birthing of the New Testament: The Intertextual Development of the New Testament Writings* (NTMon, 1: Sheffield: Sheffield Phoenix, 2004), pp. 206–35; and D. C. Sim, 'Matthew and the Pauline Corpus: A Preliminary Intertextual Study', forthcoming *JSNT*. Despite their agreement that Matthew was probably familiar with the Pauline corpus, these authors disagree over the issue of the evangelist's use of them. Both Goulder and Brodie affirm that Matthew used the Pauline letters because he found them informative and authoritative, while Sim argues the opposite view that he alludes to certain Pauline passages as part of his anti-Pauline polemic.

contrast of these independent Christian authors is still a valuable historical and theological exercise. It should be noted that Mohrlang's important discussion worked on the assumption that Matthew betrayed no Pauline influence whatsoever.

Even less attention has been devoted to a comparison between Matthew and other New Testament authors. In the case of Matthew and Mark, where an obvious comparison presents itself because of the former's use of the latter, all too little has been done. Matthaean scholars of course note Matthew's use of Mark and his editing of this major source, but there is all too little effort given to comparing Mark's particular theological perspective with Matthew's.[15] Even the recent work of A. M. O'Leary on Matthew's judaizing of Mark,[16] despite the promising nature of the title, is concerned with the evangelist's insertion of Old Testament allusions into the Markan narrative and not with Matthew's tendency to judaize Mark's portrait of Jesus. In the case of Matthew and the Epistle of James, the discussion has been concerned less with a comparison of their theological perspectives than with the parallel Jesus traditions found in each text and which are more often than not viewed as James/Q overlaps.[17] Since the time of the Reformation and Luther's rather unkind description of James as 'an epistle of straw', scholars have understandably focused on the relationship between James and Paul.

This very brief overview of the situation in Matthaean scholarship provides the context for the nature and purpose of the present volume. It is intended to address a real gap in the field by providing meaningful comparisons between the evangelist with his distinctive Christian viewpoint and other early Christian authors. What do Matthew and these Christian writers hold in common and where do they depart from one another? If it is legitimate to envisage a dialogue involving the Jewish Matthew and the Jewish Johannan ben Zakkai, then how much more appropriate is it to envisage similar conversations between the Christian Matthew and his Christian contemporaries? In this volume Matthew is compared with many of the important canonical authors – Paul, Mark, Luke, John, James, and the author of Hebrews – as well as the writers of important non-canonical texts, the author of the *Didache* and Ignatius of

---

15.   An exception is Luz, *Matthew 1-7*, pp. 41–3 who explores the issue of Matthew's theological relationship to both Mark and Q, but his discussion is necessarily brief. Also worthy of mention is the study of identity formation in both Mark and Matthew by J. K. Riches (see note 5 above), but Riches' discussion is also limited in scope.

16.   A. M. O'Leary, *Matthew's Judaization of Mark: Examined in the Context of the Use of Sources in Graeco-Roman Antiquity* (JSNTSup, 323; London: T&T Clark International, 2006).

17.   See, for example, P. J. Hartin, *James and the Q Sayings of Jesus* (JSNTSup, 47; Sheffield: Sheffield Academic Press, 1991). Hartin accepts that the author of James was also aware of Matthew's special source, the so-called M tradition.

Antioch. A final chapter is devoted to Matthew and the historical Jesus. While Jesus of Nazareth cannot be considered in any sense to be a 'Christian', important comparisons can be made between this historical figure and Matthew's determined attempt to depict him in strictly Jewish terms, especially in those areas where the evangelist edits and overturns the portrait in Mark.

As much as the editors would have liked to include all of Matthew's Christian contemporaries, this was not possible within a single volume. Therefore a process of selection was inevitable. In terms of the canonical authors, the choice of Paul needs no justification, nor does the selection of the other three evangelists. James and the writer of Hebrews assume a Jewish background and thus lend themselves to a ready comparison with Matthew's similar background. Of the non-canonical writers, the *Didache* was an obvious choice as well. Scholarly attention on this text has increased dramatically in recent times and many of these studies have been directly concerned with the relationship between the Gospel of Matthew and the *Didache* and/or their respective Jewish contexts.[18] Ignatius of Antioch was also a logical choice, given that he hailed from the same probable location as Matthew (Antioch) but represents a very different Christian tradition. The selection of these texts and authors meant the omission of others. The present volume pays no attention at all to the Deutero-Pauline literature, Colossians, Ephesians and the Pastoral epistles; and the other Catholic Epistles, notably the Petrine letters, are also absent. Nor is there any discussion of Matthew and the author of Revelation, even though these two writers share much in common in terms of eschatological concerns. Of the non-canonical literature, 1 *Clement* and the *Epistle of Barnabas* are not included. The exclusion of these authors and writings is unfortunate but unavoidable. There is no doubt that interesting results would arise were Matthew to be compared with any or all of these authors. It is our hope that this volume will instigate further research in these areas.

The studies presented in this volume are no more than the first tentative steps to initiate the dialogue between Matthew and his Christian contemporaries. All of the contributors know well that it is impossible in a single chapter to do justice to the variety and complexity of issues involved in a comparative analysis of different writers. Again, it is hoped that these

18.   See, for example, H. van de Sandt and D. Flusser, *The Didache: Its Jewish Sources and Its Place in Early Judaism and Early Christianity* (CRINT, 3.5; Assen: Royal van Gorcum, 2002); M. Slee, *The Church in Antioch in the First Century C.E.: Communion and Conflict* (JSNTSup, 244; London: T&T Clark International, 2003); A. J. P. Garrow, *The Gospel of Matthew's Dependence on the Didache* (JSNTSup, 254; London: T&T Clark International, 2004), and H. van de Sandt (ed.), *Matthew and the Didache: Two Documents From the Same Jewish-Christian Milieu?* (Assen: Royal van Gorcum, 2005).

provisional studies will provide an impetus for further and more detailed discussions. Each contributor has focused on certain key issues that he deemed to be of importance or relevance. Not surprisingly the issue of the Torah emerges most often throughout the various chapters, but other important subjects are discussed as well. And it is important to note that the contributors fall across the spectrum in terms of their understanding of Matthew and/or the authors with whom he is compared. For example, some of us accept that Matthew was vehemently anti-Pauline, while others are just as convinced that he was not. Some believe that the Gospel of Mark was very much influenced by Paul, while others see no direct connection between the two. The volume therefore exhibits a dialogue between the various contributors, and once more our hope is that other colleagues will enter the conversation.

Daniel Harrington takes on perhaps the most difficult assignment of all, the comparison between Matthew and Paul. Beginning with the different genres that each author uses and noting their individual historical contexts, Harrington moves on to a direct analysis of certain shared themes – christology, Law and love, the moral life, communal conflicts, and salvation and eschatology. In the course of his examination, Harrington notes the points of contact and the differences between Paul and Matthew. This discussion leads Harrington to make some observations about the relationship between these two important Christian writers. He is not convinced by the view that Matthew wrote in opposition to Paul, but he accepts that it serves as an important reminder of our collective tendency to harmonize the canonical authors.

The next contribution is a comparison of Matthew and Mark by Jesper Svartvik. He starts with a discussion of various 'circles' within the early Christian movement, and contends that Mark and Paul should be viewed as representatives of the same theological circle, and that Matthew and James belonged to a very different Christian circle. This preliminary but important discussion sets the scene for an examination of Matthew's redaction of his Markan source. Svartvik focuses attention on four key aspects – the rejudaization of Jesus, the reinforcement of *halakhah*, the rebuke of the Pharisees and the rehabilitation of Peter. In the final part of his study, Svartvik muses on the irony that many scholars have noted the theological division between Paul and James, but have ignored the similar division between Matthew and Mark.

The comparison of Matthew and Luke is undertaken by Boris Repschinski who confines his discussion to the important issue of the Gentile mission. Matthew emphasizes the people of Israel and the Jewish mission, and even when the Gentile mission is enjoined at the end of the Gospel it is a Law-observant mission that the risen Christ demands. This perspective is sharply contrasted with that of Luke who relates in his two-volume work how the mission unfolds and expands from the original mission to the Jews, to the Samaritan mission and eventually to the Law-free mission to the Gentiles. Repschinski concludes his study by noting that Matthew advocates a church of both Jews and Gentiles that remained faithful to its Jewish heritage, while Luke envisages a predominately Gentile Christian community in which the Law no longer played a significant role.

John Painter discusses Matthew and John. After noting that both texts appear to have been written within the context of a struggle with Formative Judaism, Painter argues that this led to different responses by the two evangelists. The Matthaean community still saw itself as a part of the Jewish world. This is evident from the continuing validity of the Torah as well as from the nature of the Gentile mission demanded at the end of the Gospel. In agreement with Repschinski, Painter affirms that this was a Law-observant mission. The Johannine community, by contrast, had broken with its Jewish heritage. The relevant evidence here includes John drawing a contrast between Jesus and Moses (and the Law), and the openness of this community to the world at large based upon its conviction that God loves the world and intends to save it.

The following essay by Martin Hasitschka examines Matthew and the letter to the Hebrews. The first part of the study surveys the common literary elements and motifs between these texts. These include, amongst others, a strong relationship to the Septuagint, an emphasis on Jesus' sonship and an interest in the Jewish Law. Such parallels do not suggest a direct literary connection between these writings, but they do indicate a similar Jewish Christian background. In the major part of the study, Hasitschka breaks new ground by arguing in detail and with conviction that, while other Christian texts link Jesus' sacrificial death with the forgiveness of sins, only in Matthew and Hebrews do we find the theme that the blood of Jesus seals a new covenant that encompasses the forgiveness of sins.

Jürgen Zangenberg compares Matthew with the epistle of James. He begins with the social and religious contexts of each document, before moving on to some of their more important theological parallels. These include an emphasis on observance of the Torah, the presence of Jesus traditions and ethical themes. Zangenberg does not believe there is a direct relationship between James and Matthew, but he does see them as representative of the same Christian circle, a point also made by Jesper Svartvik. As to whether these two texts were anti-Pauline, a claim often made of James and sometimes made of Matthew, Zangenberg is not convinced in either case. They belong to a different Christian tradition, but it is more accurate to describe them as un-Pauline rather than as anti-Pauline.

Huub van de Sandt begins his treatment of Matthew and the *Didache* by referring to their common traditions and the various attempts by scholars to explain these parallels. He then narrows the discussion to the topic of the Torah in both documents and notes that each emphasizes the love command, the second half of the Decalogue and the idea of perfection as the goal of Christian life. But van de Sandt notes a tension between Matthew and the *Didache* on the practical implementation of the Mosaic Law. The evangelist is absolutely clear that the Law must be upheld in its entirety, while the author of the *Didache* presents a more nuanced position. The Torah should be obeyed by all Christians, but he permits a partial compliance with the ritual demands of the Torah, an innovation that was probably introduced for the benefit of Gentile converts.

In the next contribution David C. Sim compares the evangelist with Ignatius of Antioch. Common residents of Antioch but separated by two or so decades, these two authors and their respective theologies could not be more different. The evangelist was Law-observant and advocated a Gentile mission with full adherence to the Law (so too John Painter and Boris Repschinki), a position at odds with the Pauline tradition (but see Daniel Harrington and Jürgen Zangenberg). By contrast, Ignatius was a thorough Paulinist who knew many of the apostle's letters and was heavily influenced by their theology. In direct contrast to the position of Matthew, Ignatius believed that there was a complete incompatibility between belief in Jesus and the practice of Judaism. Sim notes that Ignatius was opposed by Christian Jews in Antioch, and he suggests that they bear a striking resemblance to the members of the earlier Matthaean community.

The study of Matthew and Jesus of Nazareth, also by David C. Sim, argues that the Gospel of Matthew sometimes gives a more accurate picture of the historical Jesus than its primary source, the Gospel of Mark, a point also made by Jesper Svartvik. Sim contends that on two issues in particular, Jesus' involvement in a Gentile mission and his views on the Law, the portrait found in Matthew is much more reliable than its Markan counterpart. The major evidence cited by Sim in favour of this thesis is the practice of the original Christian community in Jerusalem, comprising the family and disciples of Jesus, which continued to live according to the Law and which showed no interest in a Gentile mission. It is much easier to account for their positions on these issues if Matthew's depiction of Jesus is accepted as more accurate than Mark's.

1. MATTHEW AND PAUL

DANIEL J. HARRINGTON SJ

1. Introduction

One of my recurrent fantasies has been to put Matthew and Paul in the same room and allow them to come out only when they had reached a joint declaration regarding Christian theology and life.[1] On the surface they represent two very different theological voices within the New Testament canon. In recent years, however, both writers have been studied by scholars from a 'new perspective' that has emphasized their roots in Judaism and their place in first-century Judaism.[2]

After discussing the particular historical context in which each author wrote, this study will compare Matthew and Paul on christology, Law and love, the moral life, communal conflicts, and salvation and eschatology. The goal is to allow both their differences and their commonalities to shine forth. In each case it treats Paul first and then Matthew, more for chronological–historical reasons than any other. Paul wrote several decades before Matthew did. Finally, it considers whether Matthew can be construed as a direct response to Paul by promoting a more traditional Jewish Christianity.

---

1.   R. Mohrlang, *Matthew and Paul: A Comparison of Ethical Perspectives* (SNTSMS, 48; Cambridge: Cambridge University Press, 1984). This work remains a valuable resource for comparing the theologies of Matthew and Paul.

2.   For the 'new perspective' on Matthew, see J. A. Overman, *Matthew's Gospel and Formative Judaism: The Social World of the Matthean Community* (Minneapolis: Fortress Press, 1990); A. J. Saldarini, *Matthew's Christian-Jewish Community* (CSHJ; Chicago: University of Chicago Press, 1994); and D. C. Sim, *The Gospel of Matthew and Christian Judaism: The History and Social Setting of the Matthean Community* (SNTW; Edinburgh: T&T Clark, 1998). For the 'new perspective' on Paul, see E. P. Sanders, *Paul and Palestinian Judaism: A Comparison of Patterns of Religion* (Philadelphia: Fortress Press, 1977); and J. D. G. Dunn, *The New Perspective on Paul: Collected Essays* (WUNT, 185; Tübingen: Mohr Siebeck, 2005).

2. *Contexts*

Paul wrote letters, while Matthew wrote a Gospel. For Paul, 'the gospel' was the proclamation of the saving significance of Jesus' life, death and resurrection (as in Rom. 1.1, 3), not a full narrative about the public career or life of Jesus. His letters concern pastoral problems (and their resolutions) that arose after the resurrection and the beginning of the church. Their literary or narrative perspective is always post-Easter. In them Paul responds to crises pertaining to Christian identity and practice. If Paul had written a Gospel (as Matthew did), it would probably have looked something like Mark's Gospel (often described as a passion narrative with a long introduction), with perhaps even more emphasis on the saving significance of Jesus' death and resurrection (along the lines of Mk 10.45).

Following the model developed by Mark, Matthew composed a narrative about the life and teaching of Jesus of Nazareth. He added an infancy narrative at the front as well as accounts of the risen Jesus' appearances and material pertaining to the empty tomb at the end. With the device of the five great speeches Matthew greatly increased the amount of actual teaching material attributed to Jesus. If Matthew wrote letters (as Paul did), they probably would have looked much like the letter of James, with a strong emphasis on practical action and drawing extensively on Jewish wisdom teachings. However, in letters from Matthew we can assume that there would be many more explicit references to the person of Jesus and more direct attributions of sayings to Jesus.

Paul wrote his seven undisputed letters in the 50s of the first century CE. His letters were written mostly from Ephesus and Corinth, which he made his bases of operations at various times. Prior to the period of his letter writing, Paul spent time in Antioch in Syria.[3] There, according to Gal. 2.11-14, Paul stood up to Peter and rebuked him for his unwillingness to continue to eat with Gentile Christians after 'certain people came from James', who questioned the practice of Jewish Christians and Gentile Christians eating together. Thus Paul is an early witness to tensions at Antioch concerning relations within the Christian community between persons of different ethnic and religious backgrounds.

It is often said by modern scholars that Matthew's Gospel was composed around 85 to 90 CE in Antioch of Syria.[4] This dating would place the composition of Matthew's Gospel 30 or more years after the writing of Paul's undisputed letters. Between the two would stand a pivotal event in

---

3.   J. Murphy-O'Connor, *Paul: A Critical Life* (Oxford: Clarendon Press, 1996), and *idem.*, *Paul: His Story* (Oxford: Oxford University Press, 2004).

4.   D. J. Harrington, *The Gospel of Matthew* (SP, 1; Collegeville: Liturgical Press, 1991), pp. 8–10.

Jewish history – the destruction of Jerusalem and its Temple in 70 CE, an event of monumental significance for all Jews, including Jewish Christians like Matthew.[5]

While Paul suggests at several points that he had endured opposition from his fellow Jews and from Roman officials, most of the problems addressed in his letters seem to have come from fellow Christians, whether so called 'judaizers' or Gentile charismatics.

If recent scholars are correct about Matthew's Gospel having been composed in the context of the crisis facing all Jews after 70 CE regarding the continuation of Israel's spiritual heritage as the people of God, then Matthew usually had an eye not only on his fellow Christians but also on his non-Christian Jewish contemporaries. The Jewish group that Matthew viewed as his own community's most serious rivals were those whom he called the 'scribes and Pharisees' (see especially Mt. 23.1-39), most likely a symbol or cipher for what we call Formative or protorabbinic Judaism.

In comparison with other New Testament writers, Paul supplied a good deal of autobiographical information, especially in Phil. 3.4-21 and Gal. 1.11–2.14. Paul put his natural talents, Jewish learning, and rhetorical training in the service of the gospel. Through his decisive encounter with the risen Christ, Paul found a new goal in life (union with Christ in his suffering and in his resurrection) and a new personal identity as a Christian Jew. Without rejecting Judaism *per se*, Paul thought that he had discovered in Jesus the key to the Jewish scriptures and the fulfilment of God's promises to his people.

The writer whom we call 'Matthew' provides little or no personal information. Without relying too heavily on 9.9 and 10.3, we can say with confidence that the author of what we call Matthew's Gospel was a Jew with a good grounding in the Jewish scriptures and Jewish traditions, and a careful editor of his sources. He too regarded the Christian movement not as a new religion separate from Judaism, but rather as the fullness of the Judaism in which he was raised and the best way to carry on Israel's heritage as the people of God now that the Jerusalem Temple had been destroyed and the land was under even greater Roman control.

3. *Christology*

In the greeting introducing the earliest extant New Testament letter (1 Thess. 1.1), Paul mentions Jesus in tandem with God the Father and refers to him as 'the Lord Jesus Christ'.[6] We can presume that this usage

---

5. Harrington, *Matthew*, pp. 10–16.
6. L. W. Hurtado, *Lord Jesus Christ: Devotion to Jesus in Earliest Christianity* (Grand Rapids: Eerdmans, 2003).

had already become commonplace in Christian circles between Jesus' death in 30 CE and Paul's letter in 51 CE. The formula affirms Jesus' identity as the 'Messiah' (Χριστός) and suggests his divinity as 'Lord' (Κύριος). Throughout his letters Paul assumes an existing set of beliefs about Jesus as Messiah, Son of David, Servant of God, Son of God and Lord. At several points he refers to existing confessions of faith (e.g. Rom. 1.3-4; 3.25) and hymns (Phil. 2.6-11) about Christ. Therefore it appears that Paul represents christological perspectives that had emerged very rapidly in early Christian circles.

The focus of Paul's christological attention was the death and resurrection of Jesus. In 1 Cor. 15.3-5 he characterizes this emphasis as based on the tradition that he had received and handed on to others. This same emphasis was at the heart of the confessions and hymns that Paul cites. However, Paul was not much interested in investigating and describing the historical details involved in Jesus' passion, death and resurrection. What concerned him most was the soteriological significance or theological implications of Jesus' death and resurrection 'according to the scriptures'. The great themes of Pauline theology, especially as they are presented in Galatians and Romans – justification, reconciliation, freedom, peace with God, access to God, atonement, new creation, salvation, and so on – are all tied to the event of Jesus' death and resurrection.

Only rarely does Paul quote or cite as authoritative the teachings of Jesus. In one of the clearest cases (1 Cor. 7.10-16) Paul refers respectfully to Jesus' (whom he calls 'the Lord') prohibition of divorce in spite of Deut. 24.1-4 (see Mk 10.2-12; Mt. 5.31-32; 19.3-12; Lk. 16.18) and presents it as normative teaching. However, Paul immediately takes it upon himself to admit an exception in the case of a Christian who is married to a non-Christian when the latter does not wish to continue in the marriage (see 7.15). In that situation 'the brother or sister is not bound'.

When writing some 30 or 40 years after Paul, Matthew used the same basic set of christological titles, along with 'Son of Man', which is probably very early and is prominent in all the Gospels but mysteriously absent from Paul's writings (unless it underlies Paul's Adam-Christ comparison in Romans 5). In his revised and expanded version of Mark's Gospel, Matthew took over much of the already traditional christology found in Mark (Jesus as Son of Man, Son of David, Messiah, Son of God, Lord, and so on) and supplemented it with the Wisdom christology suggested by the sayings source Q and various early Christian hymns (Col. 1.15-20; Jn 1.1-18; Heb. 1.3-4). Like Paul, Matthew in large part reflects the christological tradition of the early church.

The distinctive focus of Matthew's christology, however, is Jesus' role as the teacher *par excellence* (see 11.25-30). The five great speeches that Matthew has constructed (chs 5–7, 10, 13, 18, 24–25) provide large samples of the content of Jesus' teachings. They tell readers how to live in preparation for the coming kingdom of God (Sermon on the Mount), how to carry on the mission of Jesus (Missionary Discourse), how to understand and live out the mystery of the Kingdom (Parables), how to deal with problems and conflicts in community life (Community Discourse), and what to expect in 'the day of the Lord' and why to be on watch for it (Eschatological Discourse). In the narratives (as in chs 8–9 and 26–27) Matthew the careful editor omits unnecessary or confusing details in order to bring out more clearly the theological points that he regarded as decisive. His blistering attack on the scribes and Pharisees in Mt. 23.1-39 insists that the followers of Jesus have only 'one teacher' and 'one instructor, the Messiah' (23.8, 10) and therefore they ought not to take upon themselves the honorific titles of 'Rabbi', 'father', and 'instructor' that Matthew's Jewish rivals were promoting.

Like Paul, Matthew includes Jesus' prohibition of divorce (5.31-32; 19.3-12) despite its tension with Deut. 24.1-4. And like Paul, he also includes an exception for what he terms πορνεία, which most likely refers to sexual misconduct on the wife's part. The result is to assimilate Jesus' teaching on divorce to that of the House of Shammai (see *m. Gittin* 9.10) and adapt it to the circumstances and experiences of the Matthaean community.

4. *Law and Love*

Paul's positive and negative statements about the Torah make it difficult to determine exactly what his attitude was toward it.[7] However, in the final analysis it appears that Paul did not believe that any Christian (even a Jewish Christian) was required to observe every part of the Mosaic Law.

The members of the original audience for Paul's letters were for the most part Gentile Christians. From Paul's perspective these people had already entered into the paschal mystery through their faith and baptism, and had received the gifts of the Holy Spirit. While these Gentile Christians may have had some contact with the Jewish Law through their association with the synagogues as 'God-fearers', it is likely that few of them had ever observed the whole Mosaic Law. It was not part of their experience. Moreover, in Paul's view, in light of their baptism and reception of the Holy Spirit, there was no need for them to observe the Law in its entirety. This is clear from Gal. 3.1-5 where Paul addresses those Gentile Christians who now felt the need to observe the Law as 'you foolish Galatians'.

---

7.   See H. Räisänen, *Paul and the Law* (WUNT, 29; Tübingen: Mohr Siebeck, 1987); and S. Westerholm, *Israel's Law and the Church's Faith: Paul and His Recent Interpreters* (Grand Rapids: Eerdmans, 1988).

Nevertheless, in Romans Paul insists that 'we uphold the Law' (3.31) and that 'the Law is holy, and the commandment is holy and just and good' (7.12). Paul's problem with the Mosaic Law for both Gentiles and Jews was that in his mind it could not do what he believed that Christ had done, that is, bring about right relationship with God (justification). In Paul's view, the mistake made by many of his fellow Jews was their belief that observance of the Law could do so.[8]

Because of misunderstanding and misuse of the Law, the Mosaic Law in turn could become a stimulus to sin and thus an ally of Sin and Death, the powers that held humankind captive before and apart from Christ. It enticed people into sin because it defined and objectified sin, and so made it more tempting. Romans 7.7-25 is an extended Pauline meditation on humankind's enslavement to the Law and sin. However, the Law had served positively as 'a disciplinarian until Christ came' (Gal. 3.24), and revealed the need that Jews (along with Gentiles) had for the revelation of God's righteousness in Christ since they all failed to live up to the demands of the Mosaic Law (cf. Rom. 2.17–3.20).

Later in Romans (13.8-10), Paul claims that 'one who loves another has fulfilled the Law'. The idea is that if one truly loves the neighbour (Lev. 19.18), one will naturally avoid sins against the neighbour such as adultery, murder, stealing and coveting. Paul concludes that 'love is the fulfilling of the Law' (13.10). By this he meant that one who loves will fulfil the deepest and most important intentions of the Law.

Paul resisted all attempts from Jewish Christians to impose the whole Mosaic Law on Gentile Christians. In his view, they did not need the Law, since they had come to Christian faith and experienced the Holy Spirit without observing the Law. Paul never forbids Jewish Christians to observe the Law, though it is doubtful that he himself observed it in all circumstances. Paul's attitude toward the Mosaic Law flowed from his basic insight that the Law could never do what Christ had already done, that is, bring about the possibility of right relationship with God for all humans. Thus at several points (2 Cor. 3; Gal. 3.19-20; Rom. 10.4-5) Paul subordinates or even denigrates the Mosaic covenant and the Law in comparison with the new covenant represented by Christ. For Paul, fulfilling the Law by love did not necessarily entail for Gentile Christians circumcision, sabbath observance, food laws and ritual purity.

Most of Matthew's original audience were Jewish Christians, and so they would have grown up with the Torah as their primary religious and moral guide. Whether they had been strict observers is another matter.

---

8.   E. P. Sanders, *Paul, the Law, and the Jewish People* (Philadelphia: Fortress Press, 1983).

Thus the evangelist could assume to some extent both knowledge and practice of the Torah on the part of many of his hearers and readers. These Jews, however, had come to believe that Jesus, a Jew from Nazareth, was the authoritative interpreter of the Mosaic Law.

Matthew presents Moses in a positive way, finding parallels between his infancy and that of Jesus, and between the gift of the Law at Sinai and the Sermon on the Mount. In the beginning of the highly polemical discourse in ch. 23 the Matthaean Jesus urges a respectful attitude toward the content of the teachings given by those who 'sit on Moses' seat' (23.2).

The key text is Mt. 5.17-19. Here Jesus proclaims that he has come 'not to abolish but to fulfil' the Law and the prophets, that this meant that every letter and every part of a letter in them was to be observed, and that those who broke even the most insignificant of the 613 precepts and taught others to do the same would be called 'least in the kingdom of heaven'. These verses from the Sermon on the Mount constitute the most straightforward and powerful affirmation of the Mosaic Law in the New Testament.

If we take Mt. 5.17-19 at face value and do not try to explain it away, the antitheses that follow in 5.21-48 cannot be understood as abolishing any of the Mosaic Law's precepts ('not to abolish but to fulfil'). Rather, by going to the root of these commandments (as in the case of murder) or building a fence around them (as in the case of adultery and divorce), the Matthaean Jesus shows how they are to be fulfilled.

This strict attitude carries through Matthew's Gospel. In the two passages about sabbath observance in Mt. 12.1-14, Matthew is careful to portray Jesus as in conflict not with the Biblical commandment itself but rather with the traditions surrounding it that were developed by the Pharisees. Likewise in Mt. 15.1-20, Jesus criticizes not the Biblical food laws and concern for ritual purity but rather the traditions that the Pharisees attached to them. In the Eschatological Discourse in Mt. 24.20 the Matthaean Jesus tells his audience to pray that the day of the Lord may not come on a sabbath lest it pose a crisis of conscience for observant Jews regarding how far they might travel on the sabbath.

Like Paul, Matthew also makes a connection between the Torah and love. In the last of the controversies situated in Jerusalem (22.34-40), the Matthaean Jesus answers the question about the 'greatest' commandment in the Mosaic Law (a question typically posed to Rabbis) by quoting Deut. 6.4-5 ('You shall love the Lord your God') and Lev. 19.18 ('You shall love your neighbour as yourself'). And then he adds; 'On these two commandments hang all the Law and the prophets' (22.40). The point seems to be similar to Paul's idea that if one truly loves God and neighbour, one will naturally do what the Law intends. However, it is likely that Matthew expected full compliance with the whole Law, at least on the part of Jewish Christians. It is doubtful that Matthew regarded Torah observance as a matter of indifference as Paul seems to have done.

Matthew's Gospel ends with the risen Jesus' command to 'make disciples of all nations' (28.19). I understand πάντα τὰ ἔθνη here to mean 'all the Gentiles' as the uses of ἔθνη elsewhere in Matthew's Gospel suggest.[9] In the context of Matthaean redaction this command seems to be a mandate directed to the evangelist's largely Jewish Christian audience to be more active in spreading the gospel to non-Jews. There is no indication that Matthew expected these Gentiles to convert to Judaism formally and to be circumcised. But it is possible in view of Mt. 5.17-19 that he did expect them to observe the Mosaic Law, at least as it was interpreted by Jesus. That observance may well have entailed the Biblical rules pertaining to sabbath rest, forbidden foods and ritual purity (cf. Mt. 12.1-14 and 15.1-20).

5. The Moral Life

In his thanksgiving, at the very beginning of his earliest extant letter, Paul refers to the Thessalonians' accomplishments in manifesting the triad of Christian theological virtues: 'your work of faith and labour of love and steadfastness of hope' (1 Thess. 1.2). The object of faith for Paul is God's offer of justification and salvation through Jesus' life, death and resurrection ('faith in Christ'). At the same time, Jesus' fidelity to his Father's will and to his mission provides the best example of faith ('the faith of Christ'). Love is the virtue that empowers and energizes all of Christian life. When in the kingdom of God faith and hope will no longer be needed (since their object is realized), love will remain as the greatest of all virtues (1 Cor. 13.13). What Paul hopes for is fullness of life with the risen Christ in the kingdom of God; 'the prize of the heavenly call of God in Christ Jesus' (Phil. 3.14). This is the goal or *telos* that shapes all of Christian life according to Paul. These three theological virtues – faith, love and hope – have their origin and object in God. As gifts from God made available through the paschal mystery, they give shape and dynamism to all of Christian life.

Within the context of the three theological virtues, Paul also stresses the importance of striving for 'natural' virtues and avoiding vices.[10] Like many of his Jewish and Graeco-Roman contemporaries, Paul provides several lists of vices (Rom. 1.29-31; 1 Cor. 5.9-10; 6.9-10; 2 Cor. 12.20; Gal. 5.19-21) and virtues (Rom. 5.3-5; Gal. 5.22-23).

---

9.   D. R. A. Hare and D. J. Harrington, '"Make Disciples of All the Gentiles" (Mt 28:19)', *CBQ* 37 (1975), pp. 359–69.

10.   W. A. Meeks, *The Origins of Christian Morality: The First Two Centuries* (New Haven: Yale University Press, 1993), pp. 63–90.

In Gal. 5.16-26, Paul characterizes the vices as the 'works of the flesh' and under this heading includes 'fornication, impurity, licentiousness, idolatry, sorcery, enmities, strife, jealousy, anger, quarrels, dissensions, factions, envy, drunkenness, carousing, and things like these' (5.19-21). By contrast, Paul describes the virtues as the 'fruit of the Spirit' and under that heading includes 'love, joy, peace, patience, kindness, generosity, faithfulness, gentleness, and self-control' (5.22-23).

These lists are illustrative rather than exhaustive. Their content is not far different from the lists produced by contemporary Jewish writers and Graeco-Roman moralists.[11] What is most important about them is the Christian theological context in which the virtues (and vices) have been placed by Paul. It is their context in the paschal mystery and in the framework of faith, love, and hope that makes them Christian virtues.

Matthew's approach to the virtues focuses more on righteousness or justice (δικαιοσύνη) than faith, love and hope.[12] In 5.20 the Matthaean Jesus challenges his followers to seek the righteousness that 'exceeds that of the scribes and Pharisees'. And in 6.33 he urges them to 'strive first for the kingdom of God and his righteousness, and all these things will be given to you'.

Matthew's understanding of what righteousness entails is spelt out in the Sermon on the Mount. The list of beatitudes in 5.3-12 first notes the virtues, attitudes and actions that are appropriate to those who are seeking God's kingdom and his righteousness: poverty of spirit, compassion, hunger and thirst for righteousness, mercy, integrity, peacemaking, and willingness to undergo persecution for it. Their second parts describe in various ways what are in the final analysis synonyms for the goal or *telos* of the Christian life of virtue: life in the kingdom of Heaven.

The antitheses in Mt. 5.21-48 encourage aspirants to God's kingdom to go to the root of various Biblical commandments as a way of avoiding their infringement and of fulfilling their deepest purposes. The section devoted to acts of piety in 6.1-18 urges that almsgiving, prayer and fasting be carried out not to gain a reputation for personal holiness but rather as acts of worship directed toward the God 'who sees in secret (and) will reward you' (6.4, 6, 18). The miscellaneous wisdom teachings gathered in 6.19–7.12 show how wise and virtuous conduct can and should be part of the better righteousness pursued by the followers of Jesus.

The concluding exhortation in 7.13-27 stresses the challenge posed by the life of Christian virtue (the narrow gate and the hard road), the

---

11.   A. Malherbe, *Moral Exhortation: A Greco-Roman Sourcebook* (Philadelphia: Westminster, 1986).
12.   Mohrlang, *Matthew and Paul.*

relationship between internal character and external actions, the need for both confession of faith ('Lord, Lord') and action, and the importance of building one's life on firm foundations (such as the wisdom presented in the Sermon on the Mount). For Matthew, the Biblical and Jewish virtue of righteousness or justice is the key to the life of Christian virtue as well as what leads one to the goal of fullness of life in God's kingdom.

6. *Communal Conflicts*

As the founding apostle of the churches addressed in his letters (except Romans), Paul exercised a great deal of moral authority. Indeed, large parts of 1 Corinthians consist of Paul's responses to pastoral questions put to him by the Corinthians themselves. And in turn Paul's letters were pastoral vehicles that allowed the founding apostle to continue teaching and advising those whom he had brought to Christian faith.

Paul is most authoritative and judgemental in the case of the incestuous man (1 Cor. 5.1-5).[13] That man was living with his stepmother or father's concubine, an action forbidden by both the Jewish Law (Lev. 18.8) and Roman law. He may well have justified his action by the slogan 'All things are lawful' (6.12; 10.23) and so garnered support from some of the more 'progressive' advocates of Christian freedom at Corinth. In this case Paul rejects this reasoning and demands that the incestuous man be excommunicated, not only to spare the community further scandal but also to shock the incestuous man into recognition of his sin in the hope that 'his spirit may be saved in the day of the Lord' (5.5).

At the opposite end of the spectrum is Paul's very sensitive treatment of the communal conflict over eating food sacrificed to 'idols' in 1 Cor. 8.1–11.1 (cf. also the somewhat similar case in Rom. 14.1–15.13). The problem here is the fact that much of the meat sold in the markets had previously some connection with rituals carried out in pagan temples. For those designated as the 'strong' this practice posed no real problem and was a matter of indifference since 'no idol in the world exists' and 'there is no God but one' (8.4). On the intellectual and theological levels Paul agreed with the 'strong'. However, on the pastoral level he was sensitive to the concerns (scruples?) of the 'weak' for whom eating meat sacrificed to pagan gods seemed to be a form of participation in pagan worship, something that they had left behind with their baptism.

---

13. R. F. Collins, *First Corinthians* (SP, 7; Collegeville: Liturgical Press, 1999), pp. 205–16.

Paul's advice was that the 'strong', while intellectually and theologically correct, should nevertheless respect the conscience of the 'weak' and be careful not to be an occasion for 'scandal' (literally, a stumbling block or obstacle) to them. In the market they may buy or they may eat at someone else's home whatever is presented to them, and need not ask about the status of the meat. However, if a fellow Christian raises a question about the meat's status, then the 'strong' should refrain from eating the meat if it had been sacrificed to pagan deities and their eating might scandalize their fellow Christians.

In adjudicating communal conflicts Paul is not simply appealing to or acting upon his own moral authority as an apostle. Rather, he frequently appeals to the person or example of Christ. With regard to the problems of factions within the Corinthian Christian community Paul asks rhetorically, 'Has Christ been divided?' (1.13). With regard to Christians visiting prostitutes, he reminds them of their status as members of the body of Christ (6.15). In commenting on Christians participating in meals at pagan temples, he appeals to the significance of sharing in the Lord's Supper for Christians (10.14-22). In treating disorder in the gatherings associated with the Lord's Supper he quotes what very likely had become the liturgical 'words of institution' (11.23-26) and thus recalled the example of Jesus' life and death. In trying to put more order into the Christian assembly Paul repeatedly in chs 12 and 14 appeals to the concept of the church as the body of Christ. And in ch. 15 he is careful to ground the Christian's hope for life after death in the death and resurrection of Jesus. While in 1 Corinthians and other letters Paul often draws on his own moral authority as the founding apostle, for him and his readers the ultimate theological authority and norm was the risen Christ.

By choosing to write a Gospel, a narrative about Jesus from his birth to his death and resurrection and stressing his teachings, Matthew necessarily presented Jesus as the moral exemplar and authority *par excellence* for his community. Moreover, by arranging traditions associated with Jesus into what has been aptly described as 'Matthew's Advice to a Divided Community' in 18.1-35, the evangelist gives some insights into conflicts within his community and how he might have dealt with them.[14]

In 18.1-5 the Matthaean Jesus first of all insists on humility as a necessary virtue for all aspirants to the kingdom of Heaven and thus to the Christian community. When all regard the kingdom as a gift and receive it as children receive gifts (without pretensions to earning or

---

14. W. G. Thompson, *Matthew's Advice to a Divided Community: Mt 17,22–18,35* (AnBib, 44; Rome: Biblical Institute Press, 1970).

owning it), then they are more likely to give respect and deference to their fellow Christians.

Next, in 18.6-9 the Matthaean Jesus emphasizes with some drastic examples the importance of avoiding scandal within the community and in particular being an obstacle or stumbling block to those other Christians referred to as 'these little ones'. From the parable of the lost sheep in 18.12-14 it appears that Christians leaving the community (going 'astray') presented a real problem. Matthew has edited the parable (cf. Lk. 15.3-7) to highlight the importance of seeking after the strays in the hope of making sure that they are not lost entirely.

The procedure outlined in 18.15-20 for correcting an erring or offending member has roots in the Old Testament (Lev. 19.17; Deut. 19.15) and is paralleled in part by the Qumran *Community Rule* (1QS 5.24–6.2). The final step is excommunication (as in 1 Cor. 5.1-5). Before that, however, there must be the opportunity for correction at the individual, small group and communal levels. The Matthaean community instruction ends with a demand for practically unlimited opportunity for forgiveness (18.21-22) and a parable that links God's unlimited willingness to forgive sinners and their willingness in turn to forgive those who have offended them (18.23-35; cf. 6.12, 14-15).

Despite the differences in genre, time frame, and relation to the community (founding apostle versus evangelist), both Paul and Matthew acknowledge the reality of communal conflicts, the danger of scandal, the possibility of apostasy, the value of humility and mutual respect, the need for forgiveness and reconciliation, and the use of excommunication as a possible extreme procedure. They differ in the literary frameworks in which they operate, with Paul confronting the issues directly by letter and Matthew rooting them in the ministry of the earthly Jesus.

7. Salvation and Eschatology

In Romans especially, Paul seems to presuppose something like the modified apocalyptic dualism described with greatest clarity in the Qumran *Community Rule* (1QS 3.13–4.26). God is sovereign over all creation. In the present, however, God has allowed the world to be dominated by two spirits, the Angel of Light and the Prince of Darkness. The children of light do the deeds of light, and the children of darkness do the deeds of darkness. But in the impending divine visitation the powers of darkness will be wiped away, and the children of light will be vindicated and rewarded.

Paul is both more pessimistic and more optimistic than his Qumran contemporaries. For Paul (cf. Rom. 7.7-25), all those before and apart from Christ are under the dominion of Sin, Death and the Law (the Pauline equivalent of the Prince of Darkness). But now through Jesus' death and resurrection and the experience of the Holy Spirit (the equiv-alent of the Angel of Light), it is possible for all persons of faith to be led by Christ and his Spirit and to walk in the light (cf. Rom. 8.1-39).

One of the major aims of Paul's theology was to help believers recognize what they have become through Christ (children of God, co-heirs with Christ). In this sense Paul emphasizes realized eschatology and the presence of salvation. According to U. Schnelle, 'the eschatological presence of God's salvation in Jesus Christ is the basis and center of Pauline thought'.[15] In this regard Paul was very much the optimist.

Paul's ethical teaching is primarily concerned to challenge believers to act in ways that are consonant with their new identity in Christ. This approach is neatly summarized by the Latin dictum *agere sequitur esse* ('action follows being'). The ethical commands (the imperatives) that Paul proposes are the attitudes and actions that are in accord with and flow from the identity of those who are 'in Christ' (the indicative).[16]

Nevertheless, Paul develops his theology against the horizon of the last judgement and the future fullness of God's kingdom. He insists that on the day of the Lord 'God's righteous judgment will be revealed', and that God 'will repay according to each one's deeds' (Rom. 2.5-6).

Matthew places more emphasis on the future dimension of salvation and future eschatology than Paul does. Again, their respective literary genres are partly responsible for this difference. Paul writes explicitly in the full afterglow of Easter, whereas Matthew is writing what purports to be a narrative of Jesus' earthly life up to his death and resurrection.

Matthew summarizes the preaching of Jesus in 4.17; 'Repent, for the kingdom of Heaven has come near' (see Mk 1.15). The present or antic-ipated dimension of the kingdom is glimpsed especially in Jesus' mighty actions or miracles (11.4-5) and in the parables that stress the beginnings of the kingdom in Jesus' ministry (13.31-32, 44-46). The kingdom is enough of a present reality to suffer violence from its opponents (12.12), and Jesus' ability to cast out demons is taken as proof that 'the kingdom of God has come to you' (12.28).

Nevertheless, the thrust of Matthew's eschatology is toward the future. The various rewards promised in the beatitudes (5.3-12) are to be enjoyed in the future fullness of God's kingdom. The parables in 13.1-52 promise a far greater future than any of the kingdom's present manifestations can ever bring. The Eschatological Discourse in chs 24–25 offers a scenario for the full coming of God's kingdom comparable to what one finds in

---

15.   U. Schnelle, *Apostle Paul: His Life and Theology* (Grand Rapids: Baker Academic, 2005), p. 389.

16.   B. S. Rosner (ed.), *Understanding Paul's Ethics: Twentieth Century Approaches* (Grand Rapids: Eerdmans, 1995).

Jewish apocalypses such as Daniel, *1 Enoch*, *4 Ezra* and *2 Baruch*. Moreover, with the many parables in 24.37–25.30 it instils a constant watchfulness in the face of the certain coming of the kingdom and the uncertainty regarding the precise time of its arrival.

The last judgement plays an important role in Matthew's future eschatology. From the parables of the weeds and wheat (13.24-30, 36-43) and the dragnet (13.47-50), it is clear that 'at the end of the age' Matthew (following Jesus) expects a divine judgement in which the righteous will be vindicated and the wicked will be punished. The climax of the Eschatological Discourse is the great judgement scene in Mt. 25.31-46. With the Son of Man as judge, 'all the nations' will be assembled and either rewarded or punished on the basis of their acts of loving kindness to 'the least'. In the context of Matthew's emphasis on future eschatology and the last judgement it is easy to understand how the ethical teachings of Jesus could be taken as imperatives and viewed as necessary for one's eternal salvation.

8. *The Relationship Between Matthew and Paul*

It is possible that Paul and Matthew never crossed paths, and that they simply represent two different, parallel Christian traditions. But might there have been some more direct relationship between the two? Given the difference in dating, Paul obviously could not have used Matthew's Gospel. However, it is conceivable that Matthew's Gospel was intended as a response to Paul by promoting a more traditional, Jewish kind of Christianity with Jesus as the one and only teacher.[17] There is no clear reference to Paul (as in 2 Pet. 3.15) or allusion to his theology (see Jas 2.14-26). But then given Matthew's genre, we could hardly expect one (though Mt. 5.17-19 could be one). And if Antioch really was the place where Matthew composed his Gospel, his work might be a witness to the continuation of the controversy there about relations between Jewish Christians and Gentile Christians glimpsed in Gal. 2.11-21.

It is not impossible that Matthew wrote his Gospel to 're-judaize' the portrait of Jesus in Mark's Gospel and to counter the influence of Pauline theology. In that event, Matthew would be not merely non-Pauline but rather anti-Pauline. And texts such as Mt. 5.19 ('whoever breaks one of the least of these commandments, and teaches others to do the same, will be called least in the kingdom of Heaven') and 7.21 ('not everyone who

17. S. Byrskog, *Jesus the Only Teacher: Didactic Authority and Transmission in Ancient Israel, Ancient Judaism and the Matthean Community* (CBNTS, 24; Stockholm: Almqvist & Wiksell, 1994).

says to me, "Lord, Lord", will enter the kingdom of Heaven') could be construed as not-so-veiled criticisms of Paul and the Law-free Christian movement that he inspired.

In a series of publications, David C. Sim has argued that Matthew and Paul are neither theologically close nor even complementary but rather stand in opposition.[18] Sim contends that Mt. 5.19 was formulated by Christian Jews in response to the Law-free gospel of Paul (and others), and that these Christian Jews would have excluded outright the Law-free Pauline Christians from having any place in the kingdom of Heaven unless they changed their ways and fully observed the Mosaic Law.

Sim regards the evangelist Matthew as a Law-observant Christian Jew who advocated a Law-observant Gentile mission, and in this respect stood closer to Paul's Christian Jewish opponents in Galatia than to Paul himself. He finds cases of Matthaean anti-Paulinism not only in Mt. 5.19 but also in 5.17 ('not to abolish but to fulfil'; cf. Rom. 10.4), the instructions at the end of the Sermon on the Mount (7.13-27), the enemy mentioned in the parable of the wheat and the weeds (13.24-30, 36-43), and the promise to Peter (16.17-19) as the one who had received divine revelations and was chosen to lead the church (rather than Paul). According to Sim, Matthew was engaged 'in a bitter and sustained polemic against Paul himself'.[19] While the evidence for Sim's hypothesis may not seem totally convincing to all, at the very least he has provided a stimulus for us to rethink our largely canon-influenced tendency to harmonize Paul and Matthew.

The Jewish Christianity promoted by Matthew did not win out. The success of Christianity among Gentiles, facilitated in part by the theological and practical foundations supplied by Paul, quickly drove out the more traditional Jewish Christianity of Matthew. However, Paul did not win out either. It is doubtful that Paul would have accepted a Christianity conceived without the strong presence of Jews like himself providing the root (cf. Rom. 9–11) or as a religion different and separate from Judaism.[20] In the New Testament canon both Paul's letters and Matthew's Gospel were integrated into a larger and different entity called the 'great' or 'catholic' church in the second and third centuries.

---

18. See Sim, *Matthew and Christian Judaism*, pp. 188–211; *idem.*, 'Are the Least Included in the Kingdom of Heaven? The Meaning of Matthew 5:19', *HTS* 54 (1998), pp. 573–87; *idem.*, 'The Social Setting of the Matthean Community: New Paths for an Old Journey', *HTS* 57 (2001), pp. 268–80; *idem.*, 'Matthew's Anti-Paulinism: A Neglected Feature of Matthean Studies', *HTS* 58 (2002), pp. 767–83, and *idem.*, 'Matthew 7.21-23: Further Evidence of Its Anti-Pauline Perspective', *NTS* 53 (2007), pp. 325–43.

19. Sim, 'Matthew's Anti-Paulinism', p. 777.

20. D. J. Harrington, *Paul on the Mystery of Israel* (Collegeville: Liturgical Press, 1992).

Although Paul and Matthew differed on many matters, it is conceivable that they could have produced a joint declaration of common theological principles at the end of their discussions. But I suspect that their debates would have been much more lively and interesting than whatever their joint statement might have revealed.

2. MATTHEW AND MARK[1]

JESPER SVARTVIK

> Consult yourself, and if you find
> A powerful impulse urge your mind,
> Impartial judge within your breast
> What subject you can manage best;
> Whether your genius most inclines
> To satire, praise, or humorous lines;
> To elegies in mournful tone,
> Or prologue 'sent from hand unknown'.
> The rising with Aurora's light,
> The muse invoked, sit down to write;
> Blot out, correct, insert, refine,
> Enlarge, diminish, interline. (Jonathan Swift, 'On Poetry')

In his justly famous poem 'On Poetry' Jonathan Swift (describing himself as 'an old experienced sinner') instructs an implicit colleague (addressed as 'a young beginner') how to compose a text: 'blot out, correct, insert, refine, enlarge, diminish, interline'.[2] These seven Swiftean recommendations on how to create a text may help us understand the Matthaean redaction – or should we rather say his *re-creation*? – of the Markan narrative.[3] The overall purpose of the present volume is to draw attention to Matthaean distinctiveness by comparing it to other early Christian texts and authors; the chief concern of this chapter is to address the specific issue of the Markan-Matthaean axis.

---

1. I am most grateful for constructive comments from the two editors of the present volume, B. Repschinski and D. C. Sim. I am also indebted to two colleagues, Jan Hermanson and Göran Larsson, for reading and commenting on this article in draft.

2. See J. Swift, 'On Poetry', in P. Rogers (ed.), *The Complete Poems* (New Haven: Yale University Press, 1983), pp. 522–36 (524 = lines 87-88).

3. For a recent study on this subject, see A. M. O'Leary, *Matthew's Judaization of Mark: Examined in the Context of the Use of Sources in Graeco-Roman Antiquity* (JSNTSup, 323; London: T&T Clark International, 2006). She describes Matthew's redaction as 'far more creative and sophisticated than is often presented by scholars who comment on Matthew's modifications of his Markan source' (p. 2). It should perhaps be noted that in this study, as in most scholarly literature, the two-source hypothesis is taken for granted, i.e. it is assumed that Matthew is dependent on Mark (or a proto-Markan text) and on a second source, conventionally termed Q. For an alternative understanding of the relation between Matthew and Mark, see C. S. Mann, *Mark: A New Translation with Introduction and Commentary* (AB, 27; New York: Doubleday, 1986).

Matthew is a text whose absence in the history of Christianity cannot be imagined. Due to its prominent role in the formation of Christian theology and liturgy, however, there is a risk that we assume that the most common interpretations of the text are the only possible readings. *This study seeks to show to what extent Matthew has been read eclectically.* Whereas some parts of this text, seemingly at least, have become indispensable ingredients in Christian theological and homiletic discourse, Matthew's interpretation of other facets of the teaching of Jesus has not attracted a similar attention. The study consists of two parts. We will first ponder the significant circumstance that the writings of Matthew and Paul are more influential than are those of Mark and James. Secondly, on the basis of that observation, we will seek to identify four aspects of the Matthaean strategy when he remodelled the message of his predecessor.

1. *Matchmaking in the New Testament*

Before the particulars of Matthew are analysed, it might prove fruitful to ponder the textual and theological pluralism within the covers of the New Testament, and before taking that argument any further, we need to transcend simplifying and disobliging dichotomies. In this study, it is not a matter of either establishing historical-genetic dependence or denying the relation between various textual *corpora*. In order not to go into the certainly intriguing but in this context tangential discussion of whether and to what extent there existed 'schools' in early Christianity, the term 'circle' will be used in this study to describe the thematic-theological affinities between some of the New Testament texts.[4]

a. *The Johannine Circle*
There is an obvious linguistic and theological relationship between the Gospel of John and the Johannine epistles. Although A. D. Callahan in a recent and thought-provoking book has recently questioned the traditional chronology of the four Johannine writings, it is likely that the time-honoured chronology will also be advocated by a considerable number of scholars in the future.[5] R. E. Brown has argued that some in the Johannine circle emphasized the pre-existence motif of the Gospel Prologue to such an extent that the author of 1 John formulated the epistle's Prologue 'almost as a corrective to be read alongside the community hymn (in order)

---

4.   For this choice of word, see the title of O. Cullmann's book on the Johannine texts; *Der johanneische Kreis: Sein Platz im Spätjudentum, in der Jüngerschaft Jesu und im Urchristentum* (Tübingen: J. C. B. Mohr [Paul Siebeck], 1975). The English translation of the book was termed *The Johannine Circle* etc.

5.   A. D. Callahan, *A Love Supreme: A History of the Johannine Tradition* (Minneapolis: Fortress Press, 2005), pp. 2–3.

to prevent misinterpretation of it'.[6] In other words, Brown suggests that there exists a certain tension between the Gospel and the epistles; 'The Gospel stressed that Jesus is the *Son of God*: the Epistles stress that *Jesus* is the Son of God... It must mean that the opponents so stress the divine principle in Jesus that the earthly career of the divine principle is neglected'.[7]

It falls outside the scope of this article to discuss the precise chronological order of the Johannine texts. Suffice it here to conclude that although the careful reader may detect something of a friction between these four texts, they nevertheless all belong to one and the same theological 'circle'. A matchmaker would not hesitate to combine the Gospel of John and the three epistles.

b. *The Lukan Double Work*

Fewer, if any, scholars today would contest the theological parallels between Luke and Acts. It is most likely that the two texts were written by one person and that both texts are dedicated to another person, quite extraordinarily addressed by the author as κράτιστε ('Your Excellency'). As early as 1927, H. J. Cadbury argued that this should trigger students of the New Testament to read the two texts as 'a single continuous work. Acts is neither an appendix nor an afterthought. It is probably an integral part of the author's original plan and purpose'.[8] During the last decades of the twentieth century narrative critics fostered our understanding of how the two Lukan narratives could and should be read in the light of each other.[9] Given the distinctly Lukan nature of Acts, one rightly wonders what a Matthaean, Markan or Johannine Acts of the Apostles would look like. What would they choose, with Swift's expression, to 'blot out, correct, insert, refine, enlarge, diminish, interline'? It is quite certain that it belongs to Lukan idiosyncrasy to accentuate the importance of history and also the role of the Holy Spirit.[10] Another distinctly Lukan concern is to draw attention to the danger of relying on material goods (μαμωνᾶς, from Aramaic ממון).[11]

---

6. R. E. Brown, *The Community of the Beloved Disciple* (New York: Paulist Press, 1979), p. 97.

7. Brown, *Community of the Beloved Disciple*, pp. 111–12.

8. H. J. Cadbury, *The Making of Luke-Acts* (London: Macmillan, 1927), pp. 8–9.

9. For an extensive commentary which interprets the two Lukan texts as a unity, see R. C. Tannehill, *The Narrative Unity of Luke-Acts: A Literary Interpretation* (2 vols; Minneapolis: Fortress Press, 1994).

10. For 'A Sketch of Lukan Theology', see J. A. Fitzmyer, *The Gospel According to Luke: Introduction, Translation, and Notes* (AB, 28 and 28A; New York: Doubleday, 1981), I, pp. 143–270.

11. See Lk. 16.9, 11, 13. Cf. Mt. 6.24.

c. *Is Mark Unfolding the Beginning of the Pauline Gospel?*

But what about the oldest narrative account of the life and death of Jesus of Nazareth? Are there texts in the New Testament which are so close to Mark in terms of theological emphases that they help us understand the theological distinctiveness of the Markan narrative? The habitual answer to this question has been to rely on a Papian fragment which presents Mark as the interpreter of Peter (Μάρκος μὲν ἑρμηνευτὴς Πέτρου γενόμενος), thus locating the first Christian narrative in a Petrine frame of reference.[12] The question we need to pose is whether this actually is a good match. How well do Mark and the premier disciple go together? The answer to this question has led a growing number of scholars to doubt the traditional Papian hypothesis. They maintain that arguments in favour of a Markan-Petrine axis do not hold water. Indeed, it is difficult to understand why scholars would take Papias' statement in the second fragment as a historical fact without further discussion, while ignoring his statement in the third fragment about the fate of Judas. There Papias reports that the body of Judas after the death of Jesus had swollen to such an extent that he could not pass where a chariot could easily enter. This tale is proof enough that the information in these fragments cannot be taken as evidence without a critical discussion simply because they are old. *External* evidence outside the actual texts needs to be combined with the *internal* evidence (i.e. actual similarities between various New Testament texts). In our quest for New Testament pairs, we need better arguments than the slippery statement by Papias. It was previously mentioned that a number of scholars point to strong arguments in favour of an alternative matchmaking. They are of the opinion that Mark, as a matter of fact, should be described as *a Pauline Gospel*.

In the discussion above about the Johannine literature, the term 'circle' was used. Are there indications that Mark and Paul could have belonged to the same theological 'circle'? Once again, what is suggested here is not that the historical Paul and the author of Mark need to have been related in a historical-genetic sense, i.e. that they actually met or that Mark had access to the Pauline epistles. What is suggested, however, is that the similarities between the authentic Pauline letters and the Markan Gospel are so conspicuous that placing them together actually furthers our understanding of earliest Christianity. Whereas some students of the New Testament may think that not enough proof can be provided for identifying a Pauline theology in Mark, a number of recent scholars have argued that the similarities cry out for explanation. D. C. Sim describes Mark as 'pro-Pauline', while J. Marcus has persuasively demonstrated the correspondence between Pauline and Markan *theologiae cruces*. Similarly,

---

12. Papias, quoted in Eusebius, *H. E.* 3.39.15.

J. Painter, in a commentary on Mark, supports the Pauline-Markan theory, arguing that the Pauline mission to the nations is the social context of Mark's Gospel.[13] Since the Pauline-Markan axis is of some importance to the line of thought in this study, it might be worthwhile to ponder, albeit briefly, the arguments in favour of this thesis.

Several facts indicate that there exists a thematic correspondence between the texts of Mark and Paul. In this short essay it will suffice to mention three of them. The first is that both Paul and Mark emphasize *the importance of the cross*.[14] Indeed, it is quite impossible to remove the cross event from the Markan narrative plot without tearing it apart. Similarly, it is difficult to imagine a Pauline christology without, so to speak, 'cross-references'. A consequence of the prominence of the cross in the Markan and Pauline theologies is an astounding lack of interest in the teaching of Jesus. Mark often states *that* Jesus taught, but the reader seldom learns in *what* that teaching consists. Strictly speaking, it is only in chs 4 (about parables) and 13 (about eschatology) that the author allows the reader of his text to encounter not only the teacher but also his teaching. What R. Bultmann once stated about the Johannine Jesus is perhaps as applicable to the central character in Mark's Gospel: *the Markan protagonist is a revealer without a revelation*.[15] In short, Mark accentuates the importance of his protagonist, but prefers not to disclose his proclamation. In a similar way, Paul emphasizes the implications of the death and resurrection of Jesus rather than the teachings of Jesus. One is reminded of the other side of the spectrum of early theological responses to the message and mission of Jesus of Nazareth. Whereas the protagonist in the *Gospel of Thomas* is continuously called 'the living Jesus', his death and alleged resurrection are insignificant.[16]

---

13. D. C. Sim, *The Gospel of Matthew and Christian Judaism: The History and Social Setting of the Matthean Community* (SNTW; Edinburgh: T&T Clark, 1998), p. 198; J. Marcus, 'Mark – Interpreter of Paul', *NTS* 46 (2000), pp. 473–87, and J. Painter, *Mark's Gospel: Worlds in Conflict* (NTR; London: Routledge, 1997), pp. 4–6, 213. See also W. R. Telford, *The Theology of the Gospel of Mark* (NTT; Cambridge: Cambridge University Press, 1999), pp. 164–9; J. Svartvik, *Mark and Mission: Mk 7:1-23 in its Narrative and Historical Contexts* (CBNTS, 32; Stockholm: Almqvist & Wiksell, 2000), pp. 344–7; and J. R. Donahue and D. J. Harrington, *The Gospel of Mark* (SP, 2; Collegeville: Liturgical Press, 2002), pp. 39–40.

14. See Marcus, 'Mark – Interpreter of Paul', pp. 479–81.

15. R. Bultmann, *Theology of the New Testament. Vol. 2* (London: SCM, 1955), p. 66; He '*reveals nothing but that he is the Revealer*'. As a matter of fact, the Johannine protagonist actually reveals *more* than does the Markan central character; in John we are at least told that the Father sent him, that he came as the light, the bread of life, witness for the truth, and so on. See Bultmann, *Theology*, p. 62.

16. The name of Jesus is often contracted; see the Prologue (NHC II, 2, 32.10).

In this comparison between Paul and Mark it is also of interest and some importance that Paul is considerably less interested in the guilt question than is Mark. The two exceptions from the overall impression prove not to be relevant: (1) there are strong reasons to believe that the sudden outburst in 1 Thessalonians 2 is a deutero-Pauline gloss, and (2) good arguments suggest that the Greek sentence behind the NRSV translation 'on the night when he was betrayed' in 1 Cor. 11.23 should be translated as 'on the night when he was handed over (i.e. possibly but not necessarily by God)'.[17] I have elsewhere suggested that the difference in interests and emphases between Mark and Paul should be ascribed to the difference in genres. It is the narrative genre, emphasizing the *complot*, which has promoted the blame discourse in Christendom.[18]

Secondly, it is not difficult to discern in Mark as well as in the Pauline correspondence *a profound critique of the twelve disciples*, Peter in no way being excluded. More than three decades ago T. J. Weeden coined the unforgettable expression that

> Mark is assiduously involved in a vendetta against the disciples. He is intent on totally discrediting them. He paints them as obtuse, obdurate, recalcitrant men who at first are unperceptive of Jesus' messiahship, then oppose its style and character, and finally totally reject it. As the coup de grace, Mark closes his Gospel without rehabilitating the disciples.[19]

Mark's understanding of Jesus' parabolic language underscores this observation. The insiders (i.e. the disciples) became outsiders, and the outsiders (i.e. the minor characters) developed into insiders; part and parcel of Markan characterization is the principle that minor characters see and understand whereas the disciples do not. Narrative readings have also highlighted the omnipresence of Gentiles in the Markan text. The present writer has elsewhere suggested that Markan spatial settings, characterizations and plotting all underscore that Mark is dependent on Gentile *dramatis personae*.[20] Thus, it can be argued that *the Markan protagonist is never more himself than in relation to the Gentiles*. It is not difficult to

17. See D. E. Garland, *1 Corinthians* (BECNT; Grand Rapids: Baker Academic, 2003), pp. 545–6.

18. For further comments, see J. Svartvik, 'Forging an Incarnational Theology Two Score Years after *Nostra Aetate*', *SCJR* 1 (2005), pp. 1–13 (4–6).

19. T. J. Weeden, *Mark – Traditions in Conflict* (Philadelphia: Fortress Press, 1971), p. 50.

20. See Svartvik, *Mark and Mission*, pp. 222–305. An instructive example is Mark's geo-political and geo-theological presentation of the Sea of Galilee with a Jewish terminology in the scenes which take place on the western shore (e.g. synagogue and sabbath in 6.2), and distinctly Gentile symbols in the scenes on the eastern side of the sea (e.g. 'a great herd of swine' in 5.11, and the Decapolis in 5.20).

see that someone with such a theological position has much in common with a person who describes himself as 'the apostle to the Gentiles' (Rom. 11.13; ἐθνῶν ἀπόστολος).

Thirdly and finally, the Markan and Pauline solutions to *the problem of Christian commensality* seem to have much in common. Paul argued vehemently that Christians would remain in whatever condition they were when they were called by God (1 Cor. 7.17-24).[21] In other words, Gentiles should remain Gentiles and not adhere to Jewish *halakhah*. Hence, according to Paul, interaction between Jewish Christians and Gentile Christians was to be at the expense of the Jewish Christians, given that Jewish food laws were not applicable. In the words of J. Marcus; 'Not everyone agreed with Paul that the Law was passé for Christians – but Mark did'.[22] The present writer has elsewhere suggested that Gal. 2.1-14 testifies both that Paul did not adhere to the stipulations from Jerusalem, and that Peter's withdrawal from commensality in Antioch is best understood as a symbolic act of disapproval with the Pauline position. Furthermore, it seems reasonable to argue with H. Räisänen that Paul in Rom. 14.14 does not refer to a dominical saying. In fact, it is not only possible but also plausible that *Mk 7.1-23 draws the theological conclusions of the Pauline Gentile mission*. In short, it seems probable that Mk 7.19b ('cleansing all foods') deserves attention in relation to commensality in Pauline communities. It replicates less the teaching of the historical Jesus, and all the more the debate among Pauline Christians some 20 years later.

In order to avoid misunderstanding, it might be necessary to repeat once more that it would be a mistake to see in the foregoing paragraphs an argument in favour of a historical-genetic connection between Paul and Mark. There may well have been such an affinity – it is under all circumstances considerably more plausible than a Markan-Petrine connection à la Papias – but the texts at our disposal are too fragmentary to allow such secure conclusions. This study simply seeks (1) to recapitulate the fact that Pauline insights from missionary experiences *chronologically* precede by one or two decades the writing down of the final redaction of Mark; and (2) to establish that the Pauline and Markan texts favour the conclusion that, with the qualifications stated above, *the Gospel of Mark could and should be understood as a Pauline Gospel*. Hence, the readers of Mark knew Paul and the Pauline proclamation. When they wanted to know more about pre-Pauline times, Mark decided to write the narrative beginning of the kerygmatic Pauline Gospel. This might be the actual

---

21. For a survey of Paul and slavery, see J. Svartvik, 'How Noah, Jesus and Paul Became Captivating Figures: The Side Effects of the Canonization of Slavery Metaphors in Jewish and Christian Texts', *JGRCJ* 2 (2005), pp. 168–227.

22. Marcus, 'Mark – Interpreter of Paul', p. 486.

reason for opening his narrative with the formula ἡ ἀρχὴ τοῦ εὐαγγελίου Ἰησοῦ Χριστοῦ (Mk 1.1; 'the beginning of the Gospel of Jesus Christ'). Borrowing an expression from R. Williams, it was a matter of 'a quest for the historical church'.[23] Pauline Christians asked whether the origin of their movement was in agreement with Pauline proclamation and paraenesis. Mark answered their question affirmatively by giving them a narrative account of how it all began. Hence, in this sense it seems to be correct to state that Mark's *narrative* Gospel unfolds the beginning of Paul's *kerygmatic* gospel.

In short, it can be stated with some degree of confidence that the writings of Mark and Paul belong to a common 'circle' in early Christianity. While the epistles of Paul might be described as a pre-Markan kerygmatic articulation of the Markan narrative, the Gospel of Mark may best be described as a narrative presentation of what preceded the Pauline *kerygma*. Now, what are we to say about Matthew? Is there an עזר כנגדו ('a fitting match') for him?[24]

d. *Is James a Matthaean Epistle?*

Interestingly, it has been suggested that there is a connection – once again, thematic if not genetic – between Matthew and James. M. H. Shepherd was one of those who, several decades ago, explored the relationship between these two New Testament texts. He claimed that the series of eight 'homiletic-didactic discourses' in James are all built around – and in some cases even contain – a central *macarism* or gnomic saying.[25] Furthermore, he argued that the Matthaean parallels relate to every single section in James, and to almost every major theme.[26] One needs to remember that when James was written, Matthew was not yet regarded as scripture. The author therefore *quotes* the LXX, but only *alludes* to Matthaean tradition. This is an indication of how James regards Matthew. It is *significant* but not (yet) perceived as *scripture*. Shepherd argues that James 'avoids any parade of learning by frequent citations from his reading; yet it contains many echoes of phrases and ideas that suggest

---

23.   See R. Williams, *Why Study the Past? The Quest for the Historical Church* (London: Darton, Longman & Todd, 2005). Needless to say, this is an echo of the title of the English translation of Albert Schweitzer's critical and influential examination of *Geschichte der Leben Jesu Forschung*.

24.   Cf. Gen. 2.18.

25.   Jas 1.2-18; 1.19-27; 2.1-13; 2.14-26; 3.3-12; 3.13–4.10; 4.11-12; 4.13–5.6; 5.7-18. See M. H. Shepherd, 'The Epistle of James and the Gospel of Matthew', *JBL* 75 (1956), pp. 40–51 (41–2).

26.   See Shepherd, 'Epistle of James', p. 44; 'James knew a group of Beatitudes about the poor, the mourners, the merciful, and the afflicted, and possibly also macarisms upon the meek, the pure in heart, and the peace-makers'.

varied associations and relationships... at no point does his comprehension of the nature of Christianity contradict the Matthean Gospel'.[27] In short, the Matthaean tradition is one of James' sources, although it is not scripture in the same sense as the LXX.[28] Jesus, according to James, is rooted in the scriptures, and this is demonstrated with the help of Matthew. Hence, Matthew is 'a transcript of the tradition held in his Church concerning the life and teaching of his Lord'.[29] In this context it is especially relevant to note Shepherd's conclusion: 'every one of these discourses provide parallels to Matthew even though there is no precise quotation'.[30]

Every undergraduate student of the New Testament is acquainted with the fact that James has not had an easy time throughout history. Martin Luther's formulation from his *Vorrede auf das Neue Testament* is notorious: the epistle is 'eyn rechte stroern Epistel' ('a genuine epistle of straw').[31] The problem facing those who subscribe to a similar understanding of James is the fact that James is so strikingly similar to the Matthaean Sermon on the Mount. It is true that James does not express himself as does Paul in his theological cross-centred parts of his epistles, but does that necessarily mean that 'sie doch keyn Euangelisch art an yhr hat' ('it contains no Gospel "art"')?[32] Should not James' paraenesis be compared to Pauline paraenesis and not to Pauline theological cross-centred discussions? In short, we cannot compare some parts of some Pauline epistles with James, and then be surprised to find that James is less Pauline than some of the Pauline epistles![33] There is reason to concur with R. Bauckham; 'James is as Christological as we should expect the kind of

27. Shepherd, 'Epistle of James', pp. 40, 47.

28. This should be compared to *Barnabas*, in which Matthew is quoted as scripture with the *terminus technicus* γέγραπται ('it is written [i.e. in Scripture]'; 4.14).

29. Shepherd, 'Epistle of James', p. 48.

30. Shepherd, 'Epistle of James', p. 42. For similar conclusions, see R. Bauckham, *James: Wisdom of James, Disciple of Jesus the Sage* (NTR; London: Routledge, 1999), pp. 93, 107–8, 111.

31. M. Luther, 'Vorrede auf das Neue Testament', in D. *Martin Luthers Werke. Kritische Gesamtausgabe. Die Deutsche Bibel. 6 Band* (Weimar: Böhlaus, 1929 [1522]), pp. 2–11 (10). For further information about the prehistory and editions of the *Vorrede*, see F. Mussner, *Der Jakobusbrief* (Freiburg: Herder, 1964), pp. 42–5. For a discussion of Luther's notorious *Tischrede* on James, in which he argues that James should be thrown out of the University of Wittenberg, see R. Kugelman, *James and Jude* (NTM, 19; Dublin: Veritas, 1980), p. 7.

32. Luther, 'Vorrede auf das Neue Testament', p. 10.

33. P. W. van der Horst, 'Pseudo-Phocylides and the New Testament', ZNW 69 (1978), pp. 187–202, has argued that there is a 'spiritual affinity' between James and the *Sentences of Pseudo-Phocylides*; 'they contain many imperatives without revealing their underlying indicatives' (p. 102).

Christian literature he writes to be. We have no way of telling whether he would have been more Christological had he written a different kind of literature'.[34]

The purpose of this section of the study is to highlight the significant similarities between Matthew and James. The latter text should not be marginalized as some sort of a watered-down version of the original cross-centred kerygmatic gospel. Quite the contrary, James may represent one of the earliest layers of Christianity. R. Kugelman states that 'with the exception of the gospels, there is no other New Testament writing which rings with so many echoes of Jesus' sayings as does James'.[35] If Kugelman is correct, and we have found nothing which contradicts his statement, then readers of the New Testament should approach James with greater interest and, perhaps also in some circles, with greater respect.

In short, Matthew and James wrote texts so similar to each other in theological tenor that they could be described as a theological pair, on a par with (1) the four Johannine writings; (2) the Lukan Gospel and Acts; and (3) the texts of Mark and Paul. In other words, in terms of theology Matthew is as different from Mark as James is from Paul. These four matchmakings may help the present reader to identify and appreciate the diversity in the New Testament.

2. *Four Aspects of the Matthaean Redaction of the Gospel Tradition*

It has already been mentioned that the purpose of this study is to ponder the specific features of the Matthaean text by comparing it to its Markan predecessor. Although the synoptic problem has been part of New Testament scholarship for several hundred years, the scholarly community has only begun to appreciate the breadth of Matthew's radical revision of the pre-Matthaean gospel tradition. It is suggested here that his re-creation can be expressed with the help of four key terms: *rejudaization, reinforcement, rebuke,* and *rehabilitation.* Although all four are part and parcel of Matthaean theology, it is relevant to examine the four words in this specific sequence in order to elucidate the theological process which gave rise to the text which we know as Matthew.

a. *Rejudaization of Jesus*
Why did Matthew write his Gospel? One imperative reason seems to have been that he was of the opinion that his predecessor did not report an adequate amount of the teaching of Jesus. In the form in which Matthew

34.   Bauckham, *James*, p. 140.
35.   Kugelman, *James and Jude*, p. 9.

has been preserved, it is quite obvious that this is an important aspect; in its final chapter, Jesus commands his disciples to teach new generations of disciples everything that he has taught (28.20: τηρεῖν πάντα ὅσα ἐνετειλάμην ὑμῖν). Now if this teaching were to be based on Mark, this would create a problem since there are almost no records of what Jesus taught in the Markan account. As the Ethiopian eunuch cried 'How can I understand unless someone guides me?', the Markan readership could have exclaimed 'How can I teach what Jesus has commanded unless someone guides me?'. Hence, Matthew considered the proclamation of the Markan protagonist to be too scarce. This lack of teaching in Mark's account was an important impetus, but it was not the only reason for Matthew taking up the pen. In this study it is argued that Matthew not only regarded Mark as *insufficient* and *inadequate*, but also as *inaccurate*. Mark was, according to Matthew, clearly off the mark. The Markan presentation of the beginning of the gospel was simply not in accordance with Matthaean theological priorities. According to Matthew, the *nova lex* of Jesus did not nullify the *antiqua lex*.[36] To use Swift's recommendations, Matthew writes his Gospel not only to *insert, enlarge and refine* (as when organising his material into five speeches), but also to *blot out, diminish and correct* (as when challenging Markan antinomianism).

Thus, what is suggested is that Matthew wanted both to present the teachings of Jesus more bountifully and to express his critique of the palpable Markan antinomianism. Jonathan Swift wrote, 'Consult yourself, and if you find a powerful impulse urge your mind, impartial judge within your breast what subject you can manage best'. There is reason to believe that Matthew was led by such 'a powerful impulse' when he wrote his influential Gospel. Matthew sought to rejudaize the protagonist of Christianity.[37] He felt that Jesus of Nazareth had been stripped of his Jewishness in the Markan-Pauline interpretation of Christianity, and he wanted to present Jesus in a way that made sense to his Jewish-Christian audience. Matthew is the first known attempt to perform a *Heimholung Jesu ins Judentum*. This conclusion brings us to our next point.

b. *Reinforcement of Halakhic Observance*
Biblical passages such as the pericope on the scribe and Jesus discussing the greatest commandment in the Torah have stimulated Christians to rank

36. W. D. Davies and D. C. Allison, *A Critical and Exegetical Commentary on the Gospel according to Saint Matthew* (ICC; 3 vols; Edinburgh: T&T Clark, 1988, 1991, 1997), III, p. 686.
37. O'Leary, *Matthew's Judaization of Mark*, p. 118 n. 1, defines Matthaean judaization as 'the literary process by which Matthew, in rewriting Mark, increases the density of explicit and implicit references to Judaism and OT Scripture'. In this study it is suggested that Matthew's judaization should be described not only as such an increase, but also as a *decrease* of Markan antinomianism.

the commandments.[38] Speaking from a general point of view, Jewish tradition cannot be said to have encouraged such ranking, one important reason probably being that Jews have been suspicious of Christian attempts to convince them that there is a fundamental difference between 'ritual' commandments (which, according to most Christians are superseded *post Christum*) and 'moral' commandments (which are eternally engraved on the tablets of the Law). As the student of Rabbinic *corpora* well knows, however, there are several texts which do tend to rank the commandments, i.e. the discussion on what commandments (מצוות) Jews are allowed to breach if life is at stake (פיקוח נפש). According to *halakhah*, Jews are even *required* to infringe 610 of the 613 commandments in order to save life. Jews are never allowed, however, to violate the three remaining commandments – murder, idolatry and forbidden sexual relations (e.g. incest).[39]

These three commandments have two things in common: they are all negative ('thou shalt not...') and they are discussed in extreme situations such as פיקוח נפש. Another approach would be to explore religious behaviour in everyday life. In that context three other commandments are often singled out, the circumcision of boy children on the eighth day, the sanctification of the seventh day of the week and the food laws.[40]

The purpose now is to explore how Matthew develops the texts which discuss these three important parts of Jewish *praxis*.[41] The first of these, circumcision, is not discussed at all in the canonical Gospels.[42] It is significant that it was not until the Pauline mission to the Gentiles that this question needed to be explored by Christians. The Gospels, even the antinomian Markan account, are all silent. This raises the intriguing question why circumcision, playing as it does such an important role in Pauline discourse, is virtually absent from the canonical Gospels. As a matter of fact, circumcision is mentioned only thrice in the New Testament Gospels, and all these instances actually *affirm* the validity of circumcision. Luke recounts the circumcisions of John the Baptist and Jesus, and John mentions circumcision as a premise in a קל וחמר discussion.[43] How is

38.   Mt. 22.34-40 and Mk 12.28-31.
39.   The Biblical basis for פיקוח נפש is Lev. 18.5. For Talmudic discussions of the interpretations and implementations, see *b. Yoma* 83a–84b and *b. Sanh.* 74a-b.
40.   See J. D. G. Dunn, *The Partings of the Ways Between Christianity and Judaism and their Significance for the Character of Christianity* (London: SCM, 1991), pp. 28–31.
41.   For extensive presentations of Matthean *halakhah*, see A. J. Saldarini, *Matthew's Christian-Jewish Community* (CSHJ; Chicago: University of Chicago Press, 1994), pp. 124–64, and Sim, *Matthew and Christian Judaism*, pp. 19–27. See also Svartvik, *Mark and Mission*, pp. 116–17.
42.   See, however, *Gos. Thom.* 53.
43.   See Lk. 1.59; 2.21, and Jn 7.22-23.

this fact to be interpreted? J. J. Collins is in all likelihood right when he argues that Paul, before his calling on the way to Damascus, 'probably was at the stricter end of the spectrum in terms of the importance he attached to circumcision. After his circumcision he continued to attach greater importance to it than did many Jews of the Diaspora, but for largely negative reasons'.[44] Collins' historical reconstruction explains the discrepancy between the Gospels and the Pauline Epistles. While the 'pre-Christian Paul' (an admittedly anachronistic term used to describe his life-transforming experience on the way to Damascus) argued *in favour of* circumcision to a higher degree than did most contemporary Jews, the 'Christian Paul' (once again, anachronistically speaking) *downplayed* the importance of circumcision more than did most Jews of that period.

The epistles which constitute the *corpus paulinum* give vent to questions which arose in the Gentile mission; circumcision was one of the hotly debated issues. The *Sitz im Leben Jesu* described in the Gospels was different. Admittedly, some of the minor characters in the Gospels are Gentiles, but the narrative setting is firmly Jewish, and in such a setting circumcision need not be argued for or against – it is part and parcel of the religious discourse to such a degree that the Johannine Jesus even takes it for granted in a *halakhic* discussion about whether it is permissible to heal a person on the sabbath.[45]

The second pillar, the commandment to observe the sabbath, is referred to in the Gospels.[46] One could say that Matthew here applies Swift's seventh suggestion, i.e. to *interline*.[47] Whereas the Markan Jesus urges his followers to pray that they need not flee to the mountains *in the winter* (13.18, χειμῶνος), the Matthaean protagonist says; 'Pray that your flight might not be in winter *or on a sabbath*' (Mt. 24.20, μηδὲ σαββάτῳ, emphasis added). W. D. Davies and D. C. Allison give five possible expla-

---

44. J. J. Collins, 'A Symbol of Otherness: Circumcision and Salvation in the First Century', in J. Neusner and E. S. Frerichs (eds), *'To See Ourselves as Others See Us': Christians, Jews, 'Others' in Late Antiquity* (SPSH; Chico: Scholars Press, 1985), pp. 163–86 (186).

45. It should perhaps be pointed out that Luke takes great pains to underline that the Pauline Gentile mission did not imply that Jews should forsake Jewish *halakhah* (e.g. Acts 21.24). Needless to say, this is a distinctly Lukan portrayal of Paul, but it is nevertheless confirmed by Paul's own letters, arguably most explicitly in 1 Cor. 7.18; 'Was anyone at the time of his call already circumcised? Let him not seek to remove the marks of circumcision' (μὴ ἐπισπάσθω).

46. Mt. 12.1-12; 24.20; 28.1; Mk 1.21; 2.23-28; 3.2-4; 6.2; 15.42; 16.1; Lk. 4.16, 31; 6.1-9; 13.10-16; 14.1-5; 23.54-56; Jn 5.9-18; 7.22-23; 9.14, 16, 31.

47. Swift defines 'interline' as 'to write or insert between lines already written or printed, as for correction or addition; to write or print something between the lines of; as, to interline a page or a book', see *Webster's Revised Unabridged Dictionary*, *s.v.* http://machaut.uchicago.edu/CGI-BIN/WEBSTER.page.sh?page=777.

nations to the Matthean interlining, and correctly draw the conclusion that the most probable of these five suggestions is that the 'members of Matthew's community still observed the Sabbath; and, given the traditional travel restrictions, they would be both hesitant and unprepared for flight on the day of rest'.[48] They base this conclusion on the conviction that 'in Matthew the Sabbath remains in force'.[49]

We come now to the third pillar, the food laws. Matthew's creative skill comes to the fore in his fifteenth chapter.[50] The Matthaean disciples ask Jesus whether he knew that the Pharisees took great offence at what he said, which gives the Matthaean Jesus opportunity to condemn the Pharisees for being blind guides (see further below). This adaptation gives vent to characteristic Matthaean anti-Pharisaism. Furthermore, by replacing the Markan general and rather inexact wording (Mk 7.15, τὰ ἐκ τοῦ ἀνθρώπου ἐκπορευόμενα) with a more specific statement (Mt. 15.11, τὸ ἐκπορευόμενα ἐκ τοῦ στόματος), Matthew is more precise. Furthermore, he is more in line with developing Rabbinic theology on the peril of evil speech (לשון הרע) and the writings of the Church Fathers.[51] As a result of the Matthaean elaboration of the Markan narrative, it is more difficult to perceive the relation between Mt. 15.1-20 and the literary context (i.e. the bread miracles, the walking on the water and the healings). But it is all the more easy to see the connection with the quotation from Isaiah (cf. χεῖλός, στόμα, and καρδία). Furthermore, the above-mentioned clarification of the statement wards off the alternative understanding that it referred to excrement (i.e. what goes out of a person into the sewer).[52] By clarifying with the word στόμα, Matthew limits the focus to *food*, but avoids the Markan conclusion of a Jesus declaring *all* foods clean. In sum, Matthew has recast the Markan pericope in such a way that the antinomian Markan flavour can no longer be detected. He has managed to rewrite the Gospel tradition to such an extent that the

---

48.   Davies and Allison, *Matthew*, III, p. 349.

49.   Davies and Allison, *Matthew*, III, p. 350.

50.   This has been pointed out by Sim, *Matthew and Christian Judaism*, pp. 132–5, and B. Repschinski, *The Controversy Stories in the Gospel of Matthew: Their Redaction, Form and Relevance for the Relationship Between the Matthean Community and Formative Judaism* (FRLANT, 189; Göttingen: Vandenhoeck & Ruprecht, 2000), pp. 154–66.

51.   For more information about the Rabbinic *terminus technichus* לשון הרע, see J. Svartvik, 'The Markan Interpretation of the Pentateuchal Food Laws', in T. R. Hatina (ed.), *Biblical Interpretation in Early Christian Gospels, Vol. 1: The Gospel of Mark* (JSNTSup, 304; London: T&T Clark International, 2006), pp. 169–81 (178–80). For a survey of all the tannaitic and also of the most relevant amoraic texts, see Svartvik, *Mark and Mission*, pp. 375–402.

52.   It is true that ἀφεδρῶν ('sewer') is mentioned in Mt. 15.17, but it is marginalized by the expression ἐκ τοῦ στόματος.

Markan upheaval of the food laws (Mk 7.19, 'cleansing all foods') is trans-formed into an inner-*halakhic* discussion on how to apply the regulations in terms of the washing of hands before meals (Mt. 15.20, 'but to eat with unwashed hands does not defile'). As astonishing as it may seem, the factual result of the Matthaean recasting of the Markan pericope is that it actually stresses the *validity* of the scriptural commandments, and this is congenial to the spirit of Matthew; after all, his protagonist came 'not to destroy, but to fulfil'.[53] It is no longer *Biblical* food laws which are called into question, but *Pharisaic* interpretations of the purity laws, which is something completely different. The Matthaean Jesus takes part in the ongoing discussion of the extension and application of the devel-oping *halakhah* by using a *mashal* stating that eating with unwashed hands does not render humans impure. Arguably, Matthew would be quite surprised to hear his readers assessing that his protagonist sought to extirpate a greater part of contemporary *halakhah*. Part of the problem should be ascribed to the fact that some members of the scholarly community have not taken into account that the practice of declaring something clean was not unknown to the theological context out of which Matthew grew. Indeed, one of the most important tasks for subse-quent generations of Rabbis in the Land as well as in the Diaspora was to do exactly that, i.e. to decide whether things were pure or impure, or whether actions were permitted or not.[54]

It is not Biblical food laws, but Pharisaic traditions and interpreta-tions, which are called into question. In short, *Markan antinomianism has been transformed into Matthaean anti-Pharisaism.* This brings us to the next part of this description of the Matthaean redaction.

c. *Rebuking the Pharisees*
The word ὑποκριτής occurs 17 times in the New Testament, 13 of which can be found in Matthew.[55] Some of these instances can be traced to pre-Matthean sources, either to Mark[56] or to Q[57], but the majority of them stem from the Matthaean redaction of his sources. Six of them are found in stereotypical formulae in the Matthaean denouncing of the scribes and Pharisees (οὐαὶ δὲ ὑμῖν, γραμματεῖς καὶ φαρισαῖοι ὑποκριταί).[58]

---

53. Mt. 5.17.
54. The most illustrous example is *b. B.M.* 59a.
55. Mt. 6.2, 5, 16; 7.5; 15.7; 22.18; 23.13, 15, 23, 25, 27, 29; 24.51; Mk 7.6; Lk. 6.42; 12.56; 13.15. Cf. *Gos. Thom.* 39 and its *Vorlage* in p. Oxy 655 ii.11-23.
56. Mt. 15.7; cf. Mk 7.6.
57. Mt. 7.5; cf. Lk. 6.42.
58. All occurrences in the Matthaean *vae scribes et pharisaeis* (23.13, 15, 23, 25, 27, 29).

The three instances in ch. 6 also elucidate that the word is being used to rebuke a religious group which, according to Matthew, did not come up to standard in terms of almsgiving, prayer and fasting.[59] In short, Matthew accuses the 'scribes and Pharisees' of being deceitful and duplicitous. While reinforcing the Torah-centric teaching of the historical Jesus (as was seen in the previous section), Matthew takes the anti-Pharisaic discourse to vertiginous heights never reached in previous Christian literature.[60] We will return to this observation in the concluding remarks, but it can be mentioned here as well, albeit in passing, that there is a lesson in this: *the rejudaization of early Christianity need not necessarily result in a more broad-minded presentation of Jesus' theological context (i.e. Judaism), either in antiquity or in modern times.*

The reader of Mk 12.28-34 looks in vain for hostility against the scribe. Whereas, according to Mark, scribes *en masse* are devious, this scribe as an individual is 'not far from the kingdom of God' (v. 34; οὐ μακρὰν ἀπὸ τῆς βασιλείας τοῦ θεοῦ). Or to put it in a Clermont-Tonnerrean way, Mark's opinion seems to have been *to the scribes as a party nothing, to the scribe as an individual everything.*[61] This Markan character did not survive the transfer from Mark to Matthew; the friendly scribe is transformed into a Matthaean testing Pharisee. Matthew converted him into an insidious Pharisee, simply wanting to test Jesus (πειράζων αὐτόν).[62] The elusive Markan scribe who is commended by Jesus for his religious insights is depicted by Matthew as yet another cartoonish antagonist, a Forsterean 'flat character'.[63] This metamorphosis is hardly an editorial gaffe; it is an example of Matthew's zeal to rebuke the Pharisees.

A second example will demonstrate the importance of polemical discourse to the Matthaean narrative. Logion 26 in the *Gospel of Thomas* could, and should, be understood as a non-polemical advice to someone who is willing to help another person; 'When you take the beam out of your own eye, then you will see clearly to take the speck out of your brother's eye'. It is, so to speak, an ophthalmological handbook to a

59.   Mt. 6.2, 5, 16.

60.   Needless to say, the assertion that the anti-Pharisaic discourse plays an important role in Matthew is not new. For important studies, see Saldarini, *Matthew's Christian-Jewish Community*, pp. 44–67; J. A. Overman, *Church and Community in Crisis: The Gospel according to Matthew* (TNTIC; Valley Forge: Trinity Press International, 1996), pp. 12–16, and, extensively and exhaustively, Repschinski, *Controversy Stories in the Gospel of Matthew*.

61.   For further comments, see Svartvik, *Mark and Mission*, pp. 275–7.

62.   Sim, *Matthew and Christian Judaism*, p. 128, also emphasizes the shift from the Markan 'interested and open-minded inquirer' to the Matthaean 'hostile Pharisee'.

63.   See E. M. Forster, *Aspects of the Novel* (London: Penguin, 1990), p. 170; 'A flat character can always be recognized by the reader whenever it reappears'. See also pp. 73–7.

person who heeds Jesus' exhortation in the preceding logion; 'Love your brother like your own soul, protect him like the pupil of your eye'. By inserting a single word (ὑποκριτά in Mt. 7.5), Matthew has changed the genre of the saying. Thomas' ophthalmological instruction manual on how to help one's beloved brother has been changed into a critique of hypocritical behaviour. Nothing in logia 25-26 suggests that polemics is its original genre. Given the growing rivalry between Pharisees and Nazarenes – or, anachronistically speaking, between 'Jews' and Christians', as the members of the two movements later would be known – it seems reasonable to assume that the non-polemical version is older than the polemical one.[64] Hence, the logion in the *Gospel of Thomas* reflects an earlier stage; Matthew has clearly added a polemical element to the saying.

The reader of Matthew should not take the radicalism of his critique of the Pharisaic movement lightly. As can be seen in his fifteenth chapter, Matthew argued that the Pharisees should be compared to weeds deserving to be destroyed; 'Every plant that my heavenly Father has not planted will be uprooted. Let them alone; they are blind guides of the blind. And if one blind person guides another, both will fall into a pit'.[65]

These three examples disclose the duality in Matthaean theology. On the one hand, the Matthaean protagonist urges his followers to be *meticulous in their halakhic observance*. In 23.2 he goes as far as to instruct the crowds and disciples to do whatever the Pharisees teach them, and in the concluding commission of the disciples in Mt. 28.20, he urges them to teach new generations of disciples to obey everything that he has commanded them. Hence, Matthew's theology is profoundly *halakhic*. On the other hand, Matthew presents a protagonist who is distinctly *anti-Pharisaic in his theology*. This is quite obvious to the reader of ch. 23, but it is also apparent to those who carefully compare the Matthaean text *in toto* with its pre-Matthaean sources.

d. *Rehabilitation of Peter*
One of the most remarkable facets of the Matthaean account is the unwavering rehabilitation of some of the most important characters in the Markan narrative. Jesus' family members are presented more favourably

---

64. For arguments in favour of this conclusion, see S. J. Patterson, *The Gospel of Thomas and Jesus* (Sonoma: Polebridge, 1993), pp. 29–31. For an illuminating examination of the relation between p.Oxy. 655, Q, the *Gospel of Thomas*, Matthew and Luke, see J. M. Robinson and C. Heil, 'The Lilies of the Field: Saying 36 of the *Gospel of Thomas* and Secondary Accretions in Q 12.22b-31', *NTS* 47 (2001), pp. 1–25.

65. Mt. 15.13-14. The expression τυφλοί ... ὁδηγοί ('blind guides') also occurs in Mt. 23.16, 24.

by Matthew than by Mark, and the disciples are not criticized to the same degree as in Mark. The *primus inter pares*, Peter, can thank Matthew for being rescued from the Markan vendetta against him and his fellow disciples. In Matthew's account Peter is Πέτρος, the Rock on which the ἐκκλησία will be built. He is appointed the exclusive leader of the church. This is quite an extraordinary rehabilitation: Matthew is Peter's *Rehabiliterungsschrift*. One can hardly imagine the consequences for Christendom had Mark rather than Matthew been the more influential of the two evangelists in shaping the contours of Peter as a *persona dramatis* in the Christian master story. Matthew forged Peter as the foremost disciple of Jesus. Matthew's importance for the development of Christian high ecclesiology cannot be overestimated; it is quite similar to Luke's significance for subsequent mariology and John's for high christology.

In this section we will examine Matthew's *impetus* for this remarkable rehabilitation of Peter.[66] In the words of Edgar Lee Masters, 'how did you, Peter... worthy of blame, arise to this fame?'[67] It is suggested that we will only find the reason for Matthew's rehabilitation of Peter (1) if he is not isolated from the rest of the disciples; (2) if Matthew's understanding of the ἐκκλησία is considered; and (3) if the magnitude of Matthaean anti-Pharisaism is measured.

It is obvious that the disciples in the Matthaean account are portrayed more favourably than in the Markan narrative. They may not understand everything Jesus has to tell them, but at least they show a willingness and ability to take his teaching into consideration. In the words of D. Senior, 'Matthew does not idealise the disciples; they are still capable of failure, but much more evidently than in Mark, the disciples are able to penetrate the mystery of Jesus' identity'.[68] Scholars have for a long time recognized Mark's hidden agenda when portraying the disciples as failing and, thus, as failed followers of Jesus. In this study we need not go into the discussion whether Mark wanted his readers to *associate* themselves with the Twelve ('they too were fallible followers!') or to *dissociate* themselves from them ('I can do better!').[69] The question which needs to be posed, however, is to what extent also the Matthaean presentation is ideological by nature. The student of the New Testament might spontaneously assume that Matthew rehabilitates the disciples either because that is how they *eigentlich* were or because he pitied them.

---

66. For a thorough survey, see Sim, *Matthew and Christian Judaism*, pp. 188–99.

67. E. L. Masters, 'Simon Surnamed Peter', quoted in R. Bartel, J. S. Ackerman and T. S. Watson (eds), *Biblical Images in Literature* (Nashville: Abingdon, 1975), pp. 289–91 (289).

68. D. Senior, *What Are They Saying About Matthew?* (New York: Paulist Press, rev. edn, 1996), p. 92.

69. See Svartvik, *Mark and Mission*, pp. 270–4. Nor do we address the issue of to what extent the characterization should be understood as being determined by text-external (i.e.

In his classical essay first published as early as 1928, E. von Dobschütz presented arguments in favour of the conclusion that Matthew was a Jewish Christian who had undergone a Rabbinic schooling. This 'converted Jewish Rabbi' installs Peter as the 'Christian chief Rabbi' with the authority to bind and loose.[70] The expression 'bind and loose' should not be understood in relation to the institution of confession, but all the more as the inauguration of Peter as the *halakhic* authority to declare valid and void, to put a fence around the Torah (לעשות סיג לתורה), and to be the true interpreter of the scriptures (*ut supra* on Matthean *halakhah*).[71] Matthew's motivation to plead for a cessation of Markan hostilities against the disciples is that he needs Simon Bar Jona, Πέτρος, as the *primus inter pares*, as his chief Rabbi. Thus, the most reasonable explanation for the Matthaean rehabilitation of Peter is that *Matthew, with his anti-Pharisaic message, could not afford Peter to be a religious leader 'worthy of blame'*. Peter was rehabilitated because Matthew needed him to be a more convincing character than were the Pharisees. In other words, Matthew's Swiftean strategy – to blot out, correct, insert, refine, enlarge, diminish and interline – can be detected in the *depreciation* of the Pharisees as well as in the *appreciation* of Peter.

3. *How Odd to Choose Matthaean Polemics but to Spurn His Theology!*

This study consists of two main parts. In the first part a matchmaking was suggested which combines similar texts. A minority of Biblical scholars would question that the four Johannine texts belong to a common 'circle'. Few would call into question that Luke and Acts together form a narrative entity. A number of students of the New Testament, including the present writer, argue that there is a Markan-Pauline axis. It has also been maintained that Matthew and James are so similar to each other that they deserve to be understood as part of a common 'circle'. Hence, according to this line of thought the Gospels of Matthew and Mark are as dissimilar as are the epistles of James and Paul.

---

this is what really happened) or text-internal factors (i.e. the agenda of identification and/or repudiation).

70. E. von Dobschütz, 'Matthew as Rabbi and Catechist', in G. N. Stanton (ed.), *The Interpretation of Matthew* (IRT, 3; London: SPCK, 1983), pp. 27–38 (32, 33). This is not the context to address the anachronistic problems which his expression provokes. A number of scholars would hesitate to use the expressions 'converted' (as if Judaism and Christianity at that time were understood as separate religions, from which and to which one could convert) and 'Rabbi' (as if nomenclature which was established only later in history were applicable to first-century Judaism).

The second part specified some of the features of the Matthaean narrative, especially as it was compared to its Markan predecessor. It was suggested that the Swiftean seven recommendations to a writer with 'a powerful impulse' can help us appreciate the extent of the Matthaean re-reading and re-making of Mark.

Assuming that Matthew was written around year 80 CE – in the present context it is not necessary to fix with more precision the time for its composition – some 50 years had passed since the death of Jesus. During that momentous half-century, in the mind of the majority of his followers (and that is what has a bearing in this analysis), Jesus had already been detached from his historical and theological contexts. Influential theological texts, such as the kerygmatic Pauline epistles and the narrative Markan Gospel, were already written, spread, read, studied and sermonized. Whatever Paul and Mark wanted to say about the Jewishness of Jesus, the result was not one that encouraged his followers to appreciate Jesus in his contemporary setting. If Jesus ever were a 'marginal Jew', as suggested by J. P. Meier, or a 'Mediterranean Jewish peasant', as J. D. Crossan describes him, this was certainly no longer what his followers thought of him.[72]

It is only when we understand the historical and theological contexts of Christianity at the time of Matthew's writing his narrative presentation of the mission and passion of Jesus, that we comprehend the radicalism of Matthew's rejudaization of Jesus. In the history of interpretation, his Gospel has sometimes been presented as a concession to influential judaizing Christians. Few presentations of earliest Christianity could be more wrong. Matthew did not follow the tide; he actually went *against* the current. The veracity in this statement can be seen in the fact that even parts of Matthew's *Heimholung Jesu in das jüdische Volk* was anachronistic. The conflict between what would eventually be called 'Judaism' and 'Christianity' was at the time of his composing the Gospel so ferocious that he thought that the vitriolic and vicious anti-Pharisaic discourse was original.

A growing number of Biblical scholars admit that Matthew is right when he situates Jesus firmly in his historical and theological contexts as a

---

71. See *m. Avot* 1.1.

72. For these examples, see W. A. Meeks, *Jesus is the Question* (Louisville: Westminster John Knox, 2006), p. 39. On the other hand, one must not forget that when reading the Gospels diachronically an even older image emerges. See T. W. Manson, *The Teaching of Jesus: Studies of its Form and Content* (Cambridge: Cambridge University Press, 2nd edn, 1948), p. 101; 'We are so accustomed... to make Jesus the object of religion that we become apt to forget that in our earliest records he is portrayed not as the object of religion but as a religious man'.

Torah-observing Jew living during the late Second Temple period.[73] The question is whether students of the Bible have sharp enough perceptions to identify the anti-Pharisaic outbursts in Matthew as evidence not of the earliest stratum of Christianity, but as an imprint of the rising hostilities between those we today know as 'Jews' and 'Christians', as much an imprint of the circumstances and perspectives of the author as are the infamous Johannine Ἰουδαῖοι.

It is suggested here that it actually was the *rejudaization* of Jesus which increased Matthew's anti-Pharisaism. This process is not unlike the fate of the various quests for the historical Jesus during the last two centuries. These quests have often led scholars to assume rather than argue for the historical uniqueness of the teaching of Jesus. But there are no imperative reasons that Jesus' teaching *in toto* was anti-contextual.[74] As it is time to summarize and evaluate what has been discussed in this article, one is easily reminded of a famous couplet.

How odd of God, to choose the Jews!
But odder still of those
who chose a Jewish God
but spurn the Jews![75]

In a similar vein, one would like to exclaim; *how odd of Matthew to rewrite Mark's narrative, but odder still of those who chose the Gospel of Matthew, yet spurn the epistle of James*. If nothing else, this discrepancy plainly shows that Matthew has not always been read on its own terms.[76]

In this study it has been argued that the theological differences between the Gospels of Matthew and Mark are as inherent as those between the epistles of Paul and James. Whereas readers of the New Testament early on recognized the theological tension between Paul and James (and in addition took sides when they in their historiography decided to favour Paul over James), the friction between Matthew and Mark has hitherto

73. See, for example, the study of Matthew and Jesus of Nazareth by David C. Sim in this volume.

74. For a study devoted to the problems which such an approach creates, see J. Svartvik, 'The Quest of the Unique Jesus and Its Implications for Global Interreligious Dialogue', in W. Jeanrond and A. Lande (eds), *The Concept of God in Global Dialogue* (Maryknoll: Orbis, 2005), pp. 126–44.

75. The tradition history of this couplet is intriguing, but fortunately of minor importance in this study. It has been attributed to Ronald Knox (*in toto*), Frederic Ogden Nash (*in toto*), William Norman Ewer (former half), Cecile Browne (latter half), and so on. Since the authorship is disputed, there is no one established version of the couplet. It is quoted above as it appears in H. Ucko, *Common Roots, New Horizons: Learning about Christian Faith from Dialogue with Jews* (Geneva: WCC, 1994), p. 1.

76. For a similar conclusion, see Sim, *Matthew and Christian Judaism*, p. 302.

not been recognized to a similar extent.[77] Why have students of the New Testament not been as willing, perhaps not even been able, to identify the differences between the Gospels of Matthew and Mark? After all, as this study has sought to demonstrate, these differences are no less significant than are those between the epistles of Paul and James. One answer to that question is that they have not been recognized because both Matthew and Mark proved to be indispensable in the remarkable reception history of the Gospels; since Christians combined *Markan antinomianism* and *Matthean anti-Pharisaism*, they did not need to separate the texts from each other. Another reason is that people in the pew, the ecclesial pulpit and the scholarly podium have normally read the Gospels in order to learn more about *the authors' protagonist*. It is quite exceptional for readers of the Gospels to be interested in *the perspectives of the authors*, and therefore to seek to isolate the narratives from each other in order to appreciate their literary and theological distinctiveness. The narratives have simply been understood and treated as windowpanes with a view over the life and teaching of Jesus of Nazareth. It is only when they are read on their own terms that their idiosyncrasies are recognized, appreciated and celebrated.

This article provokes a second paraphrase of the couplet; *how odd to choose Matthew's anti-Pharisaic polemics, but to spurn his scriptural interpretation* (which was the very cause of his polemical discourse). It was mentioned above that there is a lesson to be learnt here. Christian groups which seek to rejudaize the message and mission of Jesus, as did Matthew long before our time, do not necessarily end up portraying Second Temple Judaism in a more positive way. Indeed, in the history of Jewish/Christian relations these groups have more than occasionally given vent to anti-Jewish theology.[78] They seem to think that since they are offering the Gospel as a *kosher* stew, it will be accepted by the Jewish people. When this does not happen, their now rejected love for the Jewish people sometimes turns into contempt. The fact that readers of the New Testament have tended to favour Matthaean polemics over his theology also says something about a general tendency. It is far more common to absorb polemical and easily won finger-pointing, a *tua culpa* theology if you like, than to see that Matthew's Gospel actually *challenges* the vast majority of Christianity. The Christian tradition has more often than not failed to reflect on the relation between the *nova lex* and the *antiqua lex*, between what Jews and Christians believe God had already revealed and what Christians believe God has manifested through Jesus of Nazareth.

---

77. There are exceptions; see Sim, *Matthew and Christian Judaism*, pp. 188–96.

78. See J. Rousmaniere, *A Bridge to Dialogue: The Story of Jewish-Christian Relations* (New York: Paulist Press, 1991).

Matthew was arguably the very first Christian seeking to rejudaize Jesus of Nazareth. Throughout two millennia, and undeniably most intensively during the last half-century, many students of the Bible have followed in his footsteps. Although he was successful in many respects, we must not forget who paid the price for his endeavour: the Pharisees, the proto-Rabbis and the Founding Fathers of those we know as the Jewish people, those whom Jesus knew as his own.

3. MATTHEW AND LUKE

BORIS REPSCHINSKI SJ

1. *Introduction*

The Gospel of Matthew has often been taken as a document that illustrates the difficult parting of the ways between Judaism and the Christian communities emerging from it into a Gentile world.[1] There certainly is a lot of evidence to suggest that the Gospel of Matthew is indeed a document reflecting quite grave differences with at least some strands of the Judaism it encountered. Even if the Gospel does not contain uncontested evidence that the break with Judaism is already a fact, it certainly looms large on the horizon. But there is also another parting that seems at least alluded to, if not present as distinctly as the conflict with Judaism. It is the conflict between the kind of Jewish Christianity proposed by Matthew and the Gentile Christianity in a Pauline tradition which abandons circumcision and the strict observance of the Law. Matthew's Gospel is written at a point in time where the evangelist can look back on the rich theology offered by its Jewish origin. However, he also looks into a future of a church that is inexorably becoming Gentile. Thus it is quite proper to speak of a parting of the ways that affected various traditions in the early church.[2] Matthew may have regretted this development, but the subsequent history of the Gospel and its prominent use among Gentiles like Ignatius of Antioch show that he could not stop this development. At about the same time as Matthew, the author of Luke-Acts faced a similar situation. From both the Gospel and the Acts it is quite obvious that Luke knew about a somewhat painful relationship between Jewish traditions

---

1.   G. N. Stanton, 'Matthew's Christology and the Parting of the Ways', in J. D. G. Dunn (ed.), *The Parting of the Ways A.D. 70 to 135* (WUNT, 66; Tübingen: Mohr Siebeck, 1992), pp. 99–116. For a history and a critique of this concept, see A. H. Becker and A. Y. Reed (eds), *The Ways That Never Parted: Jews and Christians in Late Antiquity and the Early Middle Ages* (TSAJ, 95; Tübingen: Mohr Siebeck, 2003).

2.   'To the abiding impoverishment of the church, the Jewish and Gentile sections of the church were going their separate ways by the turn of the century'. W. D. Davies and D. C. Allison, *A Critical and Exegetical Commentary on the Gospel according to Saint Matthew* (ICC; 3 vols; Edinburgh: T&T Clark, 1988, 1991, 1997), III, p. 722.

and the Gentile future of the greater Church. The aim of this study is, therefore, to look at the different strategies of both authors in dealing with the advent of Gentiles in their Christian communities with their Jewish heritage. This will include first and foremost a look at the approach to the Gentile mission, taking up from there issues like the observance of the Law, salvation and christology.

2. *The Gentile Mission in Matthew*

Looking at the Gospel of Matthew one cannot be but impressed by the enormous influence of Mt. 28.16-20 over Matthew's interpreters. Perhaps this was most poignantly expressed by O. Michel when he took the command of the risen Jesus to the universal mission as the key to the Gospel and went on to state, 'Seit der Erhöhung Jesu Christi fällt die Scheidewand des Gesetzes hin, wird das Evangelium zur Botschaft für "alle Völker", d. h. für alle Menschen, ohne Rücksicht auf die Gesetzesfrage'.[3] Michel is basically repeating what still seems the consensus among scholars, namely that the Gospel exhibits a positive attitude towards the Gentiles and that it consequently embraced the Gentile mission without reservations. It has even been suggested that the commission to the Gentile mission concludes the mission to Israel, so that the Jews are no longer included in πάντα τὰ ἔθνη of Mt. 28.19.[4] Still, the mission to the Gentiles comes as something of a surprise after the Gospel was concerned to portray the mission of Jesus as one to the lost sheep of the house of Israel (Mt. 15.24).[5] Such a view usually appeals to the seemingly unqualified positive appearance of the Gentiles in the Gospel.[6] There are references to Abraham as the father of all nations, to the women in the genealogy, to the appearance of the magi, to the two fulfilment quotations in Mt. 4.15 and 12.18, to the centurion and his admirable faith surpassing that of all Israel (Mt. 8.5-13), to Jesus' visit to Gadara (Mt. 8.28-34) or Tyre and

---

3.   O. Michel, 'Der Abschluß des Matthäusevangeliums', *EvT* 10 (1950), pp. 16–26 (26). Michel goes on to place the final redaction of the Gospel squarely within Gentile Christianity.

4.   See D. R. A. Hare and D. J. Harrington, '"Make Disciples of All the Gentiles" (Mt 28:19)', *CBQ* 37 (1975), 359–69 and D. J. Harrington, *The Gospel of Matthew* (SP, 1; Collegeville: Liturgical Press, 1991), p. 416.

5.   Thus D. A. Hagner writes, 'Now, after the death and resurrection of Jesus, for the first time the limitation of the gospel to Israel (cf. 10:5; 15:24) is removed'. See D. A. Hagner, *Matthew 14-28* (WBC, 33B; Dallas: Word Books, 1996), p. 887. S. Brown speaks of the Gentile mission as a 'deus ex machina'. See S. Brown, 'The Matthean Community and the Gentile Mission', *NovT* 22 (1980), pp. 193–221 (221).

6.   A good example of such a position is B. Byrne, 'The Messiah in Whose Name "The Gentiles Will Hope" (Matt 12:21): Gentile Inclusion as an Essential Element of Matthew's Christology', *ABR* 50 (2002), pp. 55–73.

Sidon (Mt. 15.21-29) where he heals the daughter of the Canaanite woman, to the Gentiles as part of the kingdom of God in Mt. 21–22, to whom the kingdom may be given after it has been taken from the Jews (Mt. 21.43), and finally to the confession of faith of the centurion under the cross (Mt. 27.54). Some scholars have argued that the affinity for the Gentiles goes so far that Matthew can no longer be considered a Jewish writing.[7] But even if one retains the majority view of the Gospel as a writing born out of a Jewish milieu, the Gentile mission can still be viewed as a result of the conflict with competing Jewish groups. These positions would at the same time often assume that the Jewish mission proposed in Mt. 10.5 and in 15.24 had come to an end or was at least unsuccessful.[8]

One attempt to challenge the assumption that Matthew takes a positive attitude towards Gentiles or a mission to them has been made by D. C. Sim.[9] Sim contends that when one looks at the relevant passages in detail it is quite hard to discern a positive attitude towards Gentiles at all. He divides the passages above into two groups and adds a third group of sayings that are hostile to Gentiles. The first group concerns passages that have traditionally been taken as indicators of Matthew's liking for the Gentiles. But Sim points out that these passages may not be concerned with the religious affiliation of the characters appearing in the narrative. This is certainly right with regard to the women in the genealogy,[10] and Sim's case with the fulfilment quotation in Mt. 4.15-16 is equally convincing. In Mt. 4.15 the expression ὁ λαός ὁ καθήμενος ἐν σκότει probably does not refer to Gentiles or a coming mission to Gentiles but to the beginning

7.   See, for example, K. W. Clark, 'The Gentile Bias in Matthew', *JBL* 66 (1947), pp. 165–72; P. Nepper-Christensen, *Das Matthäusevangelium: Ein judenchristliches Evangelium?* (ATDan, 1; Åarhus: Universitetsforlaget, 1958); J. P. Meier, *The Vision of Matthew: Christ, Church and Morality in the First Gospel* (New York: Paulist Press, 1979). This thesis has not reached anything near a scholarly consensus. The latest proponent of this theory is P. Foster, *Community, Law and Mission in Matthew's Gospel* (WUNT, 2.177; Tübingen: Mohr Siebeck, 2004).

8.   An example of such a position pushed to its extreme is given by Brown, 'The Matthean Community and the Gentile Mission'. He proposes that the Matthean community relocated from Palestine to Syria after the Jewish war and came into conflict with the local Jewish authorities. This made a Gentile mission highly attractive to parts of Matthew's group. Brown sees the purpose of the Gospel in the evangelist's attempt to persuade the community to engage in a mission that at the same time was still controversial.

9.   See D. C. Sim, 'The Gospel of Matthew and the Gentiles', *JSNT* 57 (1995), pp. 19–48. He later refined his arguments in D. C. Sim, *The Gospel of Matthew and Christian Judaism: The History and Social Setting of the Matthean Community* (SNTW; Edinburgh: T&T Clark, 1998), pp. 215–56.

10.   I think that Sim's attempts to discredit the Gentile affiliation of the women is questionable. See Sim, *Matthew and Christian Judaism*, p. 218.

ministry of Jesus in Galilee, a ministry to 'the lost sheep of the house of Israel' (Mt. 15.24). And his words of caution against an all too easy interpretation of the quotation Mt. 12.18-21 as bringing justice and salvation to Gentiles are well justified.

Sim notes a second group of stories in the Gospel where some of the protagonists are Gentile, yet not at all drawn in a positive light. Sim includes the story of the Gadarenes and their swine (Mt. 8.28-34) and interprets it as a clear rejection of Jesus.[11] A second example is the story of the Canaanite woman who is portrayed much more distastefully in Mt. 15.21-28 than in Mk. 7.24-30.[12]

The group of sayings hostile to the Gentiles include Mt. 5.46-47; 6.7-8, 31-32; and finally 18.15-17. While the first two of these are also found in Luke and thus probably are from a tradition Matthew took over, his interest in such statements can be discerned from the last two sayings which have no parallel. In these statements an attitude or behaviour within the community is contrasted with what Gentiles do. Gentiles show love to their friends, but Jesus' disciples are to love their enemies. Gentiles are concerned about food and clothing; Jesus' disciples know that the heavenly Father will provide these things. Gentiles heap up empty phrases in prayer, the disciples pray the Our Father. And lastly, if someone in the community puts themselves outside of the community's discipline, they are to be treated as a Gentile. It is interesting to note that these statements are first and foremost statements about the discipline within the community, they are not statements directly aimed against Gentiles. The Gentiles are a foil on which the demands on the community come into clearer perspective. To take these sayings as clear indications that Gentiles are 'irreligious people' and that 'contact with the Gentile world should be avoided'[13] is overstating the case.[14]

While his reconstruction of a community under siege from Gentile persecutors has not found support, Sim's caution against a too easy

---

11.   One of his arguments is that Matthew leaves out the missionary activity of the cured men in the Decapolis. Sim, *Matthew and Christian Judaism*, p. 222. Most interesting is that even though he doubles the number of the healed man, Matthew takes very little interest in the pair at all. They do not express a desire to follow Jesus, nor is there a hint that the two men go and tell either the whole Decapolis (Mk 5.20) or at least the inhabitants of their city (Lk. 8.39). The focus rests almost entirely on the destruction of the demons and the subsequent reaction of the townspeople to the report of the swineherds.

12.   Sim's treatment of the soldiers under the cross is less convincing in that he sees their confession of Jesus as the Son of God as a 'proleptic judgment scene' in which the torturers of Jesus recognize what punishment will befall them for their deed. See D. C. Sim, 'The "Confession" of the Soldiers in Matthew 27:54', *HeyJ* 34 (1993), pp. 401-24.

13.   Sim, 'The Gospel of Matthew and the Gentiles', p. 229.

14.   Criticisms have been voiced by D. Senior, 'Between Two Worlds: Gentiles and Jewish Christians in Matthew's Gospel', *CBQ* 61 (1999), pp. 1–23; Byrne, 'Messiah', among others.

acceptance of Matthew's Gospel as a reflection of a community embracing Gentiles without reservations[15] is timely. If the Matthaean community found itself in a situation where the Gentile mission was presented as enjoined by the risen Lord on the one hand, but where there also existed some reservations about Gentiles on the other, one might expect the Gospel to address this conflict. And indeed it does.

The first thing to note is what it actually is that Gentiles do in the Gospel. If one does take the women in the genealogy to be Gentiles, then one thing they do is enter into the people of Israel, contributing to the Davidic lineage. Of course the women are outsiders, but Ruth was always considered a convert to Judaism (cf. Ruth 1.15-17), while at least in later Judaism Rahab and Tamar were considered proselytes as well.[16] Even though there is no such evidence for Bathsheba the thrust of any argument from the Gentile women is clear. They are integrating into a form of Judaism already in existence; they are not forming a new people of God.

This point is subtly underlined by the Gentile magi who appear out of the East.[17] They form of course the contrast to faithless Herod and his court of chief priests and elders. And yet, before they can come to Jesus they have to stop in Jerusalem and consult with the Jewish experts in scripture concerning the newborn king. The point of the magi is not that they are Gentile, but that they listen to what the scriptures have to say about Jesus.[18] In a sense, then, they are more faithful to the scriptures than those expounding on it, a very familiar theme from Jesus' controversies with the Jewish leaders.

A similar observation can be made about the centurion's faith that surpasses anything Jesus had experienced in Israel (Mt. 8.5-13). Obviously the story comes from tradition, since Luke reports a similar incident in Lk. 7.1-10. The original form of the story is very difficult to ascertain. For Luke the centurion is obviously a proselyte and benefactor of the Jewish community. Matthew does not report this, but adds a statement found elsewhere in Luke (Lk. 13.28-29) about people coming from East and West

15. Much of Byrne's construction of a mixed community of Jews and Gentiles making up a new people of God ignores Sim's suggestions. Byrne's interpretation of the Canaanite woman as indicating a 'change in the direction of Jesus' ministry' is not convincing at all. See Byrne, 'Messiah', p. 69 n. 43.

16. The evidence is discussed in M. D. Johnson, *The Purpose of the Biblical Genealogies with Special Reference to the Setting of the Genealogies of Jesus* (SNTSMS, 8; Cambridge: Cambridge University Press, 1969), pp. 159-70. Sim, *Matthew and Christian Judaism*, p. 219, points out that such women were probably not models of a Law-free Gentile mission.

17. There really isn't much point in discussing whether they might be Jews, *pace* D. C. Sim, 'The Magi: Gentiles or Jews?', *HTS* 55 (1999), pp. 980-1000.

18. B. Repschinski, 'Of Mice and Men and Matthew 2', in K. Pandikattu and A. Vonach (eds), *Religion, Society and Economics. Eastern and Western Perspectives in Dialogue* (Frankfurt: Peter Lang, 2003), pp. 75-94.

to sit at table with Abraham, Isaac and Jacob in the kingdom of Heaven. The centurion is contrasted with those in Israel who will be thrown out of this sort of eschatological banquet celebrating the victory of God.[19] However, the point of Matthew's story is not just that the centurion's faith is greater than that found in Israel, but that this faith results in his joining into table fellowship with the Jewish patriarchs. The centurion thus becomes a convert to Judaism by his faith in Jesus. The story also is a precursor of the parable of the wicked tenants (Mt. 21.33-46). There the vineyard is taken from the opponents of Jesus and given to a new people. It is a story that the chief priests and Pharisees recognize to be about themselves (Mt. 21.45). In the story of the centurion it is those who by tradition should have been at the banquet who are replaced by people like the centurion.

The story of the Canaanite woman (Mt. 15.21-28) makes the theme of proselytism even more palpable. It is a story that also occurs in Mk. 7.24-30. But Matthew's changes are telling. Apart from making the woman a little more unlikeable,[20] Matthew also inserts a short dialogue between Jesus and the disciples. Matthew has the disciples ask Jesus to pay attention to the woman, thus establishing the story more firmly as a story about the community. That this problem was a matter of lengthy deliberations is suggested by the imperfect ἠρώτουν in Mt. 15.23. Jesus' answer to the disciples shows where the problem lies: Jesus was sent only to the lost sheep of the house of Israel (15.24), yet here an annoying Gentile intrusion into this arrangement takes place, and the woman is not to be dissuaded from her intent of worshipping (προσέκυνει, 15.25) Jesus.[21] The Matthaean solution to this conundrum betrays his sympathies quite well. As in Mark the simile of the bread for the dogs from the table of the children is used, with the woman not at all questioning the designation. However, Matthew changes her acceptance to eat, not as in Mark, the crumbs of the children, but the crumbs from the table of the masters (τῶν κυρίων, 15.27). It is the recognition of the masters that lets Jesus exclaim about the greatness of her faith. If this story is a representation of how Matthew viewed the Gentiles positively, there are several implications. First, Matthew identifies it as a longstanding problem of the community. Secondly, the Gentiles come to worship Jesus. Thirdly, they acknowledge their masters at the table, the house of Israel. Thus Matthew

---

19. This feast is anticipated in both the Old Testament and the New Testament. See, for example, Isa. 25.6; Mt. 22.1-14; 25.10; Rev. 19.9; Lk. 14.15-16; *b. Pesah* 119b; *Exod. Rab.* 25.10. See D. A. Hagner, *Matthew 1-13* (WBC, 33A; Dallas: Word Books, 1993), p. 205.

20. So noted by Sim, *Matthew and Christian Judaism*, p. 223.

21. At this point one has to question Sim's assertion that none of the Gentiles really become disciples of Jesus. Whatever is meant by this expression, the Canaanite woman is a worshipper of Jesus. See Sim, *Matthew and Christian Judaism*, p. 223.

creates not just a story about the great faith of the Gentiles. The Canaanite woman also tells of the low place of the Gentiles in the hierarchy of the community.

With the way the Gentiles appear in the Gospel several statements of Matthew suddenly become more intelligible. The mission of Jesus was perceived by Matthew as a mission to Israel, and consequently the disciples were to go nowhere near Gentiles and Samaritans. At the same time, right from the birth of Jesus there are Gentiles intruding into the story. At the great inauguration of Jesus' teaching in the Sermon on the Mount, much of which concerns the holiness of the Jewish Law, Matthew has a multitude of Jews and Gentiles in attendance, ἀπὸ τῆς Γαλιλαίας καὶ Δεκαπόλεως καὶ Ἱεροσολύμων καὶ Ἰουδαίας καὶ πέραν τοῦ Ἰορδάνου (Mt. 4.25). Quite possibly Matthew gives here an, albeit idealized, image of the community in his mind. Thus the promise of hope for the Gentiles in Mt. 12.15-21 through the meek Messiah is not unprepared, but quite definitely part of what Matthew can hold out to Gentiles.[22] It is no surprise, then, that the mission to the Gentiles is something Matthew views as part of the community's life while it waits for the end time (Mt. 24.14).

Matthew draws all these narrative threads and elements together in the final commission of the risen Jesus (Mt. 28.16-20). The first thing to note is the presentation of Jesus. He is again on a mountaintop, as he was when he began his teaching (Mt. 5.1). His disciples worship him, and Jesus describes his authority in continuation with the earthly ministry of Jesus (Mt. 9.6; 11.27) and couched in the language of Dan. 7.13-14. Already in Dan. 7.14 this kind of authority is power also over the Gentiles.[23] The universal dominion of the risen Christ now extends to the disciples in their mission to make disciples of all nations, to baptize them and to teach them to keep (τηρεῖν) all that Jesus commanded (ἐνετειλάμην) his disciples. This, of course, cannot be the beginning of the Law-free Gentile mission, as some might think. Jesus never did teach that in the Gospel of Matthew, but instead commanding obedience to the Law, its necessary fulfilment to the last iota, and its interpretation in the light of the prophets (Mt. 5.17-20) who enjoined mercy more than sacrifices (see the use of Hos. 6.6 in Mt. 9.13 and 12.7).

One striking aspect in Matthew's treatment of the Gentiles is that they appear as outsiders in the narrative. They are held up as negative

---

22. Byrne, 'Messiah', p. 69, sees this as a most important passage in defining the relationship of the Gospel to the Gentiles. While this is certainly true, the passage does not allow us to conclude that the mission to the Gentiles is a Law-free mission.

23. For the background of this passage in Daniel see J. Schaberg, *The Father, the Son, and the Holy Spirit. The Triadic Phrase in Matthew 28:19b* (SBLDS, 31; Chico: Scholars Press, 1982), pp. 111–221.

examples, they appear as individual characters in particular pericopae but then disappear again like the magi who return to the East or the centurion and the Canaanite woman who just fade. Even in the final commission Jesus commands his Jewish disciples to extend the mission to Israel (cf. Mt. 10.5) now also to the Gentiles, as if this was a completely new direction of the mission, as in fact it is within the scope of the narrative. The redaction of the story of the Canaanite woman shows how much the discussion of a Gentile mission must have been a live issue in the community, and may even have been distasteful to some of its members.

The community understood the mission to the Gentiles as a command of the risen Lord, and Matthew found ways of preparing for this command within his narrative of the earthly Jesus. The Matthaean mission to the Gentiles was, however, clearly confined to a mission that asked of the new believers in Christ to become Jewish as well, keeping to the commandments of the Law and recognizing that their participation in the community was restricted to being something of a second-class Christian Jew. In this sense, Matthew's community was not really a mixed community. It is likely that a community dominated by Jews but accepting proselytes experienced a lot of the conflicts described in Matthew 18, and the nature of those conflicts might have been akin to those described by Luke in Acts 6.

3. *The Gentile Mission in Luke*

The Gospel of Luke, together with its companion volume Acts,[24] has by a large consensus been described as originating with and addressed to a Gentile audience.[25] It is, therefore, most surprising that the Gentiles do not feature prominently in the Gospel at all. Their great entrance into salvation history, so to speak, happens only in the Acts of the Apostles. There are no Gentiles appearing at the manger of Jesus, and the Syrophoenician woman from Mk 7.24-30 does not show up in Luke's Gospel. Even the

24. The majority of scholars view Luke and Acts as a two-part narrative by one author. However, there are sometimes arguments for the independence of the Gospel of Luke from Acts, even to the point of suggesting that they are by different authors. For a moderate argument of independence, see J. Nolland, *Luke 1:1-9:20* (WBC, 35A; Dallas: Word Books, 1989), pp. xxxiii–xxxiv.

25. However, Nolland, *Luke 1:1-9:20*, p. xxxii, argues for a setting among proselytes, while J. Jervell is convinced of a Jewish Christian origin. See J. Jervell, *Die Apostelgeschichte* (KEK, 3; Göttingen: Vandenhoeck & Ruprecht, 1998), pp. 49–52. C. Stenschke notices that, despite the consensus of placing Luke-Acts within the Gentile world, there is little scholarly attention focused on the topic as a theological issue, perhaps because it has been taken for granted. See C. Stenschke, *Luke's Portrait of Gentiles Prior to Their Coming to Faith* (WUNT, 2.108; Tübingen: Mohr Siebeck, 1999), p. 3.

faithful centurion of Capernaum does not appear in person but sends emissaries to plead his case with Jesus (Lk. 7.3, 6). On top of this he is very carefully described as one who loves Israel and is a benefactor of the local community. There are few places where the Gentiles put in a personal appearance in the Gospel of Luke. At the beginning of the Sermon on the Plain it can be safely inferred that among the people from Tyre and Sidon (Lk. 6.17) there are some Gentiles present,[26] but their activity is restricted to listening to Jesus' teaching. Another appearance of Gentiles can be inferred in the story of the Gerasene demoniac (Lk. 8.26-39). Yet, as in Matthew the Gerasenes ask Jesus to leave. Like Mark, Luke notes the request of the healed man to remain with Jesus. Instead he gets a commission to tell the deed of God in his household. Luke does not yet seem to envision Gentiles among those following Jesus.[27] The man proceeds to tell his story in the whole city. The only other Gentiles who appear in Luke's Gospel are those connected with his arrest, passion and death. Of course this is a very negative appearance of the Gentiles in the story of Jesus. However, Luke manages to put a positive spin on it in the third passion prediction (Lk. 18.31-34). There are several remarkable Lukan redactions of Mk 10.32-34. The first is the introduction of the theme of fulfilment of scripture, in which Luke has a particular interest (cf. Lk. 24.26-27; 44). The second is the addition of the Gentiles, into whose hands Jesus has to be handed over. Finally, Luke formulates a remark that the disciples did not understand. It appears that the Gentiles have become part of the plan of salvation laid out in scripture, recognized by Jesus and explained to his disciples on the road to Emmaus.[28]

There are several instances where the Gentiles are the recipients of great hope arising out of the ministry of Jesus. At the presentation in the

---

26.   J. A. Fitzmyer, *The Gospel According to Luke: Introduction, Translation and Notes* (AB, 28-28A; 2 vols; New York: Doubleday, 1983), I, p. 622, sees the presence of the Gentiles here as owing to Mk 3.8. This may be so, but since the Markan context is completely different it may safely be assumed that Luke intends more than faithfulness to a source.

27.   It is doubtful whether Fitzmyer, *Luke*, I, p. 735, here speaks correctly of the first 'pagan disciple' of Jesus. After all, the man is not allowed to remain with Jesus. Nolland, *Luke 1:1-9:20*, p. 414, seems to be more correct in his statement that 'the time of the Gentiles has not yet come', particularly since the mission of the man does not extend to the whole Decapolis as in Mark but only to his own village.

28.   Fitzmyer, *Luke*, II, p. 1208, sees the lack of understanding on the part of the disciples as related to the partitioning of salvation history in Luke-Acts and draws the parallel to the Emmaus pericope where the disciples' eyes will finally be opened. I do not understand how Nolland can construe the passage into a polemic against 'the foreign overlords who controlled the government of Palestine at the highest level, and under whom the Jews were a subject people'; J. Nolland, *Luke 9:21-18:34* (WBC, 35B; Dallas: Word Books, 1993), p. 896. The introduction of the fulfilment of scripture is a very clear argument that at stake here is the plan of God from ancient times, not the apportioning of guilt. The additional remark about the disciples is a further indicator of this.

Temple, the aged Simeon gives praise because he has seen universal salvation in Jesus, a 'light for revelation to the Gentiles and for glory to your people Israel' (Lk. 2.32). John, baptizing at the Jordan, speaks of the beginning of an age that includes salvation for all Gentiles (Lk. 3.6) and follows this up with a prophecy of judgement against those coming to him at the Jordan, a judgement that will not take into account that they are children of Abraham but will ask for their deeds (Lk. 3.7-9). And John makes it explicit that it is the one coming after him who already has the winnowing fork in his hand (Lk. 3.17). This sentiment of judgement against those relying on their Jewish heritage seems to be underlying the lament of the Galilean cities as well (Lk. 10.13-16). However, if the judgement is made according to the deeds of people and not according to their heritage, this holds true for the Gentiles as well (Lk. 12.30; 17.26-30). In the programmatic appearance of Jesus in the Nazareth synagogue, Luke holds up Elijah and Elisha who worked signs of salvation among Gentiles, and the allusion to the repentance of the Ninevites and the visit of the Queen of the South (Lk. 11.30-32) is remarkably similar to the examples at Nazareth. These remarks show that Luke envisions salvation held out to Gentiles, while at the same time applying a measure to both Jews and Gentiles. It is the response to Jesus which will make or break salvation for both groups.

It remains curious, however, that on the one hand Luke clearly envisions a universal salvation including Jews and Gentiles, and at the same time removes the Gentiles so far from the narrative of the Gospel. It has been suggested that this is due to Luke's view of salvation history which depicts a thoroughly Jewish ministry of Jesus in his lifetime, while the mission in Acts takes off towards the Gentiles.[29] There is some truth to this view. The mission to the Gentiles takes off in Acts at the express command of the risen Lord, much like in Matthew. This mission is first revealed to Ananias (Acts 9.15), then entrusted to Peter in a vision that he does not understand. Only at the sight of Cornelius and his household possessed of the Holy Spirit does Peter understand the vision as well as the plans God has for the salvation of the Gentiles (Acts 10). Finally, it is Paul who takes up this mission systematically. Even though Paul is depicted as teaching in the synagogues around the cities he travels to, Luke also shows how his message is repeatedly rejected at the synagogue and in consequence he turns to the Gentiles. Furthermore, Paul's self-understanding as it is reported in Acts is that of a missionary sent to the Gentiles by the will of God himself (Acts 9.15; 15.7).

---

29.   This theory goes back to the influential study of H. Conzelmann, *Die Mitte der Zeit. Studien zur Theologie des Lukas* (BHT; Tübingen: J. C. B. Mohr [Paul Siebeck], 4th edn, 1962). Conzelmann's work was revised and updated by M. Dibelius, E. Haenchen and P. Vielhauer.

However, Luke does not leave the great separation between the Gospel and Acts unbridged. His way of bringing together the ministry of Jesus to the Jews and the ministry of Peter and Paul to the Gentiles is the introduction of another ἔθνος (Acts 8.9) that is different from the Jews (ἀλλογενής, Lk. 17.18), the Samaritans.[30] Neither Mark nor Matthew gives the Samaritans as much space as does Luke. Mark does not mention them at all, and Matthew specifically excludes them from the mission of the disciples (Mt. 10.5-6). Furthermore, Luke obviously did not deem it necessary to explain any of the differences between Samaritans and Jews.[31] The first report of the Samaritans is contained at the beginning of the big Lukan interpolation (Lk. 9.51-56), often regarded as a theological turning point within the Gospel. A Samaritan village refuses to offer hospitality to Jesus 'because his face was set toward Jerusalem' (Lk. 9.53).[32] Jesus' disciples are aggravated at this and suggest calling down fire from heaven to burn the place to the ground. However, Jesus rebukes his disciples. The story is remarkable in that it portrays the Samaritans as not receiving Jesus, who in turn protects the Samaritans from the wrath of the disciples. In a sense it may be said that just as for Jesus the time of his assumption had not yet come (Lk. 9.51), neither had the time for the Samaritans come. It is possible to view the mission of the 72 disciples in Lk. 10.1-12 as being directed to the Samaritans as well.[33] There is no change of place between Lk. 9.56 and 10.1.[34] There is nothing to suggest that the mission of the

---

30.   J. Jervell argues that the Samaritans are complete Jews, but fails to account for their unique status in Luke and Acts. See J. Jervell, 'The Lost Sheep of the House of Israel: The Understanding of the Samaritans in Luke-Acts', in J. Jervell, *Luke and the Divided People of God: A New Look at Luke-Acts* (Minneapolis: Fortress Press, 1979), pp. 113–32. Stenschke, *Gentiles*, p. 111, places the Samaritans among the Gentiles, but he needs to explain at least why he does so despite a different terminology that does not merely seem to originate with geographical variations. The debate is summarized by M. Böhm, who herself views the Samaritans as a Jewish sect. Her arguments are very persuasive. See M. Böhm, *Samarien und die Samaritai. Eine Studie zum religionshistorischen und traditionsgeschichtlichen Hintergrund der lukanischen Samarientexte und zu deren topographischer Verhaftung* (WUNT, 2.111; Tübingen: Mohr Siebeck, 1999), pp. 8–30.

31.   This is very different from Jn 4.9 which supplies editorial comments about the Samaritans' uniqueness. Otherwise the parallels with John 4 are significant, and are detailed by D. Ravens, *Luke and the Restoration of Israel* (JSNTSup, 119; Sheffield: Sheffield Academic Press, 1995), pp. 72–4.

32.   This is a striking difference to the rejection at Nazareth in 4.16-30. See J. T. Sanders, *The Jews in Luke-Acts* (Philadelphia: Fortress Press, 1987), p. 144.

33.   Nolland draws some parallels, but he is not clear on whether he actually views the mission of Lk. 10.1-12 as directed to the Samaritans. See Nolland, *Luke 9:21-18:34*, p. 533.

34.   The whole central section, or big interpolation, mentions only two indications of where Jesus is, and both of these mention Samaria: Lk. 9.52 and 17.11. The obvious conclusion to draw from this is that Samaria was the 'area of Jesus' ministry' in the central section, paralleling the earlier ministry in Galilee. See Ravens, *Luke*, p. 78.

72 is not a mission to the Samaritan towns, and there is a remarkable parallelism between the disciples sent to the Samaritan village and the 72 sent to the villages Jesus is going to visit later on. In both cases the phrase ἀπέστειλεν...πρὸ προσώπου αὐτοῦ is used (Lk. 9.52; 10.1). Lastly, the injunction to the disciples to eat what is offered them points to a situation in which Jewish purity rules might not be kept. The mission in Luke 10 is modelled on Lk. 9.1-6, where the Twelve go into the villages of Galilee. In both missions the possibility of rejection is entertained. Consequently, the rejection of Jesus in the Samaritan village is not a blanket judgement over Samaritans, but a precursor of what the disciples will have to deal with themselves. It should not be interpreted as a proleptic statement about the death of Jesus like the rejection at Nazareth, since the Samaritans are not involved in the passion.

Much more positive is the image of the Samaritans presented in the parable of the Good Samaritan (Lk. 10.25-37) and the healing of the ten lepers (Lk. 17.11-19). In both stories the Samaritans who do right are used as a foil to show up how the Jewish characters in the story fail to respond appropriately to the challenges of their respective situations. The Good Samaritan teaches the questioning lawyer that mercy is the fulfilment of the requirement to inherit eternal life and at the same time the fulfilment of the Law. He is described in contrast to the priest and the Levite with their connections to the Temple and the cult.[35] It is quite significant that a Samaritan, contrasted to the Jewish leaders at the Temple, becomes the key argument in a discussion about the Jewish Law. Similarly, the leprous Samaritan,[36] in breaking off his journey to the Temple to show himself to the priests and instead returning to Jesus to give thanks, is the one who really gives God honour. This man is characterized not only as a Samaritan, but also as ἀλλογενής, a foreigner, who distinguishes himself not by going to the Temple to fulfil the rituals required by the Law but by turning to Jesus. Both the Good Samaritan and the leper are acting in a way that is contrary to the Law, and yet judged by Luke to be doing the right thing.

The Samaritans suddenly appear in a rather positive light. While they are a people that Jesus turns to and sends his disciples to, they are also a people who are very different from the Judaism that is present elsewhere in the Gospel. The leper is not described as baulking at being sent to the

35. It is often suggested that the priest and Levite act out of fear for their purity. See the discussion in Fitzmyer, *Luke*, II, p. 887, and F. Bovon, *Das Evangelium nach Lukas* (EKKNT, 3; 3 vols; Zürich: Benziger Verlag, 1989, 1996, 2001), II, p. 90.

36. It is quite possible, as suggested by M. S. Enslin, that this story is a development of the healing of Naaman the Syrian by Elisha as narrated in Lk. 4.27. If so, Jesus here is presented as much more powerful than Elisha. M. S. Enslin, 'Luke and the Samaritans', *HTR* 36 (1943), pp. 274–97 (295–6).

Temple priests, but seeing his healing he also knows that the place to give glory to God is at the feet of Jesus. Clearly Jesus expected such behaviour from the other nine as well.

In Acts 8 the Samaritans appear again as the recipients of the first mission outside of Jerusalem. In Acts 8.1 there is still a parallelism between Judaea and Samaria.[37] However, Judaea soon disappears from sight, and in Acts 8.4 a fully-fledged mission to the Samaritans is underway with the subsequent founding of a community founded in baptism by Philip and in the Holy Spirit by the apostles Peter and John. This Samaritan mission of Philip and the apostles is the context in which finally the first Gentile[38] is baptized at the instigation of an angel of the Lord (Acts 8.26). The story of the eunuch is not the beginning of the Gentile mission in Acts. This is inaugurated in Acts 10.1. However, it draws very efficiently the line from the Samaritan to the Gentile mission. The Gentile mission is not just a mission of the early church, even if at the instigation and with the blessing of the risen Lord. It has its roots in a Samaritan mission which was already part of Jesus' ministry before his death and resurrection. The Samaritans form one of the links between the Jesus of the Gospel and the missionary church of Acts.[39] If in the Gospel there is a progression from Jesus' mission to the Jews in Galilee to the Samaritans in the big interpolation, Acts takes the progression a step further from the Samaritans to the Gentiles.

37.   Böhm, *Samarien*, p. 304, thinks that this indicates that Luke is not interested in a mission to Gentiles but in a restoration of Israel's tribes, announced in 1.6-8. However, she probably underestimates the context of the Jerusalem persecution.

38.   A. Lindemann has little doubt that the man is a Gentile. He argues that despite the inauguration of the Gentile mission in 10.1, the placement of the eunuch's story is quite apt in view of this being a story of an individual, not an ethnic group. See A. Lindemann, 'Der "äthiopische Eunuch" und die Anfänge der Mission', in C. Breytenbach and J. Schröter (eds), *Die Apostelgeschichte und die hellenistische Geschichtsschreibung. Festschrift für Eckhard Plümacher* (Leiden: Brill, 2004), pp. 109–33. Jervell, *Apostelgeschichte*, pp. 270–1, maintains that, because of his pilgrimage to Jerusalem and his reading of scripture, the man is 'Jude, aber aus einer besonderen Gruppe', namely the proselytes. It is true that the man has been on pilgrimage to Jerusalem, but the description of his origin in Ethiopia and the court of Queen Kandake are equally weighty. Furthermore, Jervell has to argue that the description of the man as a eunuch is an honorific title rather than a description of castration. In all, Jervell's case to describe the man as a Jew seems strained.

39.   The parallel has been called into question by Ravens on the grounds that there is a direct intervention necessary for the Gentile mission; however, for the Samaritan mission this is not so. 'This is a clear indication that Luke regards Jews and Samaritans as being within one fundamental group to which even the most devout God-fearer does not belong'; Ravens, *Luke*, p. 93. Since the Samaritans are Jews, they cannot be used to foretell a Gentile mission. Yet even Ravens has to acknowledge that on a narrative level the Samaritan mission is a stepping stone towards the Gentiles. Ravens does not take into account that the Samaritans in the Gospel are portrayed as a foil to show up Jewish deficiencies.

If the Samaritans in the Gospel are the forerunners of the Gentiles in Acts, they also shape the form the Gentile mission will assume. If the Samaritans of the Gospel are serving as a foil to show up the limitations of the Law, the mission to the Gentiles deals with this contrast by becoming a Law-free mission. The baptism of Cornelius and the ensuing conflict (Acts 10.1–11.18) lets this vibrantly come alive with the issue of food purity and communion with Gentiles. The really contentious issue in the Jerusalem community is not described as Peter baptizing a Gentile. What those from the circumcision (Acts 11.2) object to is that Peter lived with uncircumcized people and shared their meals (11.3). Peter describes his vision and the ensuing events to them, which seems to satisfy the Jewish Christians for a while. But this story already intimates that soon a separation between those from the circumcision and the Gentiles will occur. Paul alludes to this in his speech to the Jews in Pisidian Antioch (13.46-48). This turn of events repeats itself in Acts 18.6 and 28.26-29 and thus becomes a pattern: Jews will reject the word, while Gentiles accept it gratefully and in great numbers. This division as a reaction to the preaching of Paul will remain a feature of his missionary activity. In Lystra there is great success in a thoroughly Gentile mission, only to be disturbed and threatened by the arrival of Jews from Pisidian Antioch (Acts 14.19). The first missionary journey of Paul basically serves to show God opened the door of faith to the Gentiles (Acts 14.27).

The account of the Jerusalem council clarifies that the mission of Paul in Antioch and elsewhere did not include circumcision (Acts 15.1), and it was not deemed necessary to impose this on the Gentiles. Then some from Jerusalem arrive who think that circumcision and the concomitant keeping of the Law must be enjoined upon the Gentiles, and they get into a heated dispute with Paul and Barnabas.[40] The solution found by the council and subsequently communicated to Antioch is one that omits circumcision and the keeping of the Law but includes admonitions to purity in religious, dietary and sexual terms. Most fascinating is the explanation James gives for this solution. He first mentions that the Gentile mission originated with Peter at the command of God, and then goes on to cite Scripture to find evidence for the fact that with the calling of the Gentiles God has chosen to rebuild the fallen hut of David (Acts 15.16-17). Luke's argument is that in the Law-free mission to the Gentiles a tottering Israel is being restored. This means that Jesus and his followers are a light to the Gentiles (Lk. 2.32; Acts 13.47), even if the disciples of Jesus are slow to recognize it. But God himself has intervened to inaugurate the mission to the Gentiles, and once the disciples understand it as God's will they acknowledge such a mission joyfully (Acts 11.18; 21.20).

---

40. Jervell, *Apostelgeschichte*, pp. 388–9, notes rightly that at issue is not Gentile salvation but the conditions for community life that are part of it.

However intent Acts seems to be in describing the acceptance of the Gentile mission by the apostles and the Jerusalem church, Luke also exhibits traits of an initial parting of the ways between Jewish Christians and the new Gentile converts. Peter may be the first apostle to convert a Gentile, but he also remains the last one. Cornelius remains Peter's only Gentile convert. After the incident in Joppa Peter returns to Jerusalem, never to leave it again. While he argues for no obligations at all to be put on the Gentiles, his position does not carry the day at the Jerusalem council, and he subsequently fades from the story. The Gentile mission, however, is pursued by Paul and his various companions. Luke reports how much Paul comes under suspicion in Jerusalem for apparently propagating a mission that tries to convince Jewish Christians to abandon the Law (Acts 21.21). James and the elders in Jerusalem appear to be on Paul's side, but they cannot prevent Paul from being arrested. Whatever the historical events behind Luke's account are, he creates the impression that the Jewish Christian community in Jerusalem is left behind after Acts 15 and does not become part of the Gentile mission at all. The narrative, however, remains with the mission that makes further forays into Gentile territory, while the Jewish and non-Christian opponents to this mission are characterised as hostile and even ridiculous (Acts 17.17).

Luke's depiction of the steady growth of Christianity in Acts is a portrait of two churches. It is on the one hand a portrait of a church in Jerusalem that remains Jewish, committed to the Temple and the Law. On the other hand are the communities in Antioch and those later founded by Paul and his companions which are Gentile in character and which are no longer keeping the Law. The Jerusalem church grows out of the band of apostles that Jesus himself gathered around him. The Gentile churches grow out of a direct intervention of the Lord in the vision of Peter. But the Gentile churches can lay claim to an origin with the earthly Jesus as well. Not only is he the fulfilment of the prophecies concerning the salvation of the nations, he himself ventured to preach to a Samaritan ἔθνος that was no longer a part of the Judaism present in Jerusalem, and he sent his disciples to do likewise. The mission to the Samaritans is the precursor to the Law-free mission to the Gentiles. Luke's sympathies lie with the Gentile communities. This is the perspective of Acts. However, his Jesus is not just a light to the Gentiles, he is also the glory of his people Israel. Thus the Luke who shows the enormous growth of Christianity among Gentiles also shows deep respect for Jesus' people Israel and the Jerusalem church worshipping in the Temple. Luke is not bent on discrediting a Jewish Christian church. But his Gentile churches are very different from the Jewish church.[41]

---

41. In this sense, S. G. Wilson's sometimes criticized aphorism that Luke views the Law as an '*ethos* for a particular *ethnos*' is basically correct. See S. G. Wilson, *Luke and the Law* (SNTSMS, 50; Cambridge: Cambridge University Press, 1983), p. 103 (original emphasis).

4. *Conclusions*

In the writings of Matthew and Luke two very different approaches to the Gentile mission confront the reader. However, the problems both authors deal with are quite similar. Both live in communities in which they have to explain how a band of Jewish disciples called together by their Jewish teacher Jesus suddenly grew into a movement that was attractive not only to Jews but also Gentiles. Moreover, they had to deal with the practical consequences of this growth and the question of how Jewish the emerging church should remain. Their answers are very different. Matthew opted for a church that would remain faithful to its Jewish heritage both in spirit and in letter. He enjoins upon his community not only the necessity of keeping the Law but also its beauty as Jesus taught it. Luke, however, envisions a church whose faithfulness to the traditions of Judaism are no longer manifested in the careful keeping of the Law, but in the awareness that the community is the people of God fulfilling the prophecies of the glory of Israel as well as the eschatological inclusion of all nations. Luke's proof for this is the working of the Holy Spirit both in the community and in individuals.

Because these two competing visions are so close in their starting point and so different in their solutions, it has been suggested by proponents of the theory of Lukan dependence on Matthew[42] that Luke's version is his correction of Matthew's theology.[43] Of course it would be intriguing to know whether Matthew's allusion to those who teach others to break the commandments of the Law as the least in the kingdom (Mt. 5.19) has one of those Lukan or maybe Pauline communities in view. It would be wonderful if we could relate the judaizers in Antioch (Acts 15.1) and those zealous for the Law in Jerusalem (Acts 21.20-21) to some leading figures in the Matthaean community. However, we cannot. We can only appreciate that for the early Christians, there was more than one way in dealing with the conflict between a rich tradition and a visionary future.

---

42. I remain unconvinced even by the very careful analysis in A. J. McNicol (ed.), *Luke's Use of Matthew: Beyond the Q Impasse* (Valley Forge: Trinity Press International, 1996).
43. Ravens, *Luke*, and E. Franklin, *Luke: Interpreter of Paul, Critic of Matthew* (JSNTSup, 92; Sheffield: JSOT Press, 1994).

4. MATTHEW AND JOHN

JOHN PAINTER

Matthew and John have the dubious distinction of being recognized as two of the most anti-Jewish documents in the New Testament.[1] The Jesus of John accuses the Jews, who are said to have believed in him, of being children of the devil who seek to kill him (8.30-31, 40, 44). He accuses the Pharisees of wilful blindness and asserts that their sin remains (9.39-41). The narrator and the Jesus of John describe the intimidation (by the Jews/Pharisees) of those who confess Jesus as the Christ by the threat to cast them out of the synagogue (9.22, 34; 12.42; 16.2).[2] The Jesus of Matthew seven times condemns the scribes and Pharisees as hypocrites (23.13, 15, 16, 23, 25, 27, 29) and the (Jewish) people present at the hearing before Pilate call for Jesus' death and assume responsibility for it; 'His blood be upon us and on our children' (27.24-25). At the same time, a strong interpretative tradition of each Gospel has argued that these two texts are the product of Jewish authors writing for Jewish believers in Jesus who were in some sort of power struggle with the leadership of the broader Jewish community.[3]

1.   For recent discussions of this problem in John and extensive bibliography, see the interdisciplinary academic seminar held in Leuven on 17–18 January 2000 and the selection of papers now to be found in R. Bieringer, D. Pollefeyt, and E. Vandecasteele-Vanneuville (eds), *Anti-Judaism and the Fourth Gospel* (Louisville: Westminster John Knox, 2001).

2.   In John 9 the antagonists of Jesus are first called 'the Pharisees' (9.13-17), then 'the Jews' (9.18-39) and finally 'the Pharisees' (9.40-41). The narrator identifies the Jewish opposition with the Pharisees in a way that is relevant to the readers of John's day. In 12.42 the threat of the Pharisees is said to intimidate even the rulers who believed in Jesus, while in 16.2 Jesus foretells the casting out of believers from the synagogue. The future tense (ποιήσουσιν), understood from the perspective of Jesus' ministry, locates the action in the time of the evangelist. In 11.45-53, especially 49-50, 53, John identifies the Jewish leaders in a plot to remove Jesus.

3.   An alternative approach considers Matthew to be the product of a Gentile author writing for a largely Gentile church. See K. W. Clark, 'The Gentile Bias in Matthew', *JBL* 66 (1947), pp. 165–172; and G. Strecker, *Der Weg der Gerechtigkeit* (FRLANT, 82; Göttingen: Vandenhoeck & Ruprecht, 3rd edn, 1971). The attempt to show that Matthew's understanding of scripture and Judaism precludes a Jewish context is unpersuasive, though reception history leads to reading Matthew through the eyes of a Gentile Church. That is

Both works are commonly dated between 80-100 CE in the period of Jewish reconstruction following the Jewish War. They reflect a struggle with Formative Judaism but are addressed to readers sympathetic to their message rather than to Jewish opponents. In each case the Gospel portrays a vision of faith and life in contrast to the dominant Judaism of the day. For Matthew the contrast is with the scribes and Pharisees, the predecessors of Formative Judaism. For John the contrast is with the Jews, who alternate with the Pharisees in Jn 9.13, 18, 22, 40.

John's varied use of 'the Jews' has created serious problems for scholars. Some problems are alleviated by recognizing that the use of 'the Jews' is influenced by the perspective of the speaker. The evidence suggests that Palestinian 'Jews' refers to Israel and Israelites unless speaking to Gentiles or Samaritans. In their conversation Jesus and Nathaniel use the terms 'Israel' and 'Israelite' (1.47, 49), but Pilate, a Gentile, refers to Jews in his conversation with Jesus (18.33-34), as does the Samaritan woman (4.9a) and Jesus replies using 'the Jews' (4.22). Nathaniel (1.49) and the pilgrim crowd (12.13) confess Jesus to be the king of Israel but Pilate asks him 'Are you the king of the Jews?' (18.33). In the light of this usage it is notable that the Johannine narrator commonly refers to 'the Jews'.[4] The narrator introduces Nicodemus as 'a ruler of the Jews' (3.1), but in his conversation with Nicodemus Jesus refers to him as 'the teacher of Israel' (3.10).[5] The language of the narrator implies that the Gospel is addressed to Gentiles or Diaspora Jews who, in this respect, adopted the language of their world, referring to 'the Jews'.[6]

It is a well-known Johannine puzzle that the evangelist has assimilated the different groups within the Judaism of Jesus' day in the characteristic reference to the Jews. In John 'the Jews' can refer to the people generally but often seems to identify the leaders in a hostile relationship to Jesus and his followers, as in 9.18, 22. These references occur within the *inclusio* of

not reading Matthew in its compositional context, for which the question of whether Matthew is a document of believing Jews or reflects a break from Judaism (as G. N. Stanton amongst others argues) is important.

4. See, for example, 1.19; 2.6, 13, 18, 20; 3.1; 4.9b; 5.1, 10, 15, 18; 6.4, 41, 52. The expression is used 71 times in John. Contrast the five uses in Matthew, 6 in Mark, and five in Luke. Acts uses the term 79 times, which is more or less comparable to the 71 uses of the shorter John. The different balance of use in Luke and Acts is notable, given common authorship.

5. The narrator in John does not use the terms 'Israel' or 'Israelite'. For the other use of 'Israel' in John, see 1.31 where the speaker is John the Baptist.

6. See J. Painter, 'Christ and the Church in John 1.45-51', in M. de Jonge (ed.), *L'Évangile de Jean* (Leuven: Peeters, 1977), pp. 359–62 and *idem.*, 'The Church and Israel in the Gospel of John', *NTS* 25 (1978), pp. 102–12. The author almost certainly writes from the Diaspora after 70 CE. See also J. Painter, *The Quest for the Messiah* (Edinburgh: T&T Clark, 2nd edn, 1993), pp. 29–31, 125–31.

9.13, 40, which identifies them with the Pharisees.[7] Elsewhere the narrator mentions priests and Levites as well as the chief priests, Pharisees, the High Priest, and the Sanhedrin (cf. 1.19; 11.47, 49, 51). There is no mention of the Sadducees, Zealots, or Essenes. The latter are not named in the entire New Testament.

In John 9 the assimilation of Pharisees and 'the Jews' occurs because the Jewish authorities, with whom John is engaged in a power struggle, are the successors of the Pharisees of Jesus' day. Interestingly, the case for something like this position in relation to one of the Gospels was first made *persuasively* for Matthew. An earlier work by J. Parkes (1934) dealt with the Gospel of John in a chapter entitled 'The Parting of the Ways', because John contains 'more elements of the situation around A.D. 100 than of the situation in the lifetime of Jesus'.[8] Parkes' work has not received the attention it deserves. In 1968, without reference to Parkes, J. L. Martyn published his revolutionary study, and Johannine studies became receptive to his thesis, which became the dominant interpretative paradigm.[9]

Earlier (1964), W. D. Davies argued that Matthew was a product of the church in Syria or Palestine between 70-100 CE.[10] The position was refined in the three-volume commentary of W. D. Davies and D. C. Allison, which narrows the probable date to between 80-95 CE,[11] and names Syrian Antioch as the probable place of origin; 'Although we have found the evidence for placing Matthew in Antioch to be considerable, we

7.   The Jews and Pharisees are first connected in 1.19, 24. The genitive (τῶν φαρισαίων) probably means that the emissaries were from the Pharisees, identifying them with the Jews of 1.19, which is likely in the light of 9.13, 18, 22, 40.

8.   See ch. 3, 'The Parting of the Ways', in J. Parkes, *The Conflict of the Church and the Synagogue: A Study of the Origins of Anti-Semitism* (London: Soncino, 1934). The quotation is on p. 28.

9.   J. L. Martyn, *History and Theology in the Fourth Gospel* (New York: Harper & Row, 1968). Second and third editions appeared respectively in 1979 and 2003. Between the works of Parkes and Martyn commentators such as C. K. Barrett referred to *birkat ha-minim* in relation to the interpretation of Jn 9.22, but did not make it a key to the understanding of John. Following the publication of Martyn's study, Parkes' book was republished in New York by Atheneum in 1969 but failed to attract attention. See J. Painter, *1, 2, and 3 John* (SP, 18; Collegeville: Liturgical Press, 2002), pp. 10–12.

10.   See W. D. Davies, *The Setting of the Sermon on the Mount* (Cambridge: Cambridge University Press, 1964), pp. 191, 256.

11.   See W. D. Davies and D. C. Allison, *A Critical and Exegetical Commentary on the Gospel according to Saint Matthew* (ICC; 3 vols; Edinburgh: T&T Clark, 1988, 1991,1997), I, p. 138. U. Luz, *Matthew 1-7* (Augsburg: Minneapolis, 1989), pp. 88–9, 92–3, dates the Gospel some time between 70 CE and not long after 80 CE. Not before 70 because Matthew presupposes the destruction of Jerusalem and the availability of Mark, but not long after 80 because Matthew reflects the recent traumatic break from the Jewish synagogue system.

must plainly state that we do not claim… a high degree of certainty… So while, in our judgement, the First Gospel was probably put together for the church of Antioch, this conclusion remains no more than the best educated guess'.[12] The period and the place (somewhere not remote from the influence of Jamnia) are significant because they understand Matthew in relation to the Judaism of the Jamnian period. In 1964 Davies was clear that 'chronologically that period cannot be precisely charted'.[13] In their commentary Davies and Allison are at pains to insist that for them Jamnia indicates a process. Referring to the role of the Pharisees after 70 CE they state, 'They set in motion a process… a word we emphasize… we have applied the term 'Jamnia' after the place where, according to tradition, the Pharisaic sages congregated after the war'.[14] Matthew reflects that process and is a response to it.[15]

The primary work of Jamnia was to unify and give a sense of cohesion and identity to a Judaism that had been fragmented by sectarianism, scattered by the destructive forces of a disastrous war, and had lost its sense of identity with the destruction of the Jerusalem Temple. The work of Jamnia, as understood by Davies (and by Davies and Allison), has been described in terms of Formative Judaism by J. Neusner.[16] Formative Judaism, symbolized by the work of Jamnia, was responsible for the transformation of the chaos, in which post 70 CE Judaism found itself, to the possibilities opened up by Rabbinic Judaism. The formation and

12. Davies and Allison, *Matthew*, I, pp. 146–7. See also J. Painter, *Just James: The Brother of Jesus in History and Tradition* (Colombia: University of South Carolina Press, 2nd edn, 2004), pp. 88–90. Though the case for Antioch is not strong, no better alternative case has been made. Luz, *Matthew 1-7*, p. 92, also notes that Antioch fits the profile for the origin of Matthew but so would other cities in Syria.

13. Davies, *Sermon*, p. 256.

14. Davies and Allison, *Matthew*, III, p. 692. See too *Matthew*, I, p. 134 n. 106 and Davies, *Sermon*, p. 292 n. 2.

15. Davies and Allison, *Matthew*, III, p. 698. Davies argued that the Sermon on the Mount is a response to and critique of the Rabbinic development at Jamnia. See *Sermon*, pp. 304–15, and Davies and Allison, *Matthew* I, pp. 133–8. G. N. Stanton is critical of Davies' argument. See his *A Gospel for a New People: Studies in Matthew* (Edinburgh: T&T Clark, 1992), pp. 307–9. Davies and Allison, *Matthew*, III, pp. 698–704, responded to this and other critiques, noting that Stanton 'reckons as a "strong possibility" the proposition that Matthew was composed in the shadow of Jamnia' (p. 698 n. 32). Actually Stanton rated this 'a strong probability' (*Gospel for a New People*, p. 145), though the context implies some reserve. The Davies and Allison response has strengthened Davies' earlier argument. All I suppose is the relationship of Matthew to the work of Formative Judaism in the Jamnian period.

16. Neusner's work was taken up by J. A. Overman, *Matthew's Gospel and Formative Judaism: The Social World of the Matthean Community* (Minneapolis: Fortress Press, 1990), pp. 2–3.

publication of the Mishnah by Rabbi Judah the Prince consolidated the foundation of Rabbinic Judaism. What Formative Judaism did for the broader Jewish community after 70 CE, Matthew did for his community. Because Matthew constituted a challenge to the unified Judaism Jamnia sought to promote, Jamnia also posed a problem for Matthew. Davies and Allison argue that the reformulation of the twelfth benediction under Rabban Gamaliel II 'had a significant impact on Jewish-Christian relations', and that 'Matthew's Gospel fits perfectly into the Jamnian period of Jewish reconsolidation'.[17] From this perspective, *birkat ha-minim* threatened groups like the Matthaean community.[18] According to Davies and Allison, the use of *birkat ha-minim* against Matthaean Christian Jews would not 'have meant exclusion from Judaism' but failure to comply 'was presumably punished only by not being permitted to lead prayer (*b. Ber.* 28b-9a)'.[19]

This understanding of the setting of Matthew has much in common with the interpretation of John that dominated the last quarter of the twentieth century. Both Gospels are understood in the context of Jamnia's attempt to unify a fragmented Judaism but the text of John (9.22, 34; 12.42; 16.2) asserts that the confession of faith in Jesus as the Christ was met with exclusion from the synagogue. The Davies and Allison understanding is that the community of Matthew remained within Judaism while John provides evidence of a break. Perhaps a majority of leading interpreters of Matthew perceive the Gospel from the perspective of a recent break away from Judaism and interpret it as a distinctively Christian document written for a mixed community of Jewish and Gentile readers.[20]

Those who see Matthew as the expression of a community that has broken away from Judaism generally also see a turning from the mission to Jews to the mission to the Gentiles. Involved in this may be an understanding of the destruction of Jerusalem in 70 CE as the judgement of God and the rejection

17.   Davies and Allison, *Matthew*, I, pp. 136–7.
18.   See Davies, *Sermon*, pp. 274–6, 278–9, and Davies and Allison, *Matthew*, III, pp. 695–6, 701 n. 10.
19.   Davies and Allison, *Matthew*, III, p. 695.
20.   See, for example, Stanton, *Gospel for a New People*; Luz *Matthew 1-7*; G. Bornkamm, 'The Authority to "Bind" and "Loose" in the Church in Matthew's Gospel: The Problem of Sources in Matthew's Gospel', in G. N. Stanton (ed.), *The Interpretation of Matthew* (IRT, 3; London: SPCK, 1983), pp. 85–97; J. P. Meier, *The Vision of Matthew: Christ, Church and Morality in the First Gospel* (New York: Paulist Press, 1979); and D. A. Hagner, *Matthew 1-13* (WBC, 33A; Dallas: Word Books, 1993). For important studies generally in agreement with Davies and Allison, see Overman, *Matthew's Gospel*; A. J. Saldarini, *Matthew's Christian-Jewish Community* (CSHJ; Chicago: University of Chicago Press, 1994); and D. C. Sim, *The Gospel of Matthew and Christian Judaism: The History and Social Setting of the Matthean Community* (SNTW; Edinburgh: T&T Clark, 1998).

of Israel. In outlining a position on the place of Matthew in relation to Judaism that is in many ways close to the position advocated in this chapter, U. Luz argues that Matthew's 'community, which failed with its mission to Israel, experienced the divine judgment of the destruction of Jerusalem, and now is called by the evangelist to a new undertaking'.[21] That new undertaking was the Gentile mission. Luz understands Matthew as the outworking of the experience of the destruction of Jerusalem as the judgement of God in relation to the encounter with Mark and the acceptance of the Gentile mission. This development opened up the dilemma of two divergent paths for Matthew's community, to retain its own distinctive position and remain isolated between Judaism and the Great Church or to move towards membership of the Great Church. Luz sees Matthew as a product of the time between leaving synagogue Judaism and joining the Great Church so that Matthew became both the Gospel of exclusive Jewish Christianity and of the Great Church.

Luz rightly recognizes the force of reception history on our reading of Matthew but he may allow it more weight than it deserves in reading Matthew in its own terms. My own reading of Matthew differs from his in a number of ways. First, rather than seeing Matthew conceived in a liminal situation between Judaism and the Great Church, it seems to me to be a work conceived within Diaspora Judaism. Obviously Matthew was in an uneasy relationship with the broader Jewish community but Matthew's portrayal of the central place of the Law for Jesus ensured that this relationship remained open. Matthew modifies Mark's understanding of mission so that this too, though problematical, does not reveal a fissure between Matthew and Judaism.

The Johannine evidence attests the exclusion from the synagogue of those who confess Jesus is the Christ. In the face of the absence of external evidence of such exclusion, a number of interpreters have concluded that these references mask the decision of some believers to leave.[22] At the very least we might say that they felt under pressure to leave.[23]

---

21.   Luz, *Matthew 1-7*, p. 85. For the dangers of this position, see J. A. Overman, *Church and Community in Crisis: The Gospel According to Matthew* (TNTIC; Valley Forge: Trinity Press International, 1996), pp. 404–8.

22.   See W. A. Meeks, 'Breaking Away: Three New Testament Pictures of Christianity's Separation from the Jewish Communities', in J. Neusner and E. S. Frerichs (eds), '*To See Ourselves as Others See Us*': *Christians, Jews, 'Others' in Late Antiquity* (SPSH; Chico: Scholars Press, 1985), pp. 93–116.

23.   Given the clarity of the Johannine text, it is unwise to reject the possibility that, at least in the Johannine locality, those who openly confessed Jesus as the Christ were excluded from the synagogue. The christological basis of the Johannine sabbath controversy in John 5 may mean that each side saw the matter differently, the synagogue viewing Johannine behaviour as a departure while the Johannine believers felt driven out. If John and Matthew need to be read in the light of what we know of the Judaism of their day, that Judaism also needs to be understood in the light of John and Matthew.

1. *The Law in Matthew*

Those who think that Matthew emerges from a community that had broken away from Judaism tend to argue that Matthew presupposes a modified commitment to the Law. Often they argue that Jesus fulfilled the Law so that specifically Jewish obligations were not required of Gentiles. A closer look at Matthew's treatment of the Law is necessary to throw light on this matter.[24] First we note that Matthew and Luke each use the term νόμος eight or nine times and John 15 times.[25] Mark does not use νόμος at all! Yet some Markan narratives have a bearing on Jesus' attitude to the Law. Matthaean editing of Mark suggests different understandings of Jesus' attitude to the Law in these two Gospels.

Matthew's use of Mk 7.1-23 in 15.1-20 provides good evidence of their different views of the Law. If, as I think, Mt. 15.1-20 is based on Mk 7.1-23, differences caused by Matthew's editing are illuminating. Although Matthew, like Mark, notes that the washing of hands before eating is a tradition of the elders, Matthew omits Mark's reference to the fact that this practice is observed by the Pharisees and all the Jews (Mk 7.3). Because Matthew rejected this tradition without repudiating his Jewishness, it was in his interest to reduce the weight of Jewish support for it. Likewise, although Matthew shares with Mark the argument put forward by Jesus that food that goes into the belly and passes out of the body cannot defile a person but rather what proceeds out of the heart defiles a person, the conclusions that are explicitly drawn by Matthew and Mark are quite different. In each Gospel the argument was put forward to counter the accusation arising from the failure of the disciples to observe the tradition of the elders. The explicit conclusion drawn by the narrator in Mark is that, by his argument, Jesus declared all food to be clean (Mk 7.19), thus rejecting the Jewish food laws. This conclusion is absent from Matthew and, given that Matthew has made use of Mark, we must assume that Matthew has rejected this conclusion. The explicit conclusion drawn by the narrator in Matthew that 'to eat with unwashed hands does not defile a person' (Mt. 15.20), is explicitly absent from Mark, though it is implied by the words of Jesus common to both Gospels. Matthew's rejection of Mark's conclusion implies the continuing force of the food laws for Matthew and his community.[26] But Matthew's rejection of the tradition of the elders, which required hand-washing to preserve purity, signals a confrontation with Formative Judaism.

24.   See 5.17, 18; 7.12; 11.13; 12.5; 22.36, 40; 23.23. In 15.6 the textual evidence favours the use of λόγον rather than νόμον.

25.   John would have 16 uses if the occurrence in 8.5 is counted.

26.   This discussion of 15.1-20 lends support to the recognition of a Law-observant mission in 28.19-20.

The word νόμος in Matthew is used by Jesus in all but one of its uses. The exception is a question asked of Jesus by a lawyer (νομικός) from amongst the Pharisees.[27] He asked him which commandment in the Law is greatest (22.36). This question allows Jesus to elaborate his understanding of the way the confusing detail of the Law is to be perceived as a coherent unity. First, Jesus unequivocally asserts that the command of Deut. 6.5 is the greatest and first commandment (22.37). This forms an alternative to the first of the ten commandments in which God commands Israel, 'You shall have no other gods but me', a command which is elaborated in the second commandment which is based on the affirmation of the jealousy of God and of God's mercy shown to those who love him and keep his commandments. The Deuteronomic form of the command asserts, 'You shall love the Lord your God with your whole (ὅλης) heart, your whole (ὅλης) life, and your whole (ὅλης) mind'. Deuteronomy represents a prophetic interpretation of the Law.[28] Second, Jesus asserts that there is a second commandment like the first and quotes from Lev. 19.18; 'You shall love your neighbour as yourself' (22.39). Bringing these two commandments together manifests prophetic hermeneutical insight along lines consistent with the interpretative activity of the Judaism of Jesus' day.[29] The two commandments chosen by the Jesus of Matthew are unified as expressions of the love command, of God and neighbour. Third, Jesus sums up, 'on these two commandments hang the whole (ὅλος) Law and the prophets' (22.40). Reference to the whole Law implies all of the laws entailed therein and 'the prophets' is also an inclusive reference. Jesus' mission was to fulfil the Law and the prophets (5.17). Because all of the Law and the prophets hang on these two commandments, Jesus also asserts; 'Therefore, whatever you will that people do to

27. Though Mk 12.28-34 does not use νόμος, it is close to Mt. 22.34-40, except Mark's sympathetic scribe becomes the Pharisaic lawyer, intent on trapping Jesus in Matthew.

28. On the prophetic understanding of the Law in Matthew, see K. Snodgrass, 'Matthew and the Law', in D. R. Bauer and M. A. Powell (eds), *Treasures New and Old: Recent Contributions to Matthean Studies* (SBLSS, 1; Atlanta: Scholars Press, 1996), pp. 99–127 (106–11).

29. In the closest Lukan equivalent to this story (Lk. 10.25-37), the testing question is put to Jesus by a lawyer, as in Matthew. But the question is genuine, 'what must I do to inherit eternal life?' Jesus turns the question on the questioner, the expert in the Law; 'What is written in the Law? How do you read?' The lawyer's understanding brings together the two commandments from Deut. 6.5 and Lev. 19.18 as Jesus does in Mt. 22.37-39 and Mk 12.30-31. Jesus affirms the correctness of the answer and tells the lawyer, 'Do this and you will live'. It seems that the bringing together of these commandments was not new, though the radical application of them as the hermeneutical key to reading the Law may have been obscured in Formative Judaism. That Luke's account continues with the parable of 'the good Samaritan' suggests a reluctance to apply the second of these two commandments.

you, you also do the same to them. For this is the Law and the prophets' (7.12).[30] But this appears to give priority to the second of the two great commandments, perhaps because this commandment was most obviously and widely ignored.

The first use of νόμος in Matthew is Jesus' first reference to the Law. It occurs in Matthew's most systematic and coherent account of Jesus' view of the place and significance of the Law (5.17-20). H. D. Betz argues that the Sermon on the Mount is a pre-Matthaean composition and that views found there are independent of Matthew.[31] Against this view it is noted that the Sermon on the Mount is part of the overall design of Matthew and internally shares the design of the other parts of the Gospel. Neither here nor there does this preclude the use of sources but reflects Matthew's overall authorial intention and method of working.

Matthew 5.17-20 programmatically sets out Matthew's understanding of the Law in opposition to Pauline Christianity and Formative Judaism:

> Do not suppose that I have come to destroy the Law and the prophets; I have not come to destroy but to fulfil. Truly I say to you, until Heaven and earth pass away, one small letter (ἰῶτα) or one small part of a letter (κεραία) shall certainly not pass away (παρέλθῃ) from the Law until all things come to be (ἕως ἂν πάντα γένηται).[32] Whoever breaks one of the least of these commandments and teaches the same to men, he will be called least in the kingdom of Heaven; but whoever does and teaches (these commandments) this person will be called great in the kingdom of Heaven. For I say to you, unless your righteousness exceeds that of the scribes and Pharisees, you will certainly not enter the kingdom of Heaven (Mt. 5.17-20).

J. P. Meier and others think that the qualification 'until all things come to be' means that in Matthew's interpretation of the teaching of Jesus some aspects of the Jewish Law are no longer in force, being already fulfilled, at least subsequent to the resurrection of Jesus if not as a consequence of the ministry of Jesus. The tension between the command of Mt. 10.5-6, which restricts the mission to the lost sheep of the house of Israel, and the command to embark on a universal mission in 28.19-20 is also explained on the basis that the resurrection has intervened, bringing about a change from the mission to Israel to the mission to the Gentiles. But those who adopt this view have not taken account of the fact that Matthew provides no instance of a *Biblical law* that has passed away.

30. Matthew 11.13 shares with Lk. 16.16 (Q?) Jesus' saying, 'all the prophets and the Law prophesied until John'. The order of the words (in Mt. 11.13) is 'prophets and Law' which reverses Matthew's other more conventional uses of the two words (5.17; 7.12; 22.40) and the order of Luke's parallel saying in 16.16.

31. See H. D. Betz, *The Sermon on the Mount* (Hermeneia; Minneapolis: Fortress Press, 1995).

32. Commonly translated as 'until all is accomplished'. Cf. Lk. 16.17 and see Mt. 24.35//Mk 13.31 and Lk. 21.33 for a comparable saying about the words of Jesus.

The details of 5.17-20 combine to rule out the abandonment of any part of the Law. First, Jesus asserts he did not come to do away with the Law or the prophets. Second, he indicates that not even the smallest letter or the smallest part of a letter of the Law will pass away until Heaven and earth pass away. In the parallel of this saying (Lk. 16.17) Jesus says, 'It is easier for Heaven and earth to pass away than for one stroke of a letter (κεραίαν) of the Law to be abolished'. This confirms that the saying does not mean that any part of the Law will be abandoned: 'until Heaven and earth pass away' means 'It is not going to happen'. Third, Jesus contrasts the person who breaks even the least of the commandments and teaches others to do so and is the least in the kingdom of Heaven with the person who keeps and teaches (the Law) and will be great in the kingdom of Heaven. This criticism seems to be aimed at Paul as the prime exponent of the Law-free gospel, while the reference to the one who teaches observance in word and action is probably a reference to James the Just, the brother of Jesus. [33]

For Matthew, the coming of Jesus to fulfil the Law and the prophets is to bring the reality commanded into being. It is about the keeping of the Law in its deepest sense rather than its abolition in any sense. What then does the reference to 'until all things come to be' mean? It is surely a reference back to 'until Heaven and earth pass away'. Only then will even the smallest part of a letter of the Law cease to be binding. Lk.16.17 says, 'It is easier for Heaven and earth to pass away than for one stroke of a letter (μίαν κεραίαν) of the Law to be abolished (πεσεῖν)'. Hence, 'until Heaven and earth pass away, may mean, 'don't hold your breath, it is not going to happen!'. There is no room to suggest that Jesus came to diminish the Law. Rather, Matthew's interpretation provides an understanding of the continuing and intensified demands of the Law.

In 5.17-20 Matthew is fighting on two fronts. He is confronting the continuing challenge of Pauline Christianity as perceived in his time, which did not keep the commandments and taught others to break them as well (Mt. 5.19; cf. Acts 21.21). The strand of tradition which asserts the continuing demands of the Law understood in their deepest sense, is peculiar to Matthew (M), and stems from James and Jerusalem but became embedded in what ultimately became a Petrine Gospel affirming the mission to the nations.[34]

---

33. H. D. Betz, *Essays on the Sermon on the Mount* (Philadelphia: Fortress Press, 1985), p. 20, agrees that Paul is the target of the criticism of Mt. 5.19. B. H. Streeter, *The Four Gospels: A Study of Origins* (London: Macmillan, 1924), pp. 256–7, also sees the criticism aimed at Paul while the praise has James the Just in view.

34. For the description of the two missions, many factions, including those represented by James and Peter, see Painter, *Just James*, pp. 73–8.

While Paul was a target of the M tradition, the primary target of the criticism in Matthew is the group described as the scribes and Pharisees who, in Matthew's time, are represented by Formative Judaism. Matthew makes clear that loyalty to the Law is fundamental for the followers of Jesus, and Formative Judaism falls under the critique of Matthew's understanding of the Law. Jesus rebukes the scribes and Pharisees as hypocrites who painstakingly tithe in petty matters but fail in the weightier matters of justice, mercy and faith. Jesus says, 'It is these (justice, mercy, and faith) that you ought to have done without neglecting the others' (23.23). The deeper demand is given priority but does not render obsolete what may appear to be petty tithing. The Jesus of Matthew pointedly asserts, 'unless your righteousness *exceeds* the righteousness of the scribes and Pharisees, you will certainly not enter the kingdom of Heaven' (5.20). It is not the one rather than the other, but in addition to the other! Thus, already in 5.17-20 there is an antithetical dimension to the teaching of Jesus and this becomes especially pointed in 5.21-48.

Insight into the more stringent interpretation of the Law is given in the six antitheses of Mt. 5.21-48. Some of the antitheses and the adversative form of all are peculiar to Matthew (M). The adversative form, 'You have heard that it was said to those of old... *But I say to you...*', suggests that the position of Jesus is new and is *opposed* to the old position found in the Law (the first part of the Hebrew Bible).[35] This is, to some extent, misleading. Certainly the adversative form gives expression to a polemical position, but the old is opposed only in one sense. The Law, *as interpreted by Formative Judaism*, was opposed by the Law as interpreted by the Matthaean Jesus. Even then, in these sayings the Jesus of Matthew does not propose *breaking* the Law as interpreted by 'those of old'. Rather, Jesus proposes a more radical and demanding interpretation of the Law and this is foreshadowed in the demand, 'Unless your righteousness exceeds the righteousness of the scribes and Pharisees, you will certainly not enter the kingdom of Heaven' (Mt. 5.20).

R. H. Gundry argues that Matthew's 'antithetical manner puts distance between Matthew's community and anything recognizably Judaistic'.[36] This argument overlooks that, in spite of the antithetical form, the

---

35. Cf. Mt. 5.21 and Exod. 20.13; 21.12; Deut. 5.17; Lev. 24.17; Mt. 5.27 and Exod. 20.14; Deut. 5.18; Mt. 5.31 and Deut. 24.1; Mt. 5.33 and Lev. 19.12; Num. 30.2; Deut. 23.21; Mt. 5.38 and Exod. 21.24; Lev. 24.20; Deut. 19.21; Mt. 5.43 and Lev. 19.18. The full adversative form is found only in sayings 1 and 4, suggesting two groups of three sayings in which the second and third sayings of each group have abbreviated introductions.

36. R. H. Gundry, 'A Responsive Evaluation of the Social History of the Matthean Community in Roman Syria', in D. L. Balch (ed.), *Social History of the Matthean Community: Cross-Disciplinary Approaches* (Minneapolis: Fortress Press, 1991), pp. 62–7 (65).

antitheses are not against the Law. They do not advocate breaking or dispensing with the Law but are intensifications of its inward demand. They get to the heart of the commandments using material largely peculiar to Matthew (M).

2. *Matthew and Q*

Matthew 11.12-14 (//Lk. 16.16) might seem to be in tension with the distinctively Matthaean 5.17-20. Such tension could be explained as Matthew's failure to reconcile conflicting tendencies between rather neutral Q and more Judaistic M traditions. A comparison of Mt. 11.12-14 with Lk. 16.16-17 and Mt. 5.18 opens up other readings.[37] First Mt. 11.12-14:

> From (ἀπὸ δὲ) the days of John the Baptist until now (ἕως ἄρτι) the kingdom of Heaven suffers violence and violent people attack it. For all the prophets and the Law prophesied until (ἕως) John; and if you will receive it, he is Elijah who is destined to come.

The form of this Q saying in Lk. 16.16-17 connects the saying about John to a saying about the Law found also in Mt. 5.18.

> The Law and the prophets were until (μέχρι) John; from then on (ἀπὸ τότε) the kingdom of God is preached (εὐαγγελίζεται) and every one violently enters (βιάζεται) into it. It is easier for Heaven and earth to pass away (παρελθεῖν) than for one stroke of a letter (μίαν κεραίαν) of the Law to be abolished (πεσεῖν).

Matthew and Luke have treated the saying about John quite differently. Matthew has placed it in the context of his account of Jesus' witness to the role and significance of John the Baptist (Mt. 11.7-19).[38] Matthew's composition brings together John the Baptist and Jesus, shaping the Q saying to set John the Baptist on the side of fulfilment with Jesus, not with the Law and the prophets. This is made clear by the identification of John the Baptist with the eschatological coming of Elijah (Mt. 11.14, which is without parallel in Luke). Matthew alone presents the message of the Baptist in exactly the same terms as the message of Jesus. Both are messengers of the kingdom preaching, 'Repent; for the kingdom of Heaven is at hand' (Mt. 3.2; 4.17).

---

37. The relationship of Lk.16.18 to Mt. 5.31-32 may also throw light on Matthew's compositional approach and meaning.

38. Paradoxically 11.11 says that of those born of women there is none greater than John the Baptist but that the least in the kingdom of God is greater than he! Does this mean that those in the kingdom of Heaven are not born of women?

For Matthew this means that John the Baptist has been moved in the direction of the new order. By comparison with Mark, Matthew moves his understanding of Jesus in the direction of the old by treating Jesus' interpretation of the Law and emphasizing the continuity between John and Jesus as messengers of cataclysmic judgement. The continuity continues in the account of the sending out of the Twelve with the instruction to preach, 'The kingdom of Heaven is at hand' (Mt. 10.7). This lacks only the call to 'repent', which is surely implied.

3. *Mission in Matthew*

For Davies and Allison, Matthew is post-Pauline because it assumes the Gentile mission, but pre-Johannine and pre-Ignatian in its attitude to the Jews as a whole.[39] That Matthew is post-Pauline need not be challenged, though it does not follow from Matthew's adoption of the mission to the nations that Matthew adopts the Pauline Law-free approach to the Gentile mission. Indeed, it is fundamental to our argument that Mt. 28.19-20 is understood, not as the mission to the Gentiles but as the mission to 'all the nations', including the Jews.[40] Davies and Allison contend that Matthew's treatment of the Jews is different from John's and this indicates that Matthew is pre-Johannine. But the differences are not as great as is sometimes supposed and they need not be the consequence of time. Such differences as there are may reflect different approaches to and relationships with emerging Jewish authority.

In Matthew's account of the sending out of the Twelve (Mt. 10.1-16) Jesus commands the disciples, 'Do not go into a way of the Gentiles, and do not enter a city of the Samaritans; but go rather to the lost sheep of the house of Israel' (Mt. 10.5-6). They are commanded to announce the arrival of the kingdom of Heaven (Mt. 10.7), to heal the sick, raise the dead, cleanse the lepers, and cast out demons (10.8) and to restrict the scope of their mission to Israel (10.5-6). These are the terms of the circumcision mission peculiar to Matthew (M) and an expression of the Jerusalem mission of the James faction. In Matthew this came to be understood as a limitation restricted to the time of the mission of Jesus. Matthew understood that the mission was extended to the nations after the resurrection of Jesus and was based on the necessity of circumcision and the keeping of the Law, which was the position of the Petrine faction.[41]

---

39. Davies and Allison, *Matthew*, I, pp. 137–8.

40. The formula πάντα τὰ ἔθνη virtually excludes a specific reference to the Gentiles. A reference to the Gentiles would be, 'make disciples of all the Gentiles'. Only if nations are differentiated is it necessary to say 'all the nations'. Cf. Rev. 7.9; 15.4.

41. See Painter, *Just James*, pp. 73–8.

That the mission, though based on circumcision and Law-observance, also had Gentiles in view is made clear by the narrative of the resurrection appearance and commission of Jesus to the eleven disciples to 'go and make disciples of all the nations' (Mt. 28.19-20). If the Jews are included in the description 'all the nations', it is also clear that the mission cannot be confined to Israel, as was the case in Mt. 10.5-6, now understood to apply only to the time of Jesus' ministry. The form of the later commission signals the scope of the mission of the Matthaean community and should be carefully examined. There is no command here *to proclaim the gospel* to all nations. Rather, the command is in three parts. First, make disciples of all the nations. Focus on the new universalism of the mission has obscured what the mission was to accomplish. It is the communication of a lifestyle to which the nations are to conform. Second, they are to be baptized. Baptism was important for the Matthaean community but there is nothing to suggest that it took the place of circumcision. Rather the demand for the greater righteousness suggests that the requirement of baptism was an additional, not an alternative, requirement. Third, they are to be taught *to observe* all the commandments of Jesus. This signals a Law-based mission where the commands of Jesus are to be found in his interpretation of the Law in its intensified form as found in Matthew. Overall this Law-observant position was true of both Peter and James but the active mission to the nations reflects the ultimate dominance of Peter's approach. Matthew incorporates tradition from James in such a way as to support Petrine leadership and legitimate a Law-observant mission to the nations.

It is unlikely that Matthew would have survived in what became a dominantly Gentile church unless an alternative reading was possible. Ignatius refers to Gentile Judaizers who seem to have been Christians.[42] They read Matthew in a way relevant to what had become a Gentile church and for which the teaching of Jesus had become a new Law. Many of the 'ritual' elements of the Jewish Law were disregarded, perhaps because Matthew was now read in circles that were not free from the influence of Paul. It was not noticed that Matthew did not share Paul's critique of the Law and no alternative rationale was sought for the abandonment of circumcision, Jewish food laws and other aspects of the Law. In the church of all nations Matthew was read as if the peculiarly Jewish elements no longer applied. This against the grain reading of Matthew was assisted by Matthew's critique of the scribes and Pharisees and his negative portrayal of the Jews in the crucifixion of Jesus.

---

42. W. R. Schoedel, 'Ignatius and the Reception of Matthew in Antioch', in Balch, *Social History*, pp. 129–77 (144–5).

4. *The Law in John*

In John the role of the Law is quite different from Matthew. John contrasts Jesus with Moses and the Law. Jesus confronts the Jewish authorities over the issue of sabbath observance. All of the Gospels portray Jesus in conflict over the sabbath and (especially Matthew) use Jewish strategies in an attempt to allay criticism. The Jesus of John does this also (7.23), but only after his initial 'defence' had totally alienated his critics (5.16-18).[43] In John 5.17 he defends *work* on the sabbath and this leads his critics to set his activity in opposition to Moses. Nevertheless, Jesus asserts that it is Moses who will accuse his Jewish critics (5.45). For the Jesus of John, the Law, like the scriptures as a whole, bears witness to him and this is their authentic role (5.39, 46). For the narrator, Jesus embodies the reality to which the Law bears witness (1.14, 17).

In John 1.17 the narrator affirms, 'The Law was given by (διὰ) Moses, grace and truth came by (διὰ) Jesus Christ'.[44] The mediation of Moses is contrasted with the mediation of Jesus. The concluding paragraph of the Prologue, in which this statement stands, poses certain problems, which can be resolved along the following lines. John 1.14 announces the incarnation of the λόγος, which has been foreshadowed by the first mention of John (the Baptist) as the witness to the coming of the true light into the world (1.6-13). The announcement of the incarnation of the λόγος by the narrator, speaking for the community of believers in the first person plural, follows in 1.14 ('we beheld his glory'), and the witness of John is reintroduced (1.15; cf. 1.6). In 1.6 the narrator describes John's role and purpose. In 1.15 the narrator reintroduces the witness, who speaks in his own words that foreshadow (repeat?) his saying in the narrative following the Prologue (1.30). Thus 1.15 adopts a time perspective later than and looking back to the narrative of 1.30, 'This was (ἦν) the one of whom (ὂν) I said (εἶπον), "The one coming after

---

43. See Mk 2.23-28; 3.1-6 and parallels. In these incidents Jesus uses scriptural precedent for actions he seeks to justify, as does the Jesus of John in 7.22-23. But the Jesus of John had already given a christological justification of the sabbath breach in 5.17. Mk 2.27-28 concludes with a christological justification, which follows scriptural precedent, so that his christological justification seems less confronting: 'The sabbath was made for humankind, not humankind for the sabbath; so that the Son of Man is Lord also of the sabbath'. This christological justification is less offensive than Jn 5.17 because the Jesus of Mark links the Son of Man with humanity whereas the Jesus of John appeals to the continuing work of his Father to justify his own work on the sabbath. Inherent in his argument is his claim that he speaks only what he hears from the Father and does only what he sees the Father doing (3.32, 35; 5.19-20, 30).

44. Only here and in 17.3 is the double name 'Jesus Christ' used in John. In the New Testament only John explains that 'Christ' is the translation of the Hebrew 'Messiah'. This tends to exclude the use of Christ as a personal name for Jesus, a development that took place quite early in the Gentile world.

me has become before me (ἔμπροσθέν μου γέγονεν), because he was before me (πρῶτός μου ἦν)"'.[45] At the end of 1.15, 1.16 returns to the first person plural of 1.14. As no speaker is identified there or in 1.16-18 we may say that the narrator speaks for a group of witnesses. Their witness is interrupted by John (the Baptist), whose witness leaves no doubt that these words are spoken of Jesus, identified as the incarnate Word in 1.14. The words of 1.16-18 are addressed by the narrator to the reader. Like the words of Jesus, they give a reliable, if at times enigmatic, guide to the meaning of the Gospel.

The polarization of Moses and Jesus in John is clearest in the balanced statement of 1.17. Reference to the dwelling (ἐσκήνωσεν) of the incarnate Word 'among us' (1.14) is reminiscent of images of the Law dwelling with Israel (Sir. 24.8, 10; Wis. 9.10; Bar. 3.37; Prov. 8.31). Clearly the Law is thought of as the Word of God (see Ps. 119.105).[46] The polarization of the Law given (ἐδόθη) by the agency of Moses and grace and truth coming to be (ἐγένετο) by the agency of Jesus Christ is clear. The agency of Moses and of Jesus (indicated by διά plus the genitive case) distinguishes each from the source of the Law and the source of grace and truth. The comparison of agencies gives way to contrasts between Law and grace, between giving and the creative bringing of something into being. In the opening verses of the Prologue it is said of the λόγος that all things came to be through him (πάντα δι᾿ αὐτοῦ ἐγένετο). The point of 1.17 seems to be that grace and truth come into being through the agency of Jesus Christ. In John, only in 1.14, 16-17, is the word 'grace' used and the paired grace and truth is found only in 1.14, 17. C. H. Dodd recognized that this unusual pairing represents the Hebrew phrase אמת וחסד.[47] These words describe the attributes of God and were believed to be revealed in the Law. But the Prologue asserts that grace and truth came to be and are revealed in Jesus Christ (1.14, 17).

The Jesus of John also recognizes that the Law was given by Moses.[48] He asks the Jewish crowd (7.15, 20), 'Has not Moses given you the

---

45.   Already in 1.30 John the Baptist referred back to an earlier statement; 'This is the one concerning whom (ὑπὲρ οὗ) I said (εἶπον), "After me comes a man (ἀνήρ) who has become before me, because he was before me"'. The many small variations in the two statements reveal the evangelist's love of linguistic variation in a Gospel that is thematically repetitive. The self-conscious strategy of the evangelist was to write the story of Jesus from the perspective of a later time. John 1.18 is written from the perspective of Jesus' return to the bosom of the Father.

46.   The whole of Psalm 119 is a Torah liturgy in which the Law is praised under many images. In addition to the prominent use of word, we find commandments, statutes, decrees, precepts and ordinances.

47.   C. H. Dodd, *The Interpretation of the Fourth Gospel* (Cambridge: Cambridge University Press, 1953), pp. 82, 175, 295, 299.

48.   But Jesus rejected the view that Moses *has given* the Manna (bread from heaven), arguing instead that 'my father *gives* you the true bread from heaven' (6.32). In Jewish sources bread is a symbol for the Law, perhaps arising from 'One does not live by bread alone

Law?', assuming a yes answer, but then asserts that no one does the Law and asks, 'Why do you seek to kill me?' (7.19). The crowd rejects this accusation and asserts that Jesus has a demon (7.20). But hostility to Jesus has been evident since the sabbath healing in ch. 5 and the hostility (5.16) was upgraded to the attempt to kill him (5.18) when Jesus defended his action by appealing to the continuing work of the Father in which he shares (5.17). The threat of death recurs in 7.2, and in 7.23 it becomes apparent that the making whole of the man on the sabbath in ch. 5 is the fundamental cause. Jesus notes the paradox that they will circumcise a person on the sabbath so that the Law would not be broken but they hate him because he made a man whole on the sabbath (7.23).[49] In this debate Jesus comes close to using something like the prophetic interpretation of the Law (found in Matthew) against a legalistic application of the Law, which he seeks to show has an inner flaw. Jesus asks, if the sabbath law can be set aside in order to keep the law concerning circumcision, why are the Jews angry with him because he made a man whole on the sabbath? The example of circumcision relates to resolving the problem of the clash of two laws. Thus the precedent to which Jesus appeals is different from the case he seeks to justify, which is more closely related to another attempt to justify sabbath action.

In Mk 3.4 (repeated with slight variation in Lk. 6.9 but modified in Mt. 12.10-11 and Lk. 14.3) Jesus is faced by a man with a withered hand in a hostile situation one sabbath in a synagogue. He asks, 'Is it lawful on the sabbath to do good or to do evil, to save a life or to kill?' In Matthew the testing situation is strengthened because the question is put to Jesus to test him and specifically asks, 'Is it lawful to heal on the sabbath?'. The aim was to get evidence as the basis for an accusation against Jesus. In response to their obvious hostility Jesus asks which of them, if their sheep fell into a pit on the sabbath, would not pull it out. Assuming that they would he asserts that a person is of much more value than a sheep and concludes that it is lawful to do well (καλῶς) on the sabbath. The illustration describes a crisis which occurs on the sabbath and is remedied on the sabbath. The waiving of the sabbath prohibition presumes a critical situation in which delay would be disastrous. Presumably, the man's hand had been as it was for some time and might have waited another day. The same might be said for the men Jesus healed in John 5 and John 9. Further, the man in John 5 was instructed by Jesus to take up his bed and

---

but by every word that comes from the mouth of the Lord' (Deut. 8.3). Not Moses but the Lord is the source of the giving of the Law.

49.   The language of making whole (ὑγιής) in 7.23 identifies this healing with John 5, where the word is used in 5.6, 9, 11, 14, 15. It is used nowhere else in John and rarely in the rest of the New Testament where it is found only in Mt. 12.13; 15.31; Mk 5.34; Acts 4.10, and Tit. 2.8.

to carry it off (5.8-9). He was observed in the act by the Jews and they cautioned him (5.10), 'It is the sabbath and it is not lawful for you to carry your bed'. He explained (5.11), 'The person who made me whole, he said to me, "Take up your bed and walk"'. Even if the healing could be defended, the bearing of a burden on the sabbath could not, so the Jewish response to Jesus in 5.16 is understandable and their anger would not have been mollified by the argument of 7.23. This argument is an attempt to appease his opponents, but it comes too late. Jesus' defence of his action at the time (5.17) tends to undermine the sabbath commandment. In defending the sabbath healing he asserts, 'My Father is working until now, and I am working'.[50] Because it is precisely work that is forbidden on the sabbath, Jesus' choice of words in the defence of his action is provocative. Because he appealed to God as his father and identified his work with God's work the Jews sought to kill him (5.18).

It is a puzzle that the recurring conflict issuing from the sabbath healing of John 5 should lead to a more apologetic defence only in 7.23 where it is similar to Jesus' defence of sabbath healings in the synoptics, especially Matthew. The evangelist has made the incident of John 5 the turning-point where openness to Jesus gives way to hostility, the paradigm of rejection.[51] The basis for the change is Jesus' failure to observe the sabbath and his encouragement of others to follow his practice. The waves caused by the sabbath healing of John 5 are still evident in John 7 and the issue is reignited in John 9. There the Jews/Pharisees conclude that Jesus is not from God but is a sinner because he does not keep the sabbath (9.16, 24). In opposition to the healed man, whom they name as a disciple of Jesus, they claim to be disciples of Moses (9.28-29). If the narrator sets Moses over against Jesus in 1.17, the Pharisees/Jews do so in a more hostile fashion in John 9. It is for this reason that the confession that Jesus is the Christ is, in the Johannine situation, grounds for exclusion from the synagogue (9.22, 34; 12.42; 16.2).

In John, the Law finds focus in the sabbath commandment, and is at the heart of the conflict between Jesus and the Jews, and the followers of Jesus and the Jews. The Jewish authorities declare any who follow Jesus to be ignorant of the Law and accursed (7.49). To no avail, Nicodemus objects that the Law does not judge a person without a hearing in which evidence is weighed (7.51-52). But the last word about the Law in John has to be

---

50. On the implied incomplete creation, see J. Painter, 'Earth Made Whole: John's Rereading of Genesis', in J. Painter, R. A. Culpepper and F. F. Segovia (eds), *Word, Theology, and Community* (St Louis: Chalice, 2002), pp. 65–84. For earlier readings moving in this direction, see J. Painter, 'Text and Context in John 5', *ABR* 35 (1987), pp. 28–34 and *idem.*, 'Theology and Eschatology in the Prologue of John', *SJT* 46 (1993), pp. 27–42.

51. See ch. 5, 'The Paradigm of Rejection', in Painter, *The Quest for the Messiah*, pp. 213–52.

that its validity depends on its witness to Jesus (1.45; 5.46). Indeed, according to the Jesus of John, not only the Law and the prophets, but also all of the scriptures bear witness to him (5.39). Just as Moses wrote of him (5.46) so did all of the writers of the scriptures and it is Moses who will judge those who reject him (5.45).

There are two views of the relationship of Jesus to Moses in John. There is the hostile relationship claimed by the Jews/Pharisees and there is the positive view claimed by Jesus. The narrator sees the incarnation of the λόγος as the embodiment of the reality enshrined in the Law (1.14, 17). That reality is also communicated in the new commandment (13.34-35; 15.12, 17; 1 Jn 3.23). The new commandment is rooted in the life of Jesus, 'Love one another as (καθώς) I have loved you. By this all people will know that you are my disciples, if you have love for one another'.[52] The love of Jesus is the source, motivating cause, and model for the disciples' love of one another. This love is the fulfilment of the Law. In John the disciples have been radically oriented to God revealed in Jesus. What is problematic is their love for one another. The Johannine Jesus is at pains to enable the love of God for the world, revealed in him, to become the source of the disciples' love for one another and the world (13.34-35; 15.9-13; 17.20-23, 26).

5. *Mission in John*

The καθώς ethic of the Johannine Jesus is the basis for the Johannine understanding of mission (13.34-35; 17.18, 20-23, 26; 20.21). Because the disciples love one another in response to Jesus' love for them and in the same way, the world recognizes them as Jesus' disciples, and the mission continues. In the prayer of John 17 Jesus speaks retrospectively of the commission of the disciples, 'As (καθώς) you sent (ἀπέστειλας) me into the world, I also sent (ἀπέστειλα) them into the world'. Compare the abbreviated form of the commission by the risen Jesus in 20.21; 'As (καθώς) the Father has sent (ἀπέσταλκέν) me, I also send (πέμπω) you'.[53] The mission of the disciples to the world is rooted in and arises from Jesus' mission from the Father. In two parallel verses Jesus' mission is expressed first in terms of God's gift and then in terms of his mission, being sent:

52. For discussion of the καθώς ethic of the Johannine Jesus, see Painter, *1, 2, and 3 John*, pp. 124, 142, 152-3, 168-70, 176-8, 268-70, 283-4, 406.

53. Obviously the two verbs of sending are used in the same sense as the parallel shows. John evidently uses ἀποστέλλω to provide the aorist and perfect tenses while using πέμπω to provide the present and future tenses. For the future see 14.26; 15.26. The Jesus of John also uses πέμπω for the aorist participle in the phrase ὁ πέμψας με πατήρ (e.g. 5.37).

For God loved the world in this way, he *gave* his only begotten son so that every one who believes in him would not perish but have eternal life.
For God did not *send* the Son into the world to condemn the world, but that the world may be saved through him. (3.16-17)

The purpose of the mission of the Son from the Father was to give eternal life, to save the world. The source of the mission was the love of God for the world, expressed as an act of giving. The mission to the world remains in view with the gathering of disciples by Jesus; he commands them to love one another because and in the same way as he has loved them, so that the world may know that they are his disciples (13.34-35). The mission to the world remains alive with their presence. The love of Jesus for them is specifically revealed in the footwashing, which is both a source and model for their lives together (13.14-15). It is also shown in the giving of his life for them (15.12-13; cf. 18.8). At his arrest Jesus gives himself up so that the disciples may go free.

The great prayer of Jesus is focused on the disciples and those who would come to believe through their witness. The prayer is that the mission may continue true to its source in the love of God so that the world may come to believe and to know the love which God has for the world (17.18, 20-23, 26). For John the success of the mission brings into living reality the fulfilment of the Law, expressed in the love command. While this focus explicitly names only the second of the two great commands upon which (according to the synoptics) all of the Law and the prophets hang, the fulfilment of that command presupposes living out of the love of God made present in Jesus. As the writer of 1 John was to put it, 'We love because he first loved us' (1 Jn 4.19), and 'In this is love, not that we loved God but that he loved us' (1 Jn 4.10). The Johannine understanding of God and his love for the world impelled the Gospel to adopt an openness to the world. Its relationship to Judaism, its ethnic home, made this openness uncomfortable for those committed to this journey. Openness to the world increased alienation from their ethnic home, and they found themselves under pressure from a hostile world. The distinctive christological handling of the Law by the Johannine Jesus and the openness to mission to the world set out in the farewell prayer made a break from its Jewish home inevitable.

6. *Matthew, John and Judaism*

In the long run both Matthew and John are read as Gospels of the Great Church. In the light of what we now know of the Judaism of the time from Jewish sources like the texts from Qumran, the Jewish character of John can be recognized. Matthew has long stood out as the Jewish Gospel because of Jesus' understanding of the Law. What has not always been understood is that the prophetic interpretation of the Law by the Jesus of Matthew involves no relaxation of the Law and yet it embraces the mission to the nations. In that mission the Jewish people continued to have an important place. With the Johannine view of mission to the world it is difficult to see how an effective mission to the Jewish people could be sustained. On issues like sabbath observance a polemical rather than an apologetic stance is adopted. While the polemical stance provides christological clarity, it is shocking to the Jewish reader. On the other hand, Matthew's nuanced distinction between the traditions of the elders and Biblical laws allowed an uneasy debate to continue with Formative Judaism.

Although Matthew and John probably reached final composition around the same time and each manifests evidence of a struggle with Formative Judaism, these two Gospels present very different accounts of the mission and teaching of Jesus. It is likely that each of these Gospels was composed in a different city. Matthew presupposes continuing contact with a large Jewish community. Jewish diversity at this time will have contributed to the differences between the two books. But the traditions were already shaped significantly in or around Jerusalem before 70 CE. The Johannine tradition provides evidence of the influence of a stream of Judaism now best known to us in some of the distinctive texts from Qumran.[54] In understanding the difference between Matthew and John, the influence of different streams of Judaism before 70 CE is as important as the different locations in which each of the Gospels was completed. To this we should add a recognition of the distinctive guiding influence to which we ascribe the authorship of each of these Gospels.

---

54. See Painter, *The Quest for the Messiah*, pp. 5–9, 33–52, 61–87 and *idem.* 'Monotheism and Dualism: John and Qumran', in G. Van Belle, J. G. van der Watt and P. Maritz (eds), *Theology and Christology in the Fourth Gospel* (Leuven: Peeters, 2005), pp. 225–43.

5. MATTHEW AND HEBREWS

MARTIN HASITSCHKA SJ

The Epistle to the Hebrews is a document with some elements of a letter, written by an anonymous author probably between 80 and 90 CE in Rome.[1] It can be called an exhortation, or more precisely, a 'word of consolation (παρακλήσεως)' (Heb. 13.22). The document wants to encourage second generation Christians who are in danger of weakening in the face of suffering and persecution. It does so through a new interpretation of the Easter events. The author sets the risen Lord before the eyes of his audience and shows them his soteriological significance. The main image used by the author is that of the High Priest, a metaphor borrowed from the Temple cult. Just as the High Priest performs the rites of blood sacrifice and enters the Holy of Holies of the Temple as the place of privileged access to God, so Jesus has reached through death the heavenly sanctuary and in it an intimate closeness to God. Out of his free will he gave his life for believers, he offered himself as a sacrifice 'once and for all' (Heb. 7.27) and thus surpassed all cultic sacrifices forever.

It cannot be answered with any degree of certainty whether the author of the Epistle to the Hebrews knew and used the Gospel of Matthew, or whether he assumes knowledge of Matthew among his audience. But there are twofold commonalities between both texts. The first is that the proclamation of Jesus Christ forms the central theme of both texts, even though the Epistle to the Hebrews emphasizes much more forcefully the working of the risen and exalted Christ than the Gospel of Matthew. Secondly, both texts are rooted theologically and literarily within the world and the texts of the Hebrew scriptures and are unintelligible without them.

This study comprises two parts. The first part gives a short overview of the common literary elements, ideas and motifs in these two early Christian documents. This discussion will also offer some insight into differing emphases. The second part examines more closely the concept of the forgiveness of sins in connection with the ideas of covenant and the

---

1.   U. Schnelle, *Einleitung in das Neue Testament* (Göttingen: Vandenhoeck & Ruprecht, 4th edn, 2002), pp. 411–27; and E. Grässer, *An die Hebräer* (EKKNT, 17; 2 vols; Zürich: Benziger Verlag, 1990, 1993), I, pp. 19–25.

blood sacrifice. Here a surprising theological convergence between Matthew and Hebrews becomes apparent.

1. *Common Literary Elements, Ideas and Motifs*

Most writings of the New Testament exhibit a more or less strongly developed relationship to the Hebrew scriptures. Quotations and the adaptation of concepts and ideas are, however, noticeably frequent in both Matthew and Hebrews. They play an important role in their respective theological arguments. The christology of both writings is 'according to scripture', building on the foundation of the Hebrew scriptures and drawing from its authority. Both the Gospel of Matthew and the Epistle to the Hebrews (and the latter more frequently) quote the Septuagint. It serves as proof from scripture even where it differs from the Hebrew text (e.g. Mt. 1.23 and Isa. 7.14; Mt. 21.16 and Ps. 8.2; Heb. 2.6-8 and Ps. 8.5-7; Heb. 10.5-7 and Ps. 40.7-9). The frequent use of the Septuagint suggests that both texts arose among Jewish Christians making their home in the Diaspora. The following presents themes common to Matthew and Hebrews. They are ordered in a sequence that mainly follows the structure of Matthew's Gospel.

Jesus is the Son of Abraham (Mt. 1.1) and has a mission to the people of Israel founded by Abraham (Mt. 10.5). Similarly the Epistle to the Hebrews states that Jesus became like his brothers and sisters in every respect (Heb. 2.17) and came to help the children of Abraham (Heb. 2.16).

The term 'people' (λαός) is used in Matthew (e.g. Mt. 1.21; 2.6; 4.16, 23) and in Hebrews (e.g. Heb. 2.17; 4.9; 5.3; 8.10; 11.25; 13.12) to refer to the chosen people of God, Israel. Jesus renews this λαός, to which the believers in Christ now belong.

In the narrative of the visit of the Magi in Mt. 2.1-12 the theme of homage to Jesus (προσκυνέω – Mt. 2.2, 8, 11) is introduced and continues to play a major role in the course of the Gospel (Mt. 8.2; 9.18; 14.33; 15.25; 20.20 and especially 28.9, 17). Jesus is owed homage and adoration otherwise reserved for God. In Hebrews the risen Jesus is offered adoration (προσκυνέω) not, as in Mt. 28.9 17, by humans, but by angels (Heb. 1.6).

Both Matthew and Hebrews develop a special christology revolving around the term 'Son' (e.g. Mt. 2.15, 'Out of Egypt I have called my Son'; Mt. 11.25, 27, 'and no one knows the Son except the Father, and no one knows the Father except the Son and anyone to whom the Son chooses to reveal him'; Mt. 16.16, 'You are the Messiah, the Son of the living God'; Heb. 1.2, 'But in these last days he has spoken to us by a Son, whom he appointed heir of all things, through whom he also created the world'). Both works emphasize that God reveals himself in the Son, and that Jesus possesses universal power and dominion (Mt. 28.16-20; Heb. 1.1-4, 5-14).

An important supporting role is played by angels (ἄγγελοι) in Matthew (Mt. 1.20, 24; 2.13, 19; 4.11; 18.10; 26.53; 28.2, 5) and in Hebrews (Heb. 1.4, 5-7; 2.5-9; 13.2). In different ways both writings show how Jesus is superior to the angels.

Both writings speak of the Law (νόμος) and thus show that they are theologically at home in the world of the Hebrew scriptures and Jewish thought. The Gospel of Matthew aims with the use of the term νόμος first and foremost at the ethical aspects of the Torah. The ethos of the Torah is not abolished but fulfilled by Jesus (Mt. 5.17-18) and finds its completion in the double commandment of love for God and neighbour (Mt. 22.34-40). In the Epistle to the Hebrews νόμος refers mostly to cultic legislation (Heb. 7.28; 8.4; 9.22). The lawfully ordered cult and especially the Temple cult is, however, but a 'shadow' (Heb. 10.1) of the cult in the heavenly sanctuary where Christ acts as the High Priest. The earthly cultic order has lost its efficacy and meaning through the event of the death and resurrection of Jesus.

Only in Matthew and Hebrews does the adjective 'merciful' (ἐλεήμων) appear. The beatitude of those that are merciful (Mt. 5.7) stands alongside the discourse about the merciful High Priest (Heb. 2.17). Typical for the Gospel of Matthew is the double quotation of Hos. 6.6 in Mt. 9.13 as well as in Mt. 12.7 ('I desire mercy, not sacrifice'). Comparable is the use of Ps. 40.7 in Heb. 10.5, 6 ('Sacrifices and offerings you have not desired... in burnt offerings and sin offerings you have taken no pleasure. Then I said, "See, God, I have come to do your will, O God"'). A cultic and sacrificial piety is replaced by mercy and the willingness to listen to God and his will.

Hebrews 12.14 contains two expressions ('pursue peace', 'see the Lord') calling to mind the sixth and seventh beatitudes in Mt. 5.8-9 ('to see God', 'to make peace'). The adjective 'pure' (κάθαρος) in the sixth beatitude comes from the same root as 'purify' (καθαρίζω) and 'purification' (καθαρισμός) which play such a central role in Hebrews (e.g. Heb. 1.3; 9.14).

In both writings the term 'eternity' or 'world' (αἰών) is used frequently, particularly to denote the coming αἰών (Heb. 2.5; 6.5; Mt. 12.32). The phrase 'end (or consummation) of the world' (συντέλεια τοῦ αἰῶνος) is found exclusively in Matthew and Hebrews (Mt. 13.39-40, 49; 24.3; 28.20; Heb. 9.26 with αἰών in the plural). The last words of the risen Christ in the Gospel of Matthew ('I am with you always, to the end of the age', ἕως τῆς συντελείας τοῦ αἰῶνος, Mt. 28:20) are comparable to an assertion about Christ at the end of the Epistle to the Hebrews ('Jesus Christ is the same yesterday and today and forever; εἰς τοὺς αἰῶνας; Heb. 13.8).

The parable of the vineyard contained in the synoptic tradition (Mt. 21.33-41 and its parallels) finds a reminiscence in Hebrews' use of the term 'heir' (κληρονόμος, Mt. 21.38; Heb. 1.2; 9.15), and a further similarity in the allusion to the suffering of the son taking place 'outside' (ἔξω) the vineyard in Matthew (Mt. 21.39) or the gate in Hebrews (Heb. 13.12).

The references to the temptations of Jesus and his offering up prayers and supplications with cries and tears (Heb. 2.18; 4.15; 5.7-8) are possibly allusions to the Gospel reports of the temptation in the desert and the prayer in Gethsemane (Mt. 4.1-11; 26.36-46).

Finally, smaller similarities are recognizable in the term 'the coming one' (Mt. 3.11; Heb. 11.37), in the theme of joy (χαρά, e.g. Mt. 2.10; 25.21, 23; 28.8; Heb. 12.2), in the care for prisoners (Mt. 25.36; Heb. 13.3), in the idea of the shaking of the heavens (Mt. 24.29; Heb. 12.26) and in the statements concerning the Temple curtain (καταπέτασμα). In Hebrews the tradition of the tearing of the Temple curtain, found not only in Matthew but also in Mark and Luke (Mt. 27.51; Mk 15.38; Lk. 23.45), is worked into a major theological theme (Heb. 6.19; 9.3; 10.20).

This series of noticeable similarities suggests on the one hand a surprising number of correspondences between Matthew and Hebrews. On the other hand the often diverging use or formulation of these similarities prohibit the assumption of a direct literary connection or dependence between the writings. Common to both texts is an early Christian background particularly coloured by Jewish Christian themes. Their common world of theological thought and christological ideas, however, bears very individual characteristics.

A further conclusion from the points of similarity may suggest itself. Possibly the Epistle to the Hebrews assumes an audience familiar with the Jesus traditions contained in the Gospels. These might include the temptation of Jesus, his prayer in Gethsemane, or the tearing of the Temple curtain.

But beyond the already mentioned points of contact there exists a soteriological paradigm that occurs only in Matthew and Hebrews, albeit within different and characteristic parameters. It is the thesis that through the blood of Jesus, which is his laying down of his life, a covenant is sealed that encompasses the forgiveness of sins. The forgiveness of sins through the giving of Jesus' life is an idea occurring elsewhere in the New Testament as well (see e.g. Rev. 1.5; Eph. 1.7; 1 Jn 1.7-9; indirectly also Rom. 3.25; Col. 1.20). However, the connection with the theme of the covenant occurs exclusively in Matthew and Hebrews.

2. Forgiveness of Sins and the Sealing of the Covenant in the Blood of Jesus in Matthew

a. Forgiveness of Sins in the Gospel of Matthew
We may begin with the name of Jesus in Mt. 1.21-23. The interpretation of the name of Jesus given by the angel to Joseph in a dream is programmatic for Jesus' entire public ministry; 'You will call (καλέω) his name

Jesus. For he will save his people from their sins' (Mt. 1.21). The name of Jesus derives from יְהוֹשֻׁעַ, or יֵשׁוּעַ in a later form, and means 'JHWH saves' or 'JHWH is salvation'. The root יָשַׁע contains the theme of salvation. The Septuagint often renders the Hebrew verb יָשַׁע with σῴζειν. Matthew gives this salvation a special meaning. It is Jesus who will save (σῴζω), and he will do so 'from their sins' (ἀπὸ τῶν ἁμαρτιῶν αὐτῶν). Different from the frequently occurring idea of the forgiveness of sins (Mt. 9.2, 5, 6; 12.31; 26.28), the verb 'to save' emphasizes here the occurrence of liberation. This liberation leads to freedom from the dominion of sin and its enslaving power over humans. A comparison with Mark and Luke shows the privileged use of the verb 'to save' in Matthew (Mt. 8.25; 9.22; 10.22; 14.30; 27.49).

Matthew 1.21 possibly contains an allusion to Ps. 130.8 (LXX Ps. 129.8). There JHWH 'will redeem Israel (λυτρόω) from all its iniquities (ἀνομία)'. Psalm 130.7 says that with God there is much redemption (πολλὴ... λύτρωσις). If there is indeed an allusion to Ps. 130, it is an indication that term people (λαός) in Mt. 1.21 refers to Israel. This is also borne out by the use of λαός in other places in the Gospel (e.g. Mt. 2.6; 4.16; 4.23).[2] If one accepts an allusion to Psalm 130 here, then one must conclude that Matthew actualizes and updates the concept of salvation in the Psalm with regard to his perception of the reality of sin and the longing for salvation from its domain of doom.

The naming of Jesus and its interpretation in Mt. 1.21 is amplified by a second calling and interpretation of Jesus' name. Matthew 1.22-23 contains the first of the five fulfilment quotations in Matthew 1–2. The quotations show a special theological concern of Matthew's Gospel: the life of Jesus is even before its beginning the fulfilment of the promises and hopes of scripture, and within scripture of the prophetic literature in particular. Mt. 1.22-23 views 'all this', which has been said so far in 1.18-21 about the origin and purpose of Jesus, as the fulfilment of the promises of Isa. 7.14. The prophecy in Mt. 1.23 concludes with the statement that the child born of a virgin will be given a special name; 'and they will call (καλέω) his name Emmanuel, which means God is with us'. The original of Isa. 7.14 reads; 'You (the young woman [MT] or the virgin [LXX]) will call his name Immanuel (עִמָּנוּאֵל, Ἐμμανουήλ)'. The difference between Matthew and Isaiah is that in Mt. 1.23 it is humans in a general sense that will call Jesus Emmanuel.

Matthew moves on to place an emphasis on translating the name and interpreting it; 'With us (μεθ᾽ ἡμῶν) God'. Already before his wondrous birth the presence of God becomes tangible in Jesus. Three places in the

---

2.   The allusion to Israel in Mt. 1.21 is thoroughly examined by B. Repschinski, 'For He Will Save His People from Their Sins (Matthew 1:21): A Christology for Christian Jews', *CBQ* 68 (2006), pp. 248–67 (251–7).

Gospel offer the insight that the 'being-with' is realized in a privileged way in the communion of the disciples with Jesus: Mt. 18.20 ('For where two or three are gathered in my name, I am there among them'); 26.29 ('...until that day when I drink it new with you [μεθ᾽ ὑμῶν] in my Father's kingdom'); 28.20 ('I am with you [μεθ᾽ ὑμῶν] always, to the end of the age'). Bringing together the two namings of Jesus in Mt. 1.21 and 1.22-23 offers the conclusion that salvation from sin through Jesus is at the same time the way into a new relationship with God which is marked by the experience that God is with us through the mediation of Jesus.

The interpretation of Jesus' name already before his birth is programmatic for his entire earthly ministry. In the Gospel of Matthew, similar to the Gospel of John (Jn 1.29), forgiveness of sins is not already ministered through John the Baptist,[3] but only through Jesus. In Matthew John preaches instead, 'Repent, for the kingdom of Heaven has come near' (Mt. 3.2). His baptism with water wants to motivate only to repentance (Mt. 3.11), even though the baptism of John leads people to confess their sins (Mt. 3.6).

The narrative of the healing of the paralytic (Mt. 9.1-8) emphasizes the theme of forgiveness of sins. Matthew omits the rhetorical question of the scribes transmitted by the synoptic parallels: 'Who can forgive sins except the one God?' (Mk 2.7; similar in Lk. 5.21). On the other hand, Matthew adds to the reaction of the crowds following the miracle. In Mark and Luke the crowds praise God (Mk 2.12; Lk. 5.26). Matthew amplifies the praise with the thought that people praise God 'who had given such authority to human beings' (Mt. 9.8). Matthew thus gives prominence to the remarkable fact Jesus has singular power to say to a person in the name of God, and like God, 'Your sins are forgiven' (Mt. 9.2).

b. *Willingness to Forgive Sins*

In Matthew's Gospel Jesus encourages his followers and disciples repeatedly and insistently to forgive each other. This happens first in the antitheses of the Sermon on the Mount (Matthew 5–7) and more particularly in the first antithesis (Mt. 5.23-24) and in the commentary on the prayer for forgiveness in the Our Father (Mt. 6.14-15). In the community discourse (Matthew 18) Jesus demands from Peter unconditional and limitless preparedness to forgive the members of the community (Mt. 18.21-22). Jesus justifies this attitude with the parable of the unforgiving servant (Mt. 18.23-35). At the same time the parable throws light on the prayer for forgiveness in the Our Father. The king in the parable remits (ἀφίημι) a very large debt (ὀφειλή, Mt. 18.32) that the servant would

---

3.   According to Mk 1.4 and Lk. 3.3 John the Baptist preaches a 'baptism of repentance for the forgiveness of sins'.

never be able to pay. The prayer in the Our Father asks, 'Forgive (ἀφίημι) us our debt (ὀφείλημα)'. It is perhaps no accident that Matthew uses two very similar terms (ὀφειλή, ὀφείλημα). Both instances place great emphasis on the intimate connection between divine and human forgiveness.

Finally, Mt. 26.28 points to the forgiveness of sins as the distinctive characteristic of the cup word at the Last Supper. Thus one can say, 'The passages in Matthew that summon to the forgiveness of sins (18.21-22, 23-35; cf. 6.12) receive their depth from the Lord's Supper. To forgive others their guilt is to participate in the mission of Jesus and to reflect the gift received from him'.[4]

c. *Interpretation of the Cup at the Last Supper*

Together with the Matthaean interpretation of the name of Jesus before his birth (Mt. 1.21-23), the interpretation of the cup at the Last Supper shortly before the end of Jesus' life (Mt. 26.28) frames the earthly ministry of Jesus and puts it in its entirety under the theme of the forgiveness of sins.

Specific characteristics of the Matthaean version of the words of Jesus interpreting the Last Supper and giving a prophetic perspective (Mt. 26.27-29) are more easily discerned when posed against their tradition in the Gospel of Mark (Mk. 14.23-25).

Mt. 26.27-29	Mk. 14.23-25
27 And taking a cup and giving thanks, he gave them	23 And taking a cup and giving thanks, he gave them, and all of them drank from it.
saying:	24 And he said to them:
Drink from it all, of you!	
28 For this is my blood of the covenant poured out for many	This is my blood of the covenant poured out for many.
for the forgiveness of sins	
29 I tell you, I will never again drink of this fruit of the vine until that day when I drink it new with you in my Father's kingdom.	25 Amen I tell you, I will never again drink of the fruit of the vine until that day when I drink it new in the kingdom of God.

Only Matthew introduces the interpreting words over both bread and wine with an imperative ('Take, eat' in Mt. 26.26; 'Drink from it, all of you!' in Mt. 26.27) followed by a reason. Mark reports that the disciples drink first before being given the interpretation. Matthew omits the Markan narrative of all drinking. He gives an interpretation of the cup before the disciples drink, and without mentioning their drinking.

---

4.   U. Luz, *Matthew 21-28* (Hermeneia: Minneapolis: Fortress Press, 2005), pp. 383–4.

The exhortation 'Drink from it, all of you!' receives the following reason: 'For (γάρ) this is my blood of the covenant, which for (περὶ)[5] many is poured out for the forgiveness of sins' (Mt. 26.28). In Matthew, different from Mark, the expression 'for many' is positioned before the verb 'poured out' and thus emphasizes the purpose and aim of the pouring out of Jesus' blood. This is the forgiveness of sins.

The term 'blood of the covenant' is a poignant allusion to the rite and its symbol sealing the covenant at the foot of Mount Sinai (Exod. 24.8). However, in the immediate context of the passage concerning the covenant (Exod. 24.3-8) there is no mention of the forgiveness of sins. The words of Jesus place a special emphasis on the notion of the blood of Jesus himself in the personal pronoun μου of the phrase 'my blood of the covenant'. Jesus' surrender of his own life is the symbol and seal of this new covenant. The covenant implies, among other things, the reality of a new and whole communion between people and God. This communion is made possible by the forgiveness of sins. The term 'forgiveness' (ἄφεσις) occurs only here in Matthew.[6] Of sin (ἁμαρτία) Matthew speaks in four other places as well (Mt. 1.21; 3.6; 9.2-6; 12.31).[7] With the words over the cup the Matthaean Jesus intimates that his death is both a free giving up of himself and at the same time the expression of forgiveness coming from him and from God himself.[8]

If we compare Mt. 1.21 with Mt. 26.28, there appears in both places a strong connection between the liberation from sin and the gift of a new community:

Mt. 1.21-23	Mt. 26.28
21 saving from sins	forgiveness from sins
23 'God with us'	covenant

The interpretation of Jesus' name in Mt. 1.23 ('God with us') is related to the theme of the covenant. Both expressions aim at the closeness of God and human communion with God.

Comparable to the cup word in Mt. 26.28 is the word about the ransom in Mt. 20.28. Jesus serves others (διακονέω). In the last consequence this

---

5.   Mark uses the preposition ὑπέρ (Mk 14.24). However, there is hardly any difference to περί.

6.   Mark uses the term twice (Mk 1.4; 3.29). Luke uses it more frequently (Lk. 1.77; 3.3; 24.47; Acts 2.38; 5.31; 10.43; 13.38; 26.18). Apart from these passages ἄφεσις occurs in Eph. 1.7 and Col. 1.14, as well as in two places in the Epistle to the Hebrews (Heb. 9.22; 10.18).

7.   In Hebrews the term occurs 25 times.

8.   Matthew's theology at this point is comparable to the Lukan Jesus praying for his enemies in Lk. 23.34: 'Father, forgive them for they do not know what they are doing'.

means that he gives his life. His life, however, is to be the ransom for many (λύτρον ἀντὶ πολλῶν).[9] The word 'ransom' usually connotes the idea of buying someone's freedom from captivity or slavery. More generally, it signifies the liberation from a situation of doom. Together with Mt. 1.21 and 26.28 the word about the ransom in 20.28 adds to the understanding of Jesus' death. Salvation, forgiveness of sins, and a newly forged communion with God under the auspices of a new covenant, also contain the aspect of liberation for which Jesus himself pays the ransom with his own life as the ultimate sign of his life in service to others.

The term 'blood' (αἷμα) in Mt. 26.28 is illuminated by a look at other occurrences in the Gospel. The woe in Mt. 23.29-33 is directed against those scribes and Pharisees who build and decorate the tombs of the prophets and the just. They are convinced, 'If we had lived in the days of our ancestors, we would not have taken part with them (κοινωνός) in shedding the blood of the prophets' (Mt. 23.30). However, the Matthaean Jesus sees in this conviction only the corroboration for the accusation that the scribes and Pharisees are 'sons of murderers (φονεύω) of the prophets' (Mt. 23.31). In this case, 'blood' carries the connotation of 'murder'.

In the following passage (Mt. 23.34-36), Matthew alludes to the fate not only of the disciples under persecution, but also of the scribes and Pharisees as well as the present generation as a whole; 'so that upon you (ἐφ' ὑμᾶς) may come all the righteous blood (πᾶν αἷμα δίκαιον) shed (ἐκχυννόμενον) on earth, from the blood of righteous (δίκαιος) Abel to the blood of Zechariah… whom you murdered between the sanctuary and the altar' (Mt. 23.35). The mention of the poured out blood again refers to murder in this context.[10] A special emphasis lies in the thought that the murder is aimed at those who are just (δίκαιος). Matthew mentions 'just blood', refers to Abel as a just man and picks up on the tombs of the just from 23.29. The blood poured out is the blood of people without sin and in a right relationship with God.

The thought of 'just blood' recurs in the contrition and confession of Judas, 'I have sinned by betraying innocent (ἀθῷον) blood' (Mt. 27.4). The adjective 'innocent' occurs only here and in the interpretation of Pilate's washing of hands before the public at the trial of Jesus, 'I am innocent (ἀθῷος) of this blood' (Mt. 27.24).[11] Pilate's ritual handwashing

---

9. Mk. 10.45 uses the same wording. Very similar to λύτρον is ἀντίλυτρον in 1 Tim. 2.5-6.

10. Acts 22.20 describes the violent stoning of Stephen with the expression 'while the blood of your witness Stephen was poured out (ἐξεχύννετω)'.

11. In 2 Sam. 3.28 David says; 'I and my kingdom are forever guiltless (LXX: ἀθῷος) before the Lord for the blood of Abner son of Ner'. Acts 20.26 reads; 'Clean (καθαρός) I am of the blood of any of you'.

and his proclamation of his innocence leads to the response of 'all the people' that 'his blood be on us (ἐφ' ἡμᾶς) and on our children' (Mt. 27.25). The term 'blood' in conjunction with the preposition ἐπί is a clear allusion to Mt. 23.35. This and other similar uses of blood with ἐπί in other writings[12] lead to the conclusion that the people take over the responsibility for the execution of Jesus and are willing to bear the consequences of Jesus' death.[13]

In the context of our study it suffices to ascertain that in the places where 'blood' becomes a topic in the Gospel of Matthew, the emphasis lies on the violent death of people who are called prophets and just. Thus Jesus too is placed into the pattern of prophets and the just who are violently brought to an end. His blood is poured out as a witness to his prophetic mission.

When the Gospel of Matthew uses the expression of the blood being 'poured out' (ἐκχύννω) in two differing contexts (23.36 and 26.28),[14] the following interpretation suggests itself. On the one hand, an emphasis is placed on the violent nature of the death of Jesus. Just like the murder of the prophets and the just, the death of Jesus entails a sin against God and reveals the evil of his opponents. On the other hand, Matthew connects the unique promise of salvation with the death of Jesus by linking the blood of Jesus to the covenant. In Jesus' willingness to accept his fate as the consequence of human violence and the consequence of sin, an unparalleled offer of forgiveness is made. In Jesus' death God's unlimited forgiveness of sin is made real. The covenant in the blood of Jesus creates communion between God and forgiven sinners and makes it the foundation of the new community.

d. *The Prophetic Outlook*
Much more clearly than the Gospel of Mark, Matthew connects Jesus' word over the cup with a prophetic outlook. Mark has such a prophetic perspective as well, but he disconnects it from the immediately preceding word over the cup by shaping it into an independent saying introduced by 'Amen, I tell you' (Mk. 14.25). Matthew constructs a connecting phrase (λέγω δὲ ὑμῖν) and thus emphasizes the intimate relationship of

12.   See 2 Sam. 1.16 (David): 'Your blood over your head'; Acts 5.28 (the High Priest to the apostles): 'You want to bring the blood of this man over us' (ἐφ' ὑμᾶς); Acts 18.6 (Paul to the Jews): 'Your blood be upon your head' (ἐπὶ τὴν κεφαλὴν ὑμῶν).

13.   The statement of Mt. 27.25 receives a deeper soteriological significance through its connection with Mt. 1.21. For a detailed argument for this thesis, see Repschinski, 'For He Will Save His People', pp. 260–5.

14.   W. D. Davies and D. C. Allison, *A Critical and Exegetical Commentary on the Gospel according to Saint Matthew* (ICC; 3 vols; Edinburgh: T&T Clark, 1988, 1991, 1997), III, p. 474, call the verb ἐκχύννω 'a sacrificial word which connotes a violent death'.

26.29 with the preceding word over the cup and the imperative to drink from it. Only Matthew adds ἀπ᾽ ἄρτι and creates a narrative tension concerning that which begins 'from now on' and reaches 'until that day' into a prophetic future in which Jesus will again drink from the fruit of the vine. The expression μεθ ὑμῶν places the disciples into the prophetic future and recalls the translation of the naming of Jesus in 1.23 ('with us is God') and the appearance of the risen Lord in 28.20 ('I am with you'). The communion alluded to in these passages is a communion that finds its fulfilment and realization in the eschatological meal in the coming kingdom of God (cf. Mt. 8.11-12). In Matthew Jesus calls the coming salvation 'the kingdom of my Father'. Such a term hints at the unique personal relationship between Jesus and God. The conclusion to the cup word promises the disciples participation in that relationship.

e. *Summary*

According to Matthew the reason behind Jesus' entire earthly life and ministry lies in the salvation from a situation of sin as a distorted relationship with God. Jesus enables people to enter into a new and salvific relationship to God. His purpose comes to its fullness in the free gift of his life for others. The restoration of a new communion with God finds its expression in the term 'covenant', denoting at the same time communion with Jesus now and fulfilment in the kingdom of Jesus' Father in the future. The covenant sealed by the blood of Jesus is the promise of faithfulness and irreversibility. Those trusting in Jesus can trust this covenant in all situations, even in a situation of sin.

3. *Cleansing From Sin as the Central Topic of the Soteriology of the Epistle to the Hebrews*

a. *The High Priest as Image of Christ*

The Epistle to the Hebrews has little to say about the earthly ministry of Jesus.[15] When Hebrews does mention the earthly Jesus, it does so in the context of salvation from a situation of sin. The introduction of the Epistle (Heb. 1.1-4) formulates this programmatically. First, there are statements concerning the deeds of God in creation and revelation through 'a Son' who is characterized by divine authority manifested in the universal power of his word. Then the author points to the death and resurrection of Jesus and calls to mind the purpose of this sacrifice as the καθαρισμόν

---

15.   Hebrews 2.18 and 4.15 allude to the temptation of Jesus (cf. Mt. 4.1-11). Hebrews 5.7-10 calls to mind the prayer of Jesus in Gethsemane. The theme of the covenant in Hebrews takes up the words of Jesus at the Last Supper.

τῶν ἁμαρτιῶν (Heb. 1.3). After having achieved this purpose, Jesus then 'sits down at the right hand of the majesty on high'. The idea of a purification (καθαρισμός) has roots in cultic concepts and recurs in Hebrews with the verb καθαρίζω in 9.14, 22, 23; 10.2. The day of the death of Jesus becomes the universal Day of Atonement whose liturgy, outlined in Leviticus 16, finds a new interpretation mainly in Heb. 9.1-14. The purpose of purification is the cleansing from sins (ἁμαρτία). This is a major term in Hebrews, occurring some 25 times. It denotes a failed, disturbed and clouded relationship to God.

In order to describe the salvific function of the death and resurrection of Jesus, Hebrews mainly uses the image of the High Priest. It is an image borrowed from the Temple cult. On the Day of Atonement, the High Priest enters the Holy of Holies in the Temple as a space of particular closeness to God and performs a rite with sacrificial blood (Leviticus 16). In a similar way, Jesus sheds his blood on the cross and through this rite enters through death into the heavenly Holy of Holies, into the presence of God himself. In his free giving up of his life for us Jesus sacrificed himself 'once for all' (ἐφάπαξ; Heb. 7.27; cf. 9.12; 10.10) and thus surpassed all cultic sacrifices.

Already the first mention of Jesus as the High Priest emphasizes that one of his main functions is 'to atone for the sins of the people' (Heb. 2.17). The verb ἱλάσκομαι[16] means to atone, to propitiate, or to cause to be favourably inclined. It is related to the idea of purification from sin (Heb. 1.3). The term 'people' (λαός) denotes here and elsewhere[17] the elect people of God, Israel. The believers in Christ count themselves among this people.

b. *Covenant, Pouring out of Blood and the Forgiveness of Sins*
The Epistle to the Hebrews speaks of the High Priest 'bringing gifts and sacrifices for sins' (Heb. 5.1; 7.27). But beyond such rather general statements, Hebrews emphasizes that in the process of sins being forgiven blood (αἷμα) plays a significant role. The central passage, Heb. 9.1-28, places the old and the new cult over against each other. First comes a description of the High Priest – and him alone – going into the Holy of Holies only on the Day of Atonement. He enters 'the second tent', but 'not

---

16.   The verb ἱλάσκομαι is found only here and in Lk. 18:13. The verb ἐξιλάσκομαι is identical in meaning and translates in the LXX mainly כפר, a word meaning 'wipe off' and in a cultic sense is used as 'purify', 'cover', or 'enshroud'. In the last sense it is often used in Leviticus and Numbers. Part of the same semantic field is the adjective ἵλεως with the meaning of 'merciful' or 'gracious'. It occurs in Heb. 8.22 and Mt. 16.22. The substantive ἱλαστήριον ('place of atonement') appears in Heb. 9.5 and Rom. 3.25, and usually translates כפרת (Exod. 25.17-21).

17.   See Heb. 4.9; 5.3; 7.27; 8.10; 9.7, 19; 10.30.

without (χωρὶς) blood'. This he offers for the 'sins committed unintentionally (ἀγνοημάτων)[18] by the people' (Heb. 9.7). Hebrews 9.11-14 then opposes this activity of the High Priest on the Day of Atonement to the activity of Jesus. Jesus entered the heavenly sanctuary once and definitively (ἐφάπαξ). This sanctuary is not a second tent made by human hands but a greater and more perfect tent (τῆς μείζονος καὶ τελειοτέρας σκηνῆς). Jesus enters it not with the blood of goats and calves, but with his own blood. Thus he works an eternal redemption (αἰωνίαν λύτρωσιν). The blood of Christ purifies (καθαρίζω) the conscience from dead works; a service (λατρεύω) of the living God becomes possible (Heb. 9.14). The idea of purification found in Heb. 1.3 is here developed through the theme of a new relationship with God (λατρεύω) that finds its expression in cultic imagery.

The following passage (Heb. 9.15-22) connects the blood rite of the Day of Atonement with the theme of the covenant in two ways. First, the covenant is likened to a last will which becomes legally effective after the death of its author (Heb. 9.16-17). The death of Jesus is, therefore, a necessity for the covenant to become valid. In a second step the Epistle refers to the covenant at Mount Sinai (Heb. 9.18-22). This covenant was not founded 'without (χωρὶς) blood' (Heb. 9.18). The quotation of Exod. 24.8 ('See the blood of the covenant that the Lord has made with you') serves to call to mind the rite of blood by which Moses sealed the covenant between God and his people at Mount Sinai.[19] In Exod. 24.8 this blood rite was restricted to a sprinkling of altar and people. Hebrews, however, expands the rite by narrating a sprinkling (ῥαντίζω; Heb. 9.19, 21) which extends now also to the book, the sanctuary and the liturgical implements. Thus Hebrews prepares the climactic argument in Heb. 9.22; 'Indeed, under the Law almost everything is purified (καθαρίζεται) with blood, and without the shedding of blood (αἱματεκχυσίας) there is no forgiveness of sins (ἄφεσις)'. The word αἱματεκχυσία is a *hapax legomenon* and as such probably a creation of the author.[20] The phrase

18. See Heb. 5.2; the High Priest 'is able to deal gently with the ignorant and wayward'. Comparable is also Lk. 23.34 ('Father, forgive them because they do not know what they are doing') and Acts 3.17 ('you acted in ignorance').

19. Davies and Allison, *Matthew*, III, p. 475, note that Mt. 26.28 'has a striking parallel in Heb. 9.15-22'. They also note the important detail that 'Heb. 9.20 uses the phrase, "This is the blood of the covenant which...". There is no "this is" in Exod. 24.8. The words rather come from the tradition of the Lord's Supper'.

20. H.-F. Weiss, *Der Brief an die Hebräer* (KEK, 13; Göttingen: Vandenhoeck & Ruprecht, 1991), p. 482; see also Grässer, *An die Hebräer*, II, p. 185. The phrase ἔκχυσις αἵματος in 1 Kgs 18.28 and Sir. 27.15 is very close in meaning to the term αἱματεκχυσία in referring to a violent shedding of blood.

'not without (χωρὶς) shedding of blood' corresponds to the expression 'not without (χωρὶς) blood' in Heb. 9.7 and 9.18. Indirectly it refers to the mysterious necessity of the death of Jesus.

Following the discourse over the death of Jesus, Heb. 9.23-28 points to the redemption (ἀπολύτρωσις)[21] effected in the death of Jesus and already mentioned in Heb. 9.15. Again Hebrews turns to the Day of Atonement as the image of that which Jesus surpassed. Jesus entered the heavenly sanctuary and heaven itself in order 'now to appear in the presence of God on our behalf' (Heb. 9.24). Just as in Heb. 7.25 ('since he always lives to make intercession'), Jesus is the eternal mediator who enters heaven not with foreign blood but with his own (see also Heb. 9.12).

Hebrews 9.26-28 can now be read as a summary. The redemption in Jesus is connected with a double appearance. At the end and in the fullness of time (ἐπὶ συντελείᾳ τῶν αἰώνων) Jesus appeared (φανερόω) one single time (ἅπαξ) for the annulment (ἀθέτησις) of sin. He took the sins of many upon himself. Here an idea present already in Isa. 53.12 is taken up and developed into an interpretation of the earthly life of Jesus. But he will appear a second time (ὁράω) for the redemption of those waiting for him. In the expected *parousia* the ministry of the earthly Jesus is brought to completion.

c. *The Blood Metaphor in Further Contexts*

Apart from the central thesis of Heb. 9.1-28, the Epistle interprets the death of Jesus through the metaphor of the blood in three further contexts. The paraenetic passage in Heb. 10.19-39 begins with the statement that 'therefore, my friends, we have confidence to enter the sanctuary by the blood of Jesus' (Heb. 10.19). This access to God is at the same time the 'new and living way' opened up by Jesus (Heb. 10.20). We approach God 'with a heart sprinkled pure from an evil conscience' (Heb. 10.22). The author here takes up again the idea of a conscience purified in the blood of Christ (Heb. 9.14). Similarly, Heb. 10.29 warns against spurning the 'blood of the covenant' which sanctifies (ἁγιάζω) the believer.[22]

In the context of Heb. 12.18-24 and its opposing images of Sinai and Zion as the images of the first and the new covenant, the Epistle formulates that the believers have come not just to Zion, but 'to Jesus, the mediator (μεσίτῃ) of a new covenant, and to the blood of sprinkling that

---

21.   The terms λύτρωσις (Heb. 9.12) and ἀπολύτρωσις (Heb. 9.15) find a parallel in λύτρον in Mt. 20.28.

22.   See Heb. 10.10; 'we have been sanctified through the offering of the body (διὰ τῆς προσφορᾶς τοῦ σώματος) of Jesus Christ once for all'.

speaks a better word than the blood of Abel' (Heb. 12.24). Again Hebrews returns to cultic images connected to the blood. The cultic act of sprinkling (ῥαντισμός)[23] blood is put into direct connection with the fall of humankind and its consequences (Gen. 3.1–4.16) visible in the murder of Abel. Thus Hebrews here moves beyond mere cultic and sacrificial references and remembers that both Jesus and Abel died a violent death. Jesus has to pour out his blood because his message meets with resistance and rejection. The rejection is so violent that it finally ends in his death sentence. His death manifests the consequences of sin as violence in a manner very similar to the death of Abel. Therefore Hebrews mentions Abel as the first one (Heb. 11.4) among the cloud of witnesses (Heb. 12.1) to faith; 'By faith Abel offered to God a more acceptable sacrifice than Cain's. Through this he received approval as righteous, God himself giving approval to his gifts; he died, but through his faith he still speaks' (Heb. 11.4). Abel still speaks today through his faith (Heb. 11.4) or through his blood (12.24), an idea suggested by Gen. 4.4. The 'blood of Abel' occurs also in Mt. 23.35 and Lk. 11.51. Only in Mt. 23.35 and Heb. 11.4 is Abel referred to as 'just' (δίκαιος).[24]

The Epistle to the Hebrews concludes with a paraenetical chapter. The ritual of the Day of Atonement is again invoked in the phrase describing that 'Jesus also suffered outside the city gate in order to sanctify (ἁγιάσῃ) the people (τὸν λαόν) by his own blood' (Heb. 13.12). The hint at the passion 'outside (ἔξω) the city gate' reminds us of the parable of the vineyard in Matthew. There the son is pointedly killed outside (ἔξω) the vineyard (Mt. 21.39; cf. Lk. 20.15).

In the course of the Epistle's final benediction (Heb. 13.20-21), the blood metaphor is once again connected with the covenant. God has raised Jesus from the dead 'in the blood[25] of an eternal covenant' (Heb. 13.20). The verb ἀνάγω establishes a connection with the themes of the Exodus. Just like Israel was led up out of Egypt, Jesus was led up out of the dominion of death. His blood is the constitutive element in the eternal covenant.[26] It surpasses the old Sinai covenant because it is better (Heb. 7.22; 8.6) and new (Heb. 9.15). The new covenant is founded on the

---

23.   The verb ῥαντίζω occurs in Heb. 9.13, 19, 21; 10.22. Hebrews 9.13 and 9.14 are of particular significance since they show the close connection between sprinkling (ῥαντίζω) and purifying (καθαρίζω).

24.   A further parallel is presented in 1 Jn 3.12. However, there it is not Abel himself who is pronounced just, but rather his works are called δίκαια.

25.   Possible are translations like 'with the blood' or 'because of the blood'. The use of the preposition ἐν can include an instrumental or causal connotation and thus corresponds to Hebrew constructions with the preposition ב.

26.   The theme of an 'eternal' covenant finds its roots in the Hebrew scriptures. Examples are Isa. 55.3; 61.8; Jer. 32.40; 50.5; Ezek. 16.60; 37.26.

forgiveness of sins (Heb. 10.18) and an irreversible promise of faithfulness. The new covenant is the invincible reality of communion with God.

d. *Summary*
Jesus as the High Priest purifies from sins through the giving of his own life and blood in sacrifice. The metaphor of the blood of Jesus in Hebrews covers two main aspects. Calling to mind Abel serves the purpose of calling to mind the violent nature of Jesus' death. Thus the mention of blood recalls suffering unto death (Heb. 2.9, 10) including temptation (Heb. 2.18; 4.15). In this Jesus learns obedience (Heb. 5.7-10). On the other hand, the references to the sacrificial cult during the liturgy of the Day of Atonement and the covenant celebrations at Sinai serve to develop the unique soteriological meaning of the pouring out of Jesus' blood. Blood becomes the symbol for the forgiveness (ἄφεσις) of sins and the sign for the inauguration of the new covenant. The covenant signifies the reality of a communion and a personal relationship which becomes possible at the initiative and faithfulness of Jesus. He is the 'merciful and faithful (πιστὸς) High Priest' (Heb. 2.17). Jesus' blood enables the believer to walk on the new and living way that leads to the heavenly sanctuary (Heb. 10.19-20). His blood is the access to the 'throne of grace' (Heb. 4.16); through it the believer draws near (ἐγγίζω) to the living God (Heb. 7.19) and serves (λατρεύω) him (Heb. 9.14) with a pure conscience (Heb. 10.2, 22). Jesus, violently put to death by humans and raised up by God, is the source of such singular hope (Heb. 3.6).

4. *Matthew and Hebrews*

The Gospel of Matthew and the Epistle to the Hebrews interpret the entire earthly ministry of Jesus in the light of the forgiveness of sins. Besides a number of linguistic and structural details of surprising similarity between the two writings, the particular combination of the themes covenant, blood and forgiveness deserves special attention. It is a combination found only in these two New Testament writings.[27]

---

27.   Luke (3.3 and 24.47) and John (1.29 and 20.23) use the theme of the forgiveness of sins as well to frame their Gospels. However, they do not explicitly connect the forgiveness with the metaphor of blood. A linking of covenant and forgiveness is found, however, in the institution narratives of the Last Supper in Lk. 22.20 and 1 Cor. 11.25. There the link is constructed around the prophecy of the new covenant (Jer. 31.31-34) of which forgiveness is a part (Jer. 31:34). However, neither Luke nor Paul makes the implicit connection between covenant and forgiveness explicit.

Distinctive similarities appear in the comparison of Mt. 1.21 ('to save his people from their sins') and Heb. 2.17 ('to atone for the sins of the people'). Similarly, comparable details are found elsewhere. Matthew 26.27-29 draws on the themes of the forgiveness of sins in the word over the cup and the prophetic description of the fulfilment of salvation. Hebrews 9.26-28 unfolds the forgiveness of sins through Jesus at his first coming; at his second coming he will fulfil the promised salvation for all believers. In both instances a statement about the earthly ministry of Jesus is complemented by a prophecy concerning his future work. A further similarity is the allusion to the servant of God carrying the sins of many (Isa. 53.12). Matthew develops the servant theme into 'the blood of the covenant poured out for many' (Mt. 26.28). Hebrews speaks of Jesus taking upon himself the sins 'of many' (Heb. 9.28).

The combination of the three themes of covenant, blood and forgiveness shows up a common approach with respect to the blood metaphor. Both the Gospel of Matthew and the Epistle to the Hebrews explain the metaphorical meaning of the blood on two distinct levels. On one level blood stands for the violence and the death Jesus has to suffer at the hands of people. His blood is poured out like that of the just Abel (Mt. 23.35; Heb. 11.4; 12.24). The rejection and murder of God's messenger is a sin against God himself. On a second level the connection with the liturgical framework makes plausible that the manner in which Jesus reacts to the violence of his enemies and to the death he has to suffer provokes a specific act of God in raising the crucified one from the dead. Both Jesus' obedient suffering and God's saving act are universal signs of the renunciation of retaliation, of Jesus' love of enemies (Mt. 5.38-48), and of God's unconditional and forgiving love.[28] The Gospel of Matthew and the Epistle to the Hebrews communicate in very different ways the conviction of the double meaning of Jesus' violent death. His blood is not just the sign of the forgiving love of God but also the seal of the new community of the covenant.

---

28.   In the Gospel of Luke, too, the cross is on the one hand an expression of extreme violence against Jesus, but on the other hand a sign of forgiveness. Luke explicates this in the prayer of Jesus for his enemies: 'Father, forgive them because they do not know what they are doing' (Lk. 23.34).

6. MATTHEW AND JAMES

JÜRGEN ZANGENBERG

Both the Gospel of Matthew and the Epistle of James have received much attention in recent scholarship. In the course of intensive work, positions about their respective theological character as well as their social, religious and historical contexts have became more diverse than ever. In this study, I will take up elements of this discussion and explore a number of issues relevant for speculating about a possible 'relationship' between Matthew and James. To be sure, 'relationship' is a colourful term which can, if taken too narrowly, easily lead to problematic conclusions about literary dependence and direct reference from one side to the other. Neither scenario, I think, is a viable option in our case. Explicit references, be they positive (asserting) or negative (rejecting), from one text to the other are strikingly rare in the earliest periods of Christian literature – a feature that interestingly is shared by contemporaneous Jewish literature. In both traditions, references to a very large extent are only made transparent if they deal with sources as authoritative as the Old Testament. We will have to examine a particularly telling example of inter-Christian referentiality later, but in general one should refrain from building up too neatly-cut pyramids of who copied from whom or who 'knew' whom only on the basis of observed similarites. The question of whether James is 'dependent' upon Matthew or vice versa is not the issue here, since such questions can hardly be answered with any degree of certainty. Despite rare occasions of explicit referentiality in early Christian literature, we usually have to operate with similarities and convergences of very different kinds These include, for example, simultaneous adoption of seemingly identical background traditions and the use of similar terminologies (or the lack thereof). It seems more likely to me that both similarites and dissimilarities between James and Matthew can best be described in such a context.

To compare a narrative text of 28 chapters (Matthew) with a letter of only five chapters (James) might seem somewhat daring. At first sight, form and content of both writings appear too diverse to warrant any useful results if compared. The basis for a meaningful comparison lies on a different level. Both texts share enough motifs, phrases and concepts to invite scholars to explore their relationship.[1] Any analysis of the relationship between James and

---

1.   See M. H. Shepherd, 'The Epistle of James and the Gospel of Matthew', *JBL* 75 (1956), pp. 40–51.

Matthew will have to keep in mind that both texts participate not only in one single referential system, but in several. When James and Matthew were written some time at the end of the first century (Matthew) or the beginning of the second century (James?),[2] early Christian identity formation to a very large extent still worked within a Jewish matrix. While references to Jewish concepts and practices can be expected to be frequent and prolific, their controversial and often polemical character should not blur the picture. Stressing differences and controversies with Jewish positions and practices is part of this dispute and does not contradict it.[3] The multiformity of Judaism in the fluid situation shortly after the first Jewish revolt makes it necessary to allow for a high degree of variability in the spelling out or the practice of one's Jewish identity. Theological considerations and situational requirements can make early Christian references to Judaism oscillate from fundamental attacks against an 'illegitimate claim on Biblical tradition' to qualified and limited criticism of particular, local or regional expressions of Judaism (which might well be equally controversial among other Jews). Few early Christian texts, however, take the effort to make such distinctions transparent. Apart from controversy with and about Judaism, early Christian texts of course were engaged in communication with other Christians, both within and outside their own communities. Finally, the pagan world also featured in many texts, although this discourse rarely worked directly, but often operated as debate *about* pagans. It is important to remember that each of these discourses demanded appropriate rhetorical and semantic forms, 'favourite topics' and stereotypes which influenced individual texts in form and content.

1. *The Message of the 'Author'*

Neither the Epistle of James nor the Gospel of Matthew was anonymously transmitted. Both texts are attributed to named personalities, though in quite different ways. The Epistle of James explicitly mentions a certain Ἰάκωβος (1.1), and the Gospel of Matthew was ascribed to a

---

2.   These dates are notoriously disputed, for James much more than for Matthew. H. Frankemölle, *Der Brief des Jakobus. Vol. 1* (Gütersloh: Gütersloher Verlagshaus, 1994), p. 61, dates it to the very end of the first century. By contrast, L. T. Johnson, *The Letter of James: A New Translation with Introduction and Commentary* (AB, 37A; New York: Doubleday, 1995), p. 121, sees James as 'a very early writing from a Palestinian Jewish source'. I hold a late-first-century date for Matthew, whereas James is almost impossible to date if one does not accept it as authentic. No matter if 'early' or 'late', I see James as textually independent from Matthew.

3.   See J. Zangenberg, 'A Conflict Among Brothers. Who were the *hypokritai* in Matthew?', forthcoming in M. D. Denton, B. McGing and Z. Rodgers (eds), *Festschrift S. Freyne* (Leiden: Brill).

certain Μαθθαῖος in the early Christian manuscript and exegetical tradition. What can the (alleged) authors tell us about the character of these writings?

The fact that the Epistle of James provides a named author does not make the ascription to Ἰάκωβος less complicated. James 1.1 provides no direct clue to characterize the author further or even help identify him with James the brother of Jesus, as tradition has come to do and as several exegetes claim today.[4] At least theoretically, the option remains that a different Ἰάκωβος could have been implied (one of the sons of Zebedee as described in Mk 1.19; 3.17; 5.37; 9.2; 13.3; 14.33; Acts 12.2, or another person of that name), but the question then arises as to what argumentative value such an identification would offer.[5] We have no information about the Zebedees' theology, while the letter is too general to fill that gap.

In the end, a critical enquiry will be careful not to go far beyond what H. Frankemölle or others have already said; 'Der Jakobusbrief ist ein weisheitlich geprägter Text, der nicht genau zu datieren, zu lokalisieren und einem bekannten Autor zuzuweisen ist'.[6] But even if one does not want to defend problematic historical assumptions about the 'historical James' as author of the text and accept that James is pseudepigraphical,[7] one can still acknowledge that the mention of Ἰάκωβος is an important signal of how the letter was meant to be understood: as a 'product' of James, the brother of Jesus and the leader of the Jerusalem-based branch of early Christianity. Early Christian tradition provides much information on James.[8] He was not only Jesus' brother (Mk 6.3), but also a witness

---

4. See, for example, R. Bauckham, *James: Wisdom of James, Disciple of Jesus the Sage* (NTR; London: Routledge, 1999), pp. 11–25; M. Hengel, 'Der Jakobusbrief als antipaulinische Polemik', in M. Hengel, *Paulus und Jakobus: Kleine Schriften III* (WUNT, 141; Tübingen: Mohr Siebeck, 2002), pp. 511–48 (511–23).

5. See K. Berger, *Theologie des Urchristentums: Theologie des Neuen Testaments* (Tübingen: Francke, 2nd edn, 1995), p. 186, on the possibility that James son of Zebedee was the author of James.

6. Frankemölle, *Jakobus*, p. 45 (see pp. 45–54 for his arguments). Hengel, who argues in favour of the authorship of James, adds a couple of problems that remain unresolved if the 'authenticity' is accepted. See Hengel, 'Jakobusbrief', pp. 520–3.

7. So M. Konradt, 'Der Jakobusbrief als Brief des Jakobus. Erwägungen zum historischen Kontext des Jakobusbriefs im Lichte der traditionsgeschichtlichen Beziehungen zum 1. Petrusbrief und zum Hintergrund der Autorfiktion', in P. von Gemünden, M. Konradt and Gerd Theißen (eds), *Der Jakobusbrief. Beiträge zur Rehabilitierung der 'strohernen Epistel'* (BVB, 3; Münster: LIT, 2003), pp. 16–53 (42–53); W. Popkes, *Der Brief des Jakobus* (THKNT, 14; Leipzig: Evangelische Verlagsanstalt, 2001), pp. 64–8; K.-W. Niebuhr, '"A New Perspective on James"? Neuere Forschungen zum Jakobusbrief', *TLZ* 129 (2004), pp. 1019–44 (1021–32). For a different view, see Johnson, *James*, pp. 108–21.

8. See M. Hengel, 'Jakobus der Herrenbruder – der erste "Papst"?', in Hengel, *Paulus und Jakobus*, pp. 549–82; Johnson, *James*, pp. 89–98; Konradt, 'Jakobusbrief als Brief des

to his 'resurrection' (therefore apostle in the truest sense; 1 Cor. 15.7), and
for many years the single most important leader of the Jerusalem church
and beyond (Acts 12.17; 15.13-22; 21.18; Gal. 2.9, 12-13), and an
opponent of Paul. Obviously James was highly respected as pious and just
(see Paul's outright acceptance of James' authority as one of the three
στύλοι, and the very early Christian attribute 'James the Just' in the
Gospel of Thomas 12), apparently based on his paradigmatic and uncompromising interpretation of the Torah. Josephus and the early Christian
tradition add to that by reporting James' death as a martyr (cf. *Ant.*
20.199-203).

Be that as it may, it is striking to see that the anonymous author of the
letter makes no attempt to use explicitly his implied author's authority. He
is not called 'brother of Jesus', nor does he invoke Jamesian *Lokalkolorit*
by referring to Palestine or Jerusalem. Instead, the author introduces
himself as θεοῦ καὶ κυρίου Ἰησοῦ Χριστοῦ δοῦλος, a term designating
somebody who is charged with faithfully fulfilling a task received from the
Lord. Any community receiving a letter from Ἰάκωβος θεοῦ καὶ κυρίου
Ἰησοῦ Χριστοῦ δοῦλος had to assume that nobody but the brother of Jesus
was its author. As such a 'servant', the author writes to all 'twelve tribes
in the dispersion' (1.1), a phrase we will return to later. Throughout the
letter, the author grounds his position on rhetorical forms and the plausi-
bilty of the traditions he uses. Still, James is much less explicit about his
alleged origin than are 1 or 2 Peter, and he makes much less use of
'personal features' of the implied author than the Pastoral Epistles which
employ folkloric traditions about Paul. But there is one topic that almost
leaves no alternative but to accept that the anonymous author had the
Lord's brother in mind when he ascribed his treatise to Ἰάκωβος, the
struggle concerning how to interpret the Law and to be observant of and
pious towards it (Jas 2.14-26). From all the wealth of early Christian (and
Jewish) lore about James the brother of Jesus, the anonymous author only
picks out a single motif, piety grounded in wisdom. There is no better
witness for such an agenda than James the Just. I therefore take the
'identity' of Ἰάκωβος with the Lord's brother in 1.1 not as 'historical fact',
but as a deliberate construction of an otherwise unknown author, who
wants his audience to read the letter as a contribution to an ongoing debate
in early Christian circles about the legacy of James.[9] Judging from the
designation of the imaginary adressees (1.1) and his familiarity with

Jakobus', p. 30, and W. Pratscher, *Der Herrenbruder Jakobus und die Jakobustradition*
(FRLANT, 139; Göttingen: Vandenhoeck & Ruprecht, 1987).

9.   On the role of James in later Christian literature, see B. Chilton and C. A. Evans
(eds), *James the Just and Christian Origins* (NovTSup, 98; Leiden: Brill, 1999); Pratscher,
Herrenbruder Jakobus, pp. 102–228; and Johnson, *James*, pp. 98–108.

Jewish traditions and diction, the anonymous author sees his position inspired by and faithful to Biblical traditions and in evident loyalty to Judaism.[10]

Unlike James, the Gospel of Matthew nowhere explicitly names an author. Μαθθαῖος is only mentioned in early manuscript superscriptions and in later Christian authors (the most important being Papias) that refer to the Gospel as being written by a certain Μαθθαῖος.[11] The reason for such an ascription is often seen in the fact that Matthew changes his *Vorlage* by replacing the Markan Λευὶν τὸν τοῦ Ἀλφαίου (Mk 2.14) with ἄνθρωπον... Μαθθαῖον λεγόμενον (Mt. 9.3). The same Μαθθαῖον returns shortly afterwards in the list of the δώδεκα ἀπόστολοι as Μαθθαῖος ὁ τελώνης (Mt. 10.3). Does that mean that this Μαθθαῖος is the author who wanted to write himself into the Gospel? Such a statement would immediately raise even stronger doubts, because synoptic comparison makes it evident that the author was no eyewitness but a redactor of older documents. Although the role the apostle Matthew played among his fellow apostles was not prominent, he at least could claim to have been Jewish and a witness to Jesus' life. That might have been enough to ascribe an originally anonymous Gospel that shows strong interest in Jewish affairs to this man. In any case, the attribution to Matthew is quite early, and its reception in Judaeo-Christian circles demonstrates how the Gospel was understood by many early Christians – whether or not that met the purpose of the 'real' author.[12]

It is interesting to see that early Christian tradition (in the form of an anonymous author as well as early copyists and commentators) connects these works with two characters that are notably independent of the 'Pauline circle'. Instead, 'James' and 'Matthew' have a close connection to Jesus (as a brother and as a follower), and a prominent affinity with Judaism. Despite this mutual affinity, there is an interesting difference. While the Epistle is connected to James, the brother of Jesus, Matthew clearly favours Peter as the focal character (cf. the unique traditions in 16.17-19; 17.24-27). James, the brother of Jesus, however, plays a very marginal role in Matthew (see 13.55). This observation should warn us

10. Berger, *Theologie*, p. 186, rightly calls the ascription a 'kirchenpolitische Tat'.
11. On theories of the identity of Matthew, see U. Luz, *Matthew 1-7* (Hermeneia; Minneapolis: Fortress Press, rev. edn, 2007), pp. 59–60.
12. With the vast majority of scholarship I do not think that the apostle Matthew was the real author of the Gospel. For an opposite view in favour of the authenticity, see R. H. Gundry, 'The Apostolically Johannine Pre-Papian Tradition Concerning the Gospels of Mark and Matthew', in R. H. Gundry, *The Old is Better: New Testament Essays in Support of Traditional Interpretations* (WUNT, 178; Tübingen: Mohr Siebeck, 2005), pp. 49–73. But see the critique in D. C. Sim, 'The Gospel of Matthew, John the Elder and the Papias Tradition: A Response to R. H. Gundry', *HTS* 63 (2007), pp. 283–99.

not to see 'Christian Judaism' or 'Judaeo-Christianity' as a monolithic block despite all the apparent similarities.[13]

2. The Community

The debate about James' social and religious context has begun only recently.[14] All we can know about his community has to be distilled from a couple of passages in the letter itself. According to Jas 1.1, James is directed to the δώδεκα φυλαὶ αἱ ἐν τῇ διασπορᾷ. Although this expression is, given its prominent place and traditional phraseology, certainly an important signal about how the author sees himself and his audience, it is far from certain what it exactly means. On the one hand, the author invokes a Biblically inspired intellectual tradition to identify the addressees with the ideal community of the 'twelve tribes' (though the term 'Israel' is notably avoided!). On the other hand, the author places all (!) twelve tribes in the Diaspora, thereby paradoxically excluding Palestine and transgressing well-known concepts of Biblical twelve-tribe geography. It is therefore no wonder that many exegetes assume that James was a kind of 'encyclica'[15] and has no actual connection to Judaism. I think the contrary is the case. However 'encyclical' the letter might be, it would not make sense to address a group of people as 'twelve tribes' if these people did not perceive that as an honorary title that correctly expresses their self-definition. Biblical terminology apparently played a major role for James' readers, as well as the language of the Septuagint and the Law, both theologically and ethically. Its pivotal role is not undermined by the fact that James shares many themes and argumentative styles with popular Greek philosophy (especially Stoicism). Matthew, on the other hand, seems to lack a comparable wealth of Hellenistic terminology and apparently follows a less cosmopolitan strand of Judaism.

Despite many positive references to Jewish heritage, there can be no doubt that James is exclusively directed to converted Christians (Jas 1.18, 21). It is disputed whether Jas 1.18, 21 imply that conversion and 'bringing to life through the word of truth' (the latter sounds rather 'Pauline', cf. Col. 1.5; 2 Tim. 2.15) were connected to baptism,[16] but Jas 2.3 seems to

---

13. On Matthew's Christian Judaism, see Luz, *Matthew 1-7*, pp. 45–52.

14. See the important study by W. Popkes, *Adressaten, Situation und Form des Jakobusbriefes* (SBS, 125; Stuttgart: Katholisches Bibelwerk, 1986). Also Popkes, *Jakobus*, pp. 17–22.

15. M. Hengel, 'Jakobusbrief', p. 514, calls James an 'Enzyklika an alle Christen... die unter den "Völkern" zerstreut leben und ganz überwiegend Heidenchristen sind'.

16. For the negative view, see Berger, *Theologie*, p. 186.

demonstrate that the community gathering took place in the context of a meal. James refers to his audience as συναγωγή (Jas 2.2) and ἐκκλησία (Jas 5.14). Although these terms can otherwise be used synonymously and in James certainly refer to one and the same community, they clearly express different aspects of it. The literary context in which each is placed indicates that συναγωγή means the gathering place of the community where everybody comes together to celebrate, while ἐκκλησία designates the community as a whole as represented through its πρεσβύτεροι who are vested with particular spiritual power and authority. James obviously does not know ἀπόστολοι and he does not call Christians κλητοί (or ἐκλεκτοί) or ἅγιοι. All of these terms, however, play an important role in the Pauline tradition (Rom. 1.1; 1 Cor. 1.1-2; 3.17; 4.2; 6.1-2; 2 Cor. 1.1).

Both συναγωγή and ἐκκλησία are well understandable in a Jewish context, although not exclusively so.[17] Much more important for the self-definition of the community is the observation that throughout the letter, the author simply addresses his audience as ἀδελφοί. While ἀδελφός is often best understood as a designation for the author's own peers (Jas 1.2, 16, 19; 2.1, 14; 3.1, 10, 12; 4.11; 5.7, 9, 10, 12, 19), the term and the topics connected with it (ὑπομονή, mutual support and so on) have the potential to address all fellow Christians (esp. Jas 1.9; 2.15, the latter including the only attestation of ἀδελφή). A large part of the paraenetical traditions in James focuses on putting such egalitarian structures in practice and maintaining them; no quarrelling or προσοπολημψία. Only once does the author claim a specific function as teacher (διδάσκαλος; Jas 3.1), but this position was also open to others. Here might be a bridge to Matthew. On the basis of Mt. 13.52 many interpreters see Matthew as a γραμματεύς, a function that is not explicitly mentioned in James but might in fact resemble that of a Jamesian διδάσκαλος.

Apart from these limited functional differentiations, James did not distinguish between different sub-groups within his audience (such as Jewish or Gentile Christians), but only singles out those who are characterized by particular behaviour. Only James' critique against the rich suggests that the community did have to cope with internal differentiation, but this was social and not functional.

Matthew, however, offers a much more colourful picture. He shares with James the interest in διδάσκαλοι (Jesus himself being the most prominent one) and γραμματεῖς (Mt. 8.19; 9.11; 23.8), but also knows ἀπόστολοι (10.2) and μαθηταί (clearly one of Matthew's favourites). Moreover, he not only deals with a wide range of topics of everyday life (taxation, agriculture, slaves and so on), but also emphasizes egalitarianism and compromise (Mt. 18.1-35; 23.8-12; cf. the appeal against quarrelling also in James). Nevertheless,

---

17. Popkes, *Jakobus*, p. 4. Consequently, he urges; 'Besondere Zurückhaltung ist bei der Einschätzung der Relation zum Judentum zu wahren' (6).

Matthew's community is heavily engaged in disputes with Pharisees and other Jews about matters of religious practice (prayer, fasting, purity issues, other religious obligations), all of which is at best only vaguely mentioned in James, if at all. In general, the outside world features much more prominently in Matthew than it does in James (only mentioned in passing in Jas 2.6, πλούσιοι κριτήρια). While the Jamesian community makes a functionally very homogeneous impression despite all socially motivated tensions, Matthew speaks explicitly of diverse groups of Christians that remain until the end (Mt. 13.24-30), but he also has reservations against internal hierarchy (Mt. 23.8-12). On different levels, Matthew also refers to συναγωγαί. They simultaneously provide the scenery for Jesus' preaching (Mt. 4.25; 9.18, 35) and for the flawed religious practices of the ὑποκριταί (Mt. 6.2, 5; 23.6). While a certain distance is noticeable in Matthew's usage of συναγωγή (Mt. 12.9, *their* synagogue; 23.34 *your* synagogues), he can also create a sense of closeness between Jesus and the συναγωγή of his hometown Capernaum (Mt. 13.54). Although Matthew never refers to 'our' synagogue(s), such a usage does not seem totally impossible on the basis of these passages, and the lack of such an expression might be more connected to the liminal social situation of the Matthaean community than to theological reasons.

Of prime importance for Matthaean studies is the discussion of its relationship to Judaism. A large number of studies on the *traditions-geschichtliche* background, the theological profile and its semantic expressions have brought fresh impetus to reconstructing the historical context of Matthew's Gospel.[18] The question as to what extent Matthew's debate with Judaism is led from 'inside' this Jewish matrix (Matthew has still not cut intellectual and theological ties with Judaism, thus J. A. Overman, A. J. Saldarini and D. C. Sim),[19] or from 'outside' (Matthew perceives his group as a fundamentally 'new people', thus G. N. Stanton, D. A. Hagner and P. Foster)[20] dominates the debate. Nobody, however, would deny that Matthew's

---

18. See D. C. Sim, 'Reconstructing the Social and Religious Milieu of Matthew: Methods, Sources and Possible Results', forthcoming in H. van de Sandt and J. Zangenberg (eds), *Matthew, James and the Didache: Three Related Documents in their Jewish and Christian Contexts* (SBLSS; Atlanta: Scholars Press).

19. See J. A. Overman, *Matthew's Gospel and Formative Judaism: The Social World of the Matthean Community* (Minneapolis: Fortress Press, 1990); *idem.*, *Church and Community in Crisis: The Gospel According to Matthew* (TNTIC; Valley Forge: Trinity Press International, 1996); A. J. Saldarini, *Matthew's Christian-Jewish Community* (CSHJ; Chicago: University of Chicago Press, 1994); and D. C. Sim, *The Gospel of Matthew and Christian Judaism: The History and Social Setting of the Matthean Community* (SNTW; Edinburgh: T&T Clark, 1998).

20. See G. N. Stanton, *A Gospel for a New People: Studies in Matthew* (Edinburgh: T&T Clark, 1992); D. A. Hagner, 'Matthew: Apostate, Reformer, Revolutionary?', *NTS* 49 (2003), pp. 193–209; and P. Foster, *Community, Law and Mission in Matthew's Gospel* (WUNT, 2.177; Tübingen: Mohr Siebeck, 2004).

intellectual matrix is deeply influenced by motifs and concepts that were fundamental for Jews, and that his debate with his Jewish opponents centres on this 'common ground'. Given this matrix, one might wonder if the alternative 'from outside' versus 'from inside' Judaism is too artificial. The problem is that we have no clear picture of the *type* of Judaism Matthew is in dispute with. His polemics, directed against Φαρισαῖοι and ὑπόκριται, does not provide enough detail to define what form of Judaism is his competition.[21] Should we not rather acknowledge the fact that Judaism never was a monolith but always comprised regional divergences and variations? But how can we get a hold on that type of Judaism? Everything has to be reconstructed from Matthew's version of things. Thus we cannot know how far the individual profile of Matthew's Jewish opponents deviated or agreed with other Jewish groups. A lot also depends on how *we* shape our criteria. What can or cannot be called 'Christian' or 'Jewish'? Matthew well illustrates the fact that there was no universally accepted demarcation, but that this distinction was in flux and always under negotiation.

A second aspect of Matthew's social and religious context, the Roman Empire and all who are perceived as neither Christian nor Jew, has only recently found appropriate attention.[22] Historically, religiously and socially we deal with no more than two aspects of the same world in which Matthew and his community lived. Every Jew (at least those with whom Matthew was in dialogue) was a part of his intellectual, Biblically inspired and ritually ordered world, but at the same time he also inhabited the Roman Empire with all its political, cultural, social and religious implications. A predominately Jewish matrix does not exclude debates about Gentiles.

In general, both Matthew and James present a rather egalitarian community structure with a striking lack of terminological and functional differentiation. In that respect, both texts differ from many other early Christian documents that display a sometimes extensive interest in differentiating between various functions and institutions within Christian communities (cf. the Pauline literature, including the Pastorals, and Acts and the *Didache*). Nevertheless, other traditions share this apparent egalitarianism with Matthew and James (the Johannine literature, Mark and Q). While James makes a quite 'primitive' appearance, Matthew shows a somewhat larger diversity.

---

21. Cf. Zangenberg, 'A Conflict Among Brothers'; J. A. Overman, 'Problems with Pluralism in Second Temple Judaism: Matthew, James and the *Didache* in Their Jewish-Roman Milieu', forthcoming in van de Sandt and Zangenberg, *Matthew, James and the Didache*.

22. W. Carter, *Matthew and Empire: Initial Explorations* (Harrisburg: Trinity Press International, 2001); J. Riches and D. C. Sim (eds), *The Gospel of Matthew in Its Roman Imperial Context* (JSNTSup, 276; London: T&T Clark International, 2005).

3. *Content and Terminology*

Recent research has developed a refreshing awareness of the fact that both Matthew and James produced meaningful works with their own theological agenda and contextual referentiality. James especially has been fully rehabilitated from offering a mere humdrum of paraenetical traditions without any actual function. Many scholars now rightly emphasize the rhetorical skills of the author and reject Dibelius' harsh criticism of James which 'over long passages completely lacks any intellectual cohesion'.[23] Influenced by wisdom traditions, frequently using poetic sequences, rhetorical figures and accumulations of imperatives to persuade the readers, James knows how to adapt his sources to suit his style and interests.[24] Having made this point, the following discussion will introduce three important themes in both Matthew and James – the Law, Jesus traditions and ethics.

Both Matthew and James emphasize the importance of observing the Law. To keep the Law not only by listening to it, but also actively doing what it demands is one of the fundamental tenets of Judaism (Lev. 18.5; Deut. 4.6; Sir. 19.20; *m. 'Avot* 1.17). It is not only Matthew and James that emphasize that hearing and doing the Law belong together (Jas 1.19-27; 2.14-26; Mt. 7.21-26),[25] other early Christian texts also share this position (Mt. 7.21, 26 is actually from Q; see also below on Paul).

Despite these general congruences, James lacks any reference to ritual laws. While Matthew is still busy with Jesus traditions commenting on purity regulations (Mt. 15.1-20), sabbath (Mt. 12.1-14) and Temple tax (Mt. 17.24-7), James mentions none of these.[26] Does that mean these topics were not on the agenda in his community, because everybody was in agreement? James' Diaspora situation might explain why tax and purity were not dealt with, but we know that sabbath was an issue also in the Diaspora. How relevant is the absence of these topics in a five-chapter text anyway,[27] especially when we consider that neither Matthew nor James mentions circumcision?

23.   M. Dibelius, *Der Brief des Jakobus* (ed. and suppl. H. Greeven; KEK, 15; Göttingen: Vandenhoeck & Ruprecht, 11th edn, 1964), p. 14 (my translation).

24.   See Hengel, 'Jakobusbrief als antipaulinische Polemik', pp. 513–19, and Shepherd, 'Epistle of James', pp. 41–2.

25.   Shepherd, 'Epistle of James', p. 45, writes about Jas 2.14-26; 'So much attention has been given to this passage of James in relation to the Pauline doctrine of justification, that it is commonly overlooked how exactly James's doctrine fits the teaching of Matthew'.

26.   B. Repschinski, 'Purity in Matthew, James and the *Didache*', forthcoming in van de Sandt and Zangenberg, *Matthew, James and the Didache*.

27.   James, therefore, is not an 'encyclical' in the sense that the letter strives to present a list of topics that is as complete as possible.

Motivation to keep the Law is also different. While for Matthew the Law needs to be observed simply because Jesus has commanded it (5.17-18), James seems to employ a variety of arguments taken from Jewish apologetics (wisdom theology, paradigmatic Old Testament 'saints'). Ultimately, God himself is the source of the Law for both, but in Matthew christology channels and almost obscures the role of God in this respect, while James' theocentric argumentation is more 'traditional' in a way (see further below).

Matthew and James are also both interested in the Jesus tradition. Nowhere else outside the Gospels do we find more Jesus traditions than in James. Apart from a similar outlook on the Law, James offers a number of sayings, motifs and phrases that also turn up in Q and the Matthean redaction in an often strikingly similar form.[28] How these congruences should be explained poses one of the most controversial problems of James/Matthew research. The following points need to be noted.

(1) From the synoptic tradition James especially carefully adapts material about 'empowered speech' (oaths, prayer). He shares material with 1 Peter which deals with the contrast of lowness and highness, or suffering and joy/heavenly recompense.[29]

(2) It is crucial to see that the parallels between James and Matthew are always on the level of single sayings, and betray no familiarity with the redactional level of their Matthaean (almost exclusively collected in the Sermon on the Mount) or Lukan (many but not all concentrated in the Sermon on the Plain) versions. The parallels therefore do not necessarily require one to assume that Matthew (or Luke) were dependent upon James or *vice versa*, or that James directly drew upon the Q tradition.

(3) It often appears that what Matthew (on the basis of Q) presents in his narrative framework as 'Jesus tradition' turns up as 'non-Jesus tradition' in wisdom and Torah-oriented James (e.g. oaths, love-command). The fact that the sayings are integrated differently in Matthew (and Luke) and James, and that they show considerable differences in tendency, form and content, suggest that they went through different redactional processes and were altered by the authors to fit into their individual contexts – despite all the similarities. This confirms the overall flexibility and adaptibility of the early Jesus traditions, as well as testifying to their 'creative appropriation and re-expression' by the authors.[30]

(4) The similarities should not be exclusively explained with reference to the literary level in Matthew and James. They must also be considered

28.   See the list in Popkes, *Jakobus*, pp. 32–5. Cf. too J. Schröter, 'Jesus Tradition in Matthew, James and the *Didache*: Searching for Characteristic Emphases', forthcoming in van de Sandt and Zangenberg, *Matthew, James and the Didache*.

29.   Berger, *Theologie*, p. 192.

30.   Bauckham, *Wisdom*, p. 93.

in the light of the fact that many of the issues raised in the parallel sayings resemble Jewish debates and are congruent with the overall situational context of these texts. Apart from their individual content, it is particularly the fact that the saying parallels connect Matthew and James with respect to both their traditio-historical background and their argumentative situation with forms of Christianity that are close to Judaism and Judaism itself. However, unlike in the Gospels, the Jesus material in James does not appear in *Chriai* and is not used in controversies with Judaism about observance of the Law.[31]

(5) The supposedly more primitive form of Jesus tradition in James compared to Matthew led many exegetes to assume that James represents an earlier stage in the development, and therefore is an important indication that Matthew postdates James. Often it seems that Matthew has spelt out in a narrative context concentrated on Jesus what James brings in gnomic, sapiential form. Neither version, however, simply parallels the other, nor can one be used to reconstruct the other. The sequence and context of these topics are different, but the type and content are similar enough to see Matthew and James drawing from the same literary and theological milieu. Most important for James were sapiential discussions about diverse ethical issues (piety, prayer, tribulations, justice) and it employs forms from this literary milieu (e.g. macarisms in Jas 1.12; 5.11).[32] Research in Jamesian ethics has demonstrated how deeply rooted the author is in Jewish paraenetical traditions (that often included tenets borrowed from pagan philosophy). It is not necessary to assume that he had Matthew in front of him.

Apart from these 'non-Jesus Jesus traditions', James is awkwardly uninterested in Jesus.[33] Instead, he thinks theocentrically.[34] He never refers to Jesus' incarnation, atoning death or his resurrection (although James expects the future resurrection of the Christians; 5.15), and he never calls Jesus Son of Man, Son of David or teacher. That does not mean that James advocates a particularly 'low' christology. On the contrary, James calls Jesus κύριος (Jas 1.1; 2.1), a term he also frequently uses for God (Jas 3.9; 5.4, 10-11; cf. also 4.15; 5.14-15). Further, Jesus is judge and will

---

31. Berger, *Theologie*, p. 186. Berger sees here a clear difference to the Petrine and Pauline traditions. Similarities between James and 1 Peter, however, relativize this distinction, at least with respect to 1 Peter. On James and Paul, see below.

32. I follow Shepherd, 'Epistle of James'. A fuller list of relevant passages is conveniently collected in Popkes, *Jakobus*, pp. 32–5, and Johnson, *James*, pp. 55–7. See also the discussion in Berger, *Theologie*, pp. 186–8, 191–2.

33. See Popkes, *Jakobus*, pp. 23–4. Popkes rightly sees James' christology to a large extent as part of theology ('Gotteslehre').

34. Popkes, *Jakobus*, pp. 22–3.

return at the end of days (Jas 5.8-9). Even so, God's role is spelt out much more diversely than that of Jesus.

This is in striking contrast to Matthew who pulls together all registers of early Christian christology, using the full array of titles and grounding his christological message in numerous Old Testament quotations (Mt. 1.22-23; 2.5-6, 17-18; 12.17-21; 13.14-15; 21.4-5, 42 and so on). James *does* of course quote from the Old Testament as well. He refers to Old Testament figures (Abraham in 2.21; the harlot Rahab in 2.25; Job in 5.11; and Elijah in 5.17-18, cf. Rev. 11.6), but always in the context of ethics and not christology (e.g. Jas 2.8 from Lev. 19.18; Jas 2.11 from Exod. 20.13-14; Jas 2.21 from Gen. 22.9; Jas 2.23 from Gen. 15.6; Jas 4.6 from Prov. 3.34).

The discussion of the Jesus tradition provides a bridge to the topic of ethics. Both writings apparently independently draw from a common pool of traditions, but rework and contextualize them differently. How are regulations motivated? How are ideals constructed and propagated? Which topics appear (poverty/riches, disunity, tribulation in James; a much wider range in Matthew mediated through much more diverse sources), and how are they dealt with?

Both James and Matthew show a considerable overlap in their construction of ideals (τέλειος-terminology).[35] For James, wisdom is a way to perfection and the epitome of early Christian ethical traditions. While Matthew motivates ethics through christology (Jesus' yoke in Mt. 11.29-30), James is more theocentric and promotes a positive image of the Law (Jas 2.8, 12). Both agree, however, that the Law needs to be observed, done and fulfilled (Jas 2.8, 14-26; Mt. 5.17-19). Other common topics are (1) endurance of trials and prayer in faith without doubt (Jas 1.6; Mt. 5.10-12; 6.13; 21.21); (2) rich and poor (Jas 4.13–5.6; Mt. 6.19, 34); (3) respect of persons (Jas 2.1-13; Mt. 19.16-30); (4) evil-speaking (Jas 3.1-12; Mt. 7.16-20; 12.33, 36; 15.11); (5) wrathful man (Jas 1.19-20; Mt. 5.21-22), and (6) oaths (Jas 5.12; Matt 5.34-37). Despite these general similarities both writings show many differences in practical details.[36]

35. W. J. C. Weren, 'Following Jesus: The "Ideal Community" According to Matthew, James and the *Didache*', forthcoming in van de Sandt and Zangenberg, *Matthew, James and the Didache*; Schröter, 'Jesus Tradition'; P. J. Hartin, *A Spirituality of Perfection: Faith in Action in the Letter of James* (Collegeville: Liturgical Press, 1999); and *idem.*, 'Ethics in the Letter of James, the Gospel of Matthew and the *Didache*: Their Place in Early Christian Literature', forthcoming in van de Sandt and Zangenberg, *Matthew, James and the Didache*.

36. On the attitude towards the poor, see J. S. Kloppenborg, 'Poverty and Piety in Matthew, James and the *Didache*', forthcoming in van de Sandt and Zangenberg, *Matthew, James and the Didache*. On oaths, see M. Vahrenhorst, 'The Presence and Absence of a Prohibition of Oaths in James, Matthew and the *Didache* and its Significance for Contextualization', forthcoming in van de Sandt and Zangenberg, *Matthew, James and the Didache*.

4. Contacts With Other New Testament Texts

Neither Matthew nor James existed in a vacuum. Similarities and dissimilarities between them and in comparison with other Christian writings contribute to a better understanding of their own theological profile and social background.

Particularly closely related are James and 1 Peter,[37] perhaps more than James and Matthew, by the fact that James and 1 Peter independently of each other adapt common traditions (cf. Jas 1.2-3 with 1 Pet. 1.6-7; Jas 1.18, 21 with 1 Pet. 1.22–2.3, and Jas 4.6-10 with 1 Pet. 5.5c-9), which are differently applied to their community situations (suffering in 1 Peter, ethical misbehaviour in James).[38] Matthew, however, shares a couple of motifs with 1 Peter (1 Pet. 3.14 and Mt. 5.10; 1 Pet. 2.12 and Mt. 5.16). M. Konradt has sketched the position of James and Matthew in the early Christian literary landscape as follows; 'Ist der 1. Petrusbrief der engste Verwandte des Jakobusbriefs, was Berührungen in einzelnen Traditionsstücken angeht, so gebührt dem Matthäusevangelium dieses Prädikat mit Blick auf die theologische Affinität'.[39] Following Konradt, affinities between Matthew and James are particularly evident with respect to the interpretation of the Law, the concept of perfection, in the lack of an explicit interest in pneumatology and the intensive use of eschatological concepts (judgement) in ethical contexts. Konradt sees Matthew, James and 1 Peter connected by a 'gemeinsames Traditionsfundament' and all as witnesses of Syrian Christianity.[40]

Of particular interest also is the relationship between Matthew (taken up only recently in research) and James (a classic since the Reformation) over against Paul. Many exegetes see the positive attitude towards the Law in Matthew and James as directly opposed to Paul's position as demonstrated in Romans or Galatians. For M. Hengel, James is a 'masterpiece of early Christian polemics' and 'anti-Pauline' throughout.[41] The most conspicuous witness for James' alleged anti-Paulinism is, of course, Jas 2.14-26. Scholars disagree over whether the Pauline position was directly known to James through his letters or orally transmitted through followers or opponents of Paul.

---

37. Popkes, *Jakobus*, pp. 39-40.
38. Konradt, 'Jakobusbrief als Brief des Jakobus', pp. 19–30; *idem.*, *Christliche Existenz nach dem Jakobusbrief. Eine Studie zu seiner soteriologischen und ethischen Konzeption* (SUNT, 22; Göttingen: Vandenhoeck & Ruprecht, 1998), pp. 324–7.
39. Konradt, 'Jakobusbrief als Brief des Jakobus', pp. 40–1.
40. On affinities as result of a common Syrian (Antiochene) context, see M. Zetterholm, 'The *Didache*, Matthew, and Paul: Reconstructing Historical Developments in Antioch', forthcoming in van de Sandt and Zangenberg, *Matthew, James and the Didache*.
41. Hengel, 'Jakobusbrief', pp. 524–5. Less emphatic but equally convinced that 2.14-26 should not be taken out of its context is Popkes, *Jakobus*, pp. 36–9.

The traditional consensus of James' 'anti-Paulinism', however, has recently come under critical re-examination by several scholars.[42] According to them, one should avoid reading James as an anti-Pauline document despite the apparent terminological similarities to elements of Pauline theology in Jas 2.14-26. Not only do important elements of Pauline theology go unmentioned in James, but James in turn deals with a couple of topics that are never mentioned in Paul, or are at least not dealt with in the way Paul deals with them. The epistolary form of James is different from Pauline formulae,[43] and there is little contact with Pauline community structures or situations. Nor is there any indication of controversies about Torah-observance for Jews and non-Jews in the Christian community.[44] Consequently, 'circumcision' is lacking in James.

On the basis of what was said above on James' understanding of the Law, it is evident that James shares several fundamental tenets about the Law with Paul.[45] Both James and Paul emphasize that one must not only hear, but also do the Law (Jas 1.22-23; Rom. 2.13; cf. Mt. 7.20-21), because the Law demands observance in order not to fall under its judgement (Jas 2.10, 12; Rom. 2.12, 14-6; Gal. 3.10; 5.3). Paul of course knows that faith brings forth fruits (Gal. 5.22-23). Love is the best way to completely fulfil the Law as required (Jas 2.8; Rom 13.9). Here, both Paul and James stand in the tradition of Hellenistic Judaism. They are both heirs of a widespread reception of Gen. 15.6 (Abraham as model of a proselyte who keeps his faith), and agree that faith is acknowledged as justice before God (Jas 2.23; Rom. 4.3).

Paul and James differ, however, in the function they assign to the connection between 'faith and works'. For Paul, the phrase is of central importance in his struggle against opponents who reject his unconditional acceptance of Gentiles into the people of God, a topic that plays no role in James. Accepting that faith will of course bring forth fruits, Paul is interested in setting out the anthropological and theological conditions under which the Law can be fulfilled. Paul is much more radical than James insofar as he ultimately ascribes both πίστις and works to God's saving and transforming power, the πνεῦμα (through εὐαγγέλιον Rom.

---

42. See e.g. Konradt, *Existenz*, pp. 210–13, 241–6; *idem.*, 'Jakobusbrief als Brief des Jakobus', p. 18; and *idem.*, 'Theologie in der "strohernen Epistel": Ein Literaturbericht zu neueren Ansätzen in der Exegese des Jakobusbriefes', *VF* 44 (1999), pp. 54–78. Niebuhr, 'New Perspective', p. 1019, characterizes recent scholarship as 'Absetzen der paulinischen Brille'. Johnson, *James*, pp. 58–64, sees James independent of Paul, but as authentic; 'Despite the remarkable points of resemblance, they appear not to be talking to each other by way of instruction or correction' (64).

43. D. J. Verseput, 'Genre and Story: The Community Setting of the Epistle of James', *CBQ* 62 (2000), pp. 96–110.

44. Niebuhr, 'New Perspective', p. 1021.

45. I follow Berger, *Theologie*, pp. 188–90.

1.17-18; Phil. 2.13). In James, the spirit is marginal and plays no role in actively helping people to fulfil the Law (the use of πνεῦμα in Jas 2.26 is telling; cf. 4.5). Instead, James can, in a way similar to Paul, talk about the 'fruits' of wisdom (Jas 3.13-18, cf. the Pauline *Wertepriamel*, 1 Cor. 13; Gal. 5.22-23). Paul does write about σοφία, but in a characteristically different way (1 Cor. 2–3). Insofar as James bases his ethics on σοφία instead of dynamic and charismatic πνεῦμα, James' perception of πίστις is different. On the one hand, πίστις is in James more limited to a particular starting situation as incipient trust in God. On the other hand, Christian life becomes a more processual character, thus assigning a different role to the ἔργα. It is notable how often James warns not to give up πίστις in the face of tribulations, but to hold out, endure and persevere. Therefore πίστις is also the trust that does not doubt if one prays (Jas 1.5-6). According to K. Berger, 'Die Position des Jak ist... eine unzertrennliche Einheit aus Glaube und Werken, und zwar so, daß der Bekenntnisglaube nur der Anfang eines Treue- und Bewährungsprozesses ist, dessen Resultat Geduld, Standhalten und Werke sind und an dessen Ende dann das Prädikat "gerecht" wirklich zutrifft. Diese Position ist bis auf den letzten Punkt auch die des Paulus'.[46] Paul too knows about tribulations that endanger faith (1 Thess. 3.5).

The theology of Paul and James are two structurally different, independent systems of how to counter typical problems of a *Bekehrungsreligion* (access, belonging, holding out). Each solution is dictated by specific problems resulting from different community situations (for Paul, acceptance of pagans; for James no pagans, but social differences through wealth) and the availability of theological tools to cope with them (for Paul pneuma-theology; for James wisdom tradition, eschatological motivation for ethics). To put it differently, James is not anti-Pauline, he is un-Pauline. The seemingly contrasting phrase πίστις and ἔργα is no Pauline invention and therefore its appearance in James should not be taken as proof of James' dependence on Paul;[47] the congruence between faith and practical behaviour is nothing particularly Pauline, but is motivated by James' sapiential ethics and theology. Moreover, Jas 2.14-26 needs to be placed back in its literary context and must no longer be

---

46. Berger, *Theologie*, pp. 188–9.

47. In favour, see Popkes, *Jakobus*; Hengel, 'Jakobusbrief'; F. Avemarie, 'Die Werke des Gesetzes im Spiegel des Jakobusbriefs: A Very Old Perspective on Paul', *ZTK* 98 (2001), pp. 282–309. Against, see Konradt, 'Literaturbericht', and Berger, *Theologie*, p. 186. Niebuhr, 'New Perspective', p. 1020, states; 'Wer etwa den Brief nicht von Paulus her liest, kommt schwerlich auf die Idee, dass die Argumentation zu Glaube und Werken in 2,14-26 sein theologisches Hauptstück sei und in den Zusammenhang frühchristlicher Auseinandersetzungen um die spezifisch paulinischen Argumentationen zur Rechtfertigung gehöre'.

isolated and contrasted to Paul whose theology is certainly different, but not the key to understanding James.

Even less evident is Matthew's correlation with Paul which has also recently been studied. D. C. Sim has argued that Matthew's Torah-centred theology so diametrically stood against Paul that it goes far beyond mere 'non-Paulinism'.[48] In a more recent article, Sim proposes that Mt. 7.21-23 rejects Paul and his group on the charge of lawlessness.[49] It is true that Paul employs a different approach towards the Law and it is also true that his communities prophesied, worked miracles and performed exorcisms (1 Cor. 12.3; Rom. 10.9-13), but they were not the only ones! How *specifically* anti-Pauline are these passages? It is entirely conceivable that judaizing opponents of Paul could charge him with lawlessness, but how *exclusively* Pauline is such a position (even James was executed on the charge of 'lawlessness')?

Anti-Paulinism does not dominate the content or form of the argumentation, nor is it at the roots of either Matthew or James. The fact that Matthew and James share important features that at the same time distinguishes them from Pauline tradition (pneumatology, differentiated community functions) demonstates that both writings have developed in a distinctly non-Pauline milieu, and even if they came into contact with strange and suspicious theological positions that might or might not have been known to them as 'Pauline', they commented on them and rejected them on the basis of their own, independently grown convictions. The rather vague diction of the supposed anti-Pauline passages (in Matthew even more vague than in James) raises the question of how these traditions were transmitted and became known to Matthew and James.

5. Conclusions

Despite many individual features, a common theological outlook and a common pool of semantic tools to express it clearly bind Matthew and James together. Matthew and James represent a type of Christianity that sees itself as a perfect way to fulfil the Law, in a way as 'perfect Judaism'. The formal and ideological diversities of James and Matthew demonstrate that the type of Christianity these texts represent was able to use a broad number of traditions and literary devices: Jesus tradition in narrative and logia form, topics and rhetorical figures from wisdom tradition, and so on. In that respect, Matthaean/Jamesian Christianity resembles the

48. Sim, *Matthew and Christian Judaism*, pp. 188–211; and *idem.*, 'Matthew's Anti-Paulinism: A Neglected Feature of Matthean Studies', *HTS* 58 (2002), pp. 767–83.

49. D. C. Sim, 'Matthew 7.21-23: Further Evidence of Its Anti-Pauline Perspective', *NTS* 53 (2007), pp. 325-43.

Johannine 'school' and Pauline tradition (if Acts is counted among it). Irrespective of all these congruences, it would be too simple to construe a literary dependence between Matthew and James. Such a solution could not explain why so much is lacking in the one that is central to the other, or why similar traditions are so differently presented. Despite many similarities, one should also not see the relationship between Matthew and James along the lines of the Gospel of John and the Johannine epistles, because the language, style and contents of Matthew and James are simply not close enough to each other. While the Johannine school (through its jargon and theological position) and the Pauline school through its idiosyncratic theology do not seem to represent the 'mainstream' phenomenon in earliest Christianity, Matthew (plus the *Didache* and Ignatius of Antioch) and James (plus 1 Peter and perhaps 2 Peter and Jude) seem to do just that.[50] Their common outlook is not so much a result of a common regional origin or even a common community background, but constitutes two different representations of a broad stream in early Christianity that redefined its relationship with Judaism in a fundamentally different way compared to Paul or John. The most prominent feature of this type of Christianity is that the Law retained its central theological and ethical position, although Matthew and James differ to an extent with regard to its theological motivation. Matthew bases his approach to the Law upon his christology (Christ as teacher, messiah and martyr whom God has sent and vindicated), while James is based more in baptism (indirectly) and a strong emphasis on paraenetical wisdom traditions with an eschatological outlook. But the differences between Matthew and James are only relative. They are due to the difference in genres, to the divergent availability of early Christian traditions and to the diverse situations of their addressees. Seen in a wider context, James and Matthew might be best understood (plus *Didache* and 1 Peter) as examples of a widespread, popular form of early Christianity, while perhaps John and Paul were marginal.

Very little is known about the *Rezeptionsgeschichte* of James until the early third century. More prominent was the figure of James for everybody who emulated James' justice and observance. Just the opposite was the case with Matthew, but the result was the same. The identity of the alleged author played no role, but the text was eagerly adpoted in Judaeo-

---

50. I disagree with Shepherd, 'Epistle of James', pp. 47–9, who sees James, *Didache* and Ignatius as individual appropriations of Matthew, but fails to include 1 Peter. I would rather place James and Matthew independently in the same moderate, Judaeo-Christian milieu, place 1 Peter close to James, and see *Didache* and Ignatius in closer association with Matthew. *1 and 2 Clement*, as well as *Hermas*, draw from similar paraenetical traditions, but conceptionally seem quite independent from any of the aforementioned texts.

Christian circles and eventually far beyond them. The early *Rezeptionsgeschichte* in Judaeo-Christian circles is a good indication about the milieu from which both texts originally came. The marginalization of these groups, however, is tragic, and at least with respect to Matthew, actually contradicts the openness and fluctuation of their original milieu.

7. MATTHEW AND THE *DIDACHE*

HUUB VAN DE SANDT

It has often been observed that there are significant agreements between the *Didache* and the Gospel of Matthew as concerns words, phrases and motifs. The collection of Jesus sayings in the 'Evangelical Section' of *Did.* 1.3–2.1 is very close to the Sermon on the Mount. The radical exposition about the love of one's neighbour as equal to loving one's enemies (*Did.* 1.3b-d) recalls the synoptic tradition in Mt. 5.44, 46-47 and Lk. 6.27-28, 32-33. In addition to this paragraph, the Evangelical Section includes two extra passages comparable to the synoptics which articulate the prohibition against violent resistance (*Did.* 1.4; cf. Mt. 5.39-41; Lk. 6.29) and the exhortation to be charitable (*Did.* 1.5-6; cf. Mt. 5.25c-26, 42; Lk. 6.30; 12.58c-59).

Moreover, with respect to other important elements the *Didache* reveals strong affinity with Matthaean Gospel ingredients as well. There is a correspondence between the trinitarian baptismal formula in the *Didache* and Matthew (*Did.* 7 and Mt. 28.19) as well as close agreement between the reproduction of the Lord's Prayer in *Did.* 8 and Mt. 6.5-13. In addition, both the community of the *Didache* (*Did.* 11–13) and Matthew (Mt. 7.15-23; 10.5-15, 40-42; 24.11, 24) were visited by itinerant apostles and prophets, some of whom were illegitimate. Finally, there is widespread recognition that the contents of *Did.* 15.3 closely match those of Mt. 18.15-17.[1]

In order to account for the undisputed correspondences, scholars have assumed time and again that the *Didache* draws on the final form of the Gospel of Matthew (and Luke).[2] If the document had been composed in

---

1. For references, see K. Niederwimmer, *Die Didache* (KAV, 1; Göttingen: Vandenhoeck & Ruprecht, 2nd edn, 1993), p. 245 n.10; H. van de Sandt, 'Two Windows on a Developing Jewish-Christian Reproof Practice: Matt 18:15-17 and *Did.* 15:3', in H. van de Sandt (ed.), *Matthew and the Didache. Two Documents From the Same Jewish-Christian Milieu?* (Assen: Royal van Gorcum, 2005), pp. 173–92 (173 n. 2).

2. For references, see J. S. Kloppenborg, 'The Use of the Synoptics or Q in *Did.* 1:3b–2:1', in van de Sandt, *Matthew and the Didache*, pp. 105–29 (105 n. 2). See also J. Verheyden, 'Eschatology in the *Didache* and the Gospel of Matthew', in van de Sandt, *Matthew and the Didache*, pp. 193–216 (for *Did.* 16 only).

the second half of the second century or later, as some believed,[3] the *Didache* would present a strong case indeed for the use of the Gospels as we have them. A new scholarly consensus is emerging, however, which dates the *Didache* to the turn of the first century CE.[4] If the *Didache* were redacted that early, the view of the document's dependence on one of the synoptic gospels becomes all but a certainty. An alternative solution might be that Matthew is dependent on the *Didache* as a direct source,[5] but this is problematic too as it implies that the *Didache* was composed much earlier than is generally thought. It is therefore more likely that the *Didache* and Matthew are related in their dependence on common tradition.[6] The documents may even have emanated from the same geographical, social and cultural setting.[7]

In their emphasis on a specific combination of core values, Matthew and *Didache* distinguish themselves from other contemporary Jewish writings. This contribution will compare the essentials of the Torah in both writings at a conceptual and practical level. The basics of the Torah effective in Matthew and the *Didache* on a conceptual level are the (double) love commandment, the second half of the Decalogue and ethical perfection. Yet there is dissimilarity at a practical level. While Matthew seems to focus

---

3.   R. H. Connolly, 'Canon Streeter on the Didache', *JTS* 38 (1937), pp. 364–79 (367–70), and F. E. Vokes, *The Riddle of the Didache. Fact or Fiction, Heresy or Catholicism?* (TCHS, 32; London: SPCK, 1938), pp. 51–61.

4.   H. van de Sandt and D. Flusser, *The Didache. Its Jewish Sources and its Place in Early Judaism and Christianity* (CRINT, 3.5; Assen: Royal van Gorcum, 2002), p. 48.

5.   Minus *Did.* 8.2b; 11.3b; 15.3-4 and 16.7 according to A. J. P. Garrow, *The Gospel of Matthew's Dependence on the Didache* (JSNTSup, 254; London: T&T Clark International, 2004).

6.   J. P. Audet, *La Didache: Instructions des apôtres* (Paris: Gabalda, 1958), pp.166–86; W. Rordorf, 'Does the Didache Contain Jesus Tradition Independently of the Synoptic Gospels?', in H. Wansbrough (ed.), *Jesus and the Oral Gospel Tradition* (JSOTSup, 64; Sheffield: JSOT Press, 1991), pp. 394–423; W. Rordorf and A. Tuilier, *La Doctrine des douze Apôtres (Didachè)* (SC, 248; Paris: Les Éditions du Cerf, 2nd edn, 1998), pp. 91, 232 and van de Sandt and Flusser, *The Didache*, pp. 48–50. It has been suggested too that the *Didache* depends on some other collection of sayings of Jesus; cf. P. Drews, 'Untersuchungen zur Didache', *ZNW* 5 (1904), pp. 53–79; A. Tuilier, 'La Didachè et le problème synoptique', in C. N. Jefford (ed.), *The Didache in Context. Essays on Its Text, History and Transmission* (NovTSup, 77; Leiden: Brill, 1995), pp. 110–30 and A. Tuilier, 'Les charismatiques itinérants dans la Didachè et dans l'Évangile de Matthieu', in van de Sandt, *Matthew and the Didache*, pp. 157–72 (167–9).

7.   See P. J. Tomson, 'The halakhic evidence of Didache 8 and Matthew 6 and the *Didache* community's relationship to Judaism', in van de Sandt, *Matthew and the Didache*, pp. 131–41; Tuilier, 'Les charismatiques itinérants, pp. 157–69; van de Sandt, 'Two Windows', pp. 173–92; and J. A. Draper, 'Do the *Didache* and Matthew Reflect an "Irrevocable Parting of the Ways" with Judaism?', in van de Sandt, *Matthew and the Didache*, pp. 217–41.

on the Torah's demand for perfection, understood as extensively and intensively as possible, the *Didache* stresses moderation and practical compromise.

1. *Similar Principles of Interpretation and Observance of the Torah at a Conceptual Level*

The terms and themes to be discussed below (the love commandment, the second table of the Decalogue and the way to perfection) are significant key components in Matthew's Gospel as well as in the *Didache*. They are the all-inclusive precepts of the basic moral code in both writings. The first two are leading principles of Torah interpretation while the path to perfection is concerned with doing Torah, that is, obedience to the Torah and, eventually, to the community ethos.[8]

a. *Interpretation of the Torah: the Love Command and the Second Half of the Decalogue*
In seeking the components of the Gospel and the *Didache* which permit a greater understanding of the Torah, we shall identify pivotal concepts and thematically related material. Which hermeneutic principles are applied to the traditional commandments of the Torah in Matthew and the *Didache*?

There is general agreement that for Matthew the commandment to love is the core of the Law. The love command defines the Torah. It guides the way to just social relations and fosters an attitude towards life beneficial to one's neighbour. Leviticus 19.18 is quoted three times (5.43; 19.19; 22.39), more frequently than any other text in the Gospel. In this series Mt. 22.37-40 deserves special attention. Jesus declares here that the 'whole Law and the prophets' hang upon the command to completely love God (Deut. 6.5) and to love one's neighbour as oneself (Lev. 19.18). In 22.40 Jesus claims that the love commandments are the highest, super-seding all the others. These directives constitute a coherent perspective for understanding the Law.

The same principle holds true for the middle section of the Sermon on the Mount (5.17–7.12). The formula 'the Law and the prophets' in 22.40 makes up the beginning and ending of this part of the Sermon. The middle section of the Sermon is brought to a close by the ethical maxim; 'So whatever you wish that men would do to you, do so to them' (7.12). The ensuing phrase in 7.12c ('for this is the Law and the prophets')

---

8.   For a detailed substantiation of these principles in the Jewish Two Ways and the Gospel of Matthew, see van de Sandt and Flusser, *The Didache*, pp. 140–237.

indicates that the Golden Rule can serve as an underlying principle of 'the Law and the prophets'. The Law and the prophets are thus fulfilled in a way which might be understood as the result of living by the Golden Rule. Surely this maxim is to be considered synonymous with the love command in Lev. 19.18.[9] The clause in 7.12c is missing in the parallel verse in Lk. 6.31 and may have been inserted by Matthew to create a deliberate link between the Golden Rule and the almost identical phrase in 5.17.[10]

Concluding the main body of the Sermon, the Golden Rule occupies an important position within the text. Matthew perceives the adage as the eminent summary and decisive climax of the preceding demands, prohibitions and ethical discussions in 5.17–7.12.[11] In the final resolution, the Law is reaffirmed and joined with the principle of loving one's neighbour. The significance of the latter observation increases when one sees that Matthew – unlike Mark and Luke – places the Rule in close proximity to a statement on the Two Ways in 7.13-14. Examining the Sermon on the Mount as a whole, one can see that the Two Ways motif (7.13-14) and the Golden Rule directly connected to it (7.12) are the essential scope and climax of the preceding rules of conduct for believers. These statements representing the 'Law and the prophets' (5.17 and 7.12) concisely reflect the description of the Two Ways. The Two Ways theme in 7.13-14 sets the stage for the warnings that follow in the final section of the Sermon on the Mount urging acceptance of Jesus' words (7.13-27).

---

9.   See W. Bacher, *Die Agada der Tannaiten. Vol. 1* (Strasburg: Trübner, 1884), p. 4, who states; 'Dieses Wort (the Golden Rule) ist nichts anderes, als die negative Ausdrucksweise für das biblische: 'Liebe deinen Nächsten wie dich selbst' (Lev. 19,18)...'. See also P. Borgen, 'The Golden Rule. With Emphasis on Its Usage in the Gospels', in P. Borgen (ed.), *Paul Preaches Circumcision and Pleases Men. And Other Essays on Christian Origins* (Relieff, 8; Trondheim: Tapir, 1983), pp. 99–114 (101, 110). For additional references, see D. C. Sim, *The Gospel of Matthew and Christian Judaism: The History and Social Setting of the Matthean Community* (SNTW; Edinburgh: T&T Clark, 1998), p. 128 n. 56. This assumption is supported by *Tg. Ps-Yon.* on Lev. 19.18. Here the Golden Rule is attached to the altruistic love commandment by paraphrasing the comparative pronoun כמוך with the following clause; 'so that what is hateful to you, you shall not do to him'. The commandment to love one's neighbour as oneself is explained in *Tg. Ps-Yon.* on Lev. 19.34 the same way, that is, as a reference to the Golden Rule in its negative form.

10.   One notes that the formula in 7.12c slightly differs from 5.17 in that the former has καί ('and') while the latter has ἤ ('or').

11.   G. N. Stanton, *A Gospel for a New People: Studies in Matthew* (Edinburgh: T&T Clark, 1992), pp. 303–4; R. A. Guelich, *The Sermon on the Mount. A Foundation for Understanding* (Waco: Word Books, 1982), pp. 360–3 and 379–81 and H. D. Betz, *The Sermon on the Mount* (Hermeneia; Minneapolis: Fortress Press, 1995), p. 518. See also K. Syreeni, *The Making of the Sermon on the Mount: A Procedural Analysis of Matthew's Redactoral Activity 1: Methodology and Compositional Analysis* (AASF, 44; Helsinki: Suomalainen Tiedeakatemia, 1987), pp. 158–60 and 173–80 and Sim, *Matthew and Christian Judaism*, pp. 127–30.

At this point[12] it is important to examine the Two Ways section in the first six chapters of the *Didache*. We find here two contrasting moral ways which serve as a framework for the subsequent exposition of two sets of opposing ethical characteristics or antagonistic groups of people associated respectively with the way of life (*Did.* 1–4) and the way of death (*Did.* 5). In addition to the *Didache*, the Two Ways tradition ranges across a variety of early Christian documents including the *Doctrina*, the letter of *Barnabas* 18–20 and some five later writings. Modern scholars generally explain the close resemblances between these different versions of the Two Ways (including *Did.* 1–6) as a consequence of their dependence upon an earlier Jewish Two Ways document which is no longer known to us. As compared to the *Didache* it is interesting to see that the various forms of the Two Ways demonstrate no familiarity with the Evangelical Section in *Did.* 1.3b–2.1 and the supplement in *Did.* 6.2-3. In fact, it appears that these early Christian writings attest to a separate circulation of a form of the Two Ways, closely related to *Did.* 1–6 but without the Christian materials in 1.3b–2.1 and 6.2-3.[13]

Let us now return to the *Didache* version of the Two Ways. The Way of Life is defined first by a fusion of the commandments of divine and altruistic love and the subsequent Golden Rule; 'The way of life, then, is this: you shall love first the God who created you, then your neighbour as yourself; and do not yourself do to another what you would not want done to you' (1.2). The text goes on to explain this principle with a collection of Jesus' sayings; 'Here is the teaching (that flows) from these words: Bless those who curse you and pray for your enemies...' (1.3b-6).

The Way of Life thus begins with a summary of the Law[14] consisting of the double love command (the 'love of God' and the 'love of neighbour') and the Golden Rule in its negative form ('do not yourself do to another what you would not want done to you'). The topic clause in 1.3a ('Here is the teaching [that flows] from these words') shows the following part to be an interpretation. The explanation of the essentials of the Way of Life continues all the way through three chapters before reaching its conclusion in 4.14b. It includes first a series of positive admonitions found in the Evangelical Section of 1.3b–2.1 which reflects some of the

---

12. Another core value (in addition to the love commandment) singled out by Matthew is 'mercy'. Since this important aspect parallels the love commandment and expresses a special dimension of it in Matthew, it is not explicitly dealt with here; cf. U. Luz, *Studies in Matthew* (Grand Rapids: Eerdmans, 2005), p. 200, and K. Snodgrass, 'Matthew and the Law', in D. J. Lull (ed.), *Society of Biblical Literature 1988 Seminar Papers* (Atlanta: Scholars Press, 1988), pp. 536–54 (543).

13. van de Sandt and Flusser, *The Didache*, pp. 55–72.

14. For the double love command and the Golden Rule as summaries of the Law, see van de Sandt and Flusser, *The Didache*, pp. 155–60.

radical requirements of the Sermon on the Mount. Then follows a list of precepts largely covering the second table of the Ten Commandments (2.2-7) and, finally, two chapters dealing with morals, humility and constructive social behaviour (3–4).

In sum, Matthew as well as the *Didache* consider the love commandment (or its variant version in the Golden Rule) as covering all of the Torah. The diverse precepts in the Sermon in Mt. 5.17–7.12 and the Way of Life in *Did.* 1.2–4.14 are organized by and subsumed under the love command (Mt. 7.12 and *Did.* 1.2).

In addition to the (double) love command and the Golden Rule, the second table of the Decalogue is also seen as summarizing the essentials of the Law. For Matthew these commandments are considered more essential than purity regulations (Mt. 15.17-19), as firmly binding over peculiar traditions (15.3-6), and as a precondition for salvation (19.18-19). Let us turn to Mt. 19.16-22 (cf. Mk 10.17-22; Lk. 18.18-23) first.[15] The passage describes the debate between Jesus and the rich young man about the correct fulfilment of the Torah. The man wants to achieve eternal life ('Good teacher, what must I do to inherit eternal life?'), and Jesus refers him to the commandments of the Torah; 'You know the commandments: "Do not kill, do not commit adultery, do not steal, do not bear false witness, do not defraud, honour your father and mother and you shall love your neighbour as yourself"' (Mt. 19.18-19).

The desire to perceive the Decalogue as a matrix and the fundamental essence of the Jewish Torah is linked to its honoured place within Second Temple Judaism.[16] The Nash Papyrus (probably dating from the second century BCE) contains a version of the Decalogue in combination with the *Shema*, which indicates a liturgical recitation. Josephus gives absolute priority to the Decalogue (*Ant.* 3.89), and in chs 11 and 44 of *Liber Antiquitatum Biblicarum*, the Decalogue is described as the most excellent legislation (11.1.5) and is held to be a summary of all precepts.

The second table of the Decalogue is similarly treated. It was understood as a comprehensive principle of the Law. We may refer to a passage in

15. See also D. Flusser, 'The Ten Commandments and the New Testament', in B.–Z. Segal and G. Levi (eds), *The Ten Commandments in History and Tradition* (PPFBR; Jerusalem: Magnes Press, 1990), pp. 219–46.

16. See F. E. Vokes, 'The Ten Commandments in the New Testament and in First Century Judaism', *SE* 5 (1968), pp. 146–54; K. Berger, *Die Gesetzesauslegung Jesu. Ihr historischer Hintergrund im Judentum und im Alten Testament* (WMANT, 40; Neukirchen-Vluyn: Neukirchener Verlag, 1972), pp. 258–361; Y. Amir, 'Die Zehn Gebote bei Philon von Alexandrien', in Y. Amir (ed.), *Die Hellenistische Gestalt des Judentums bei Philon von Alexandrien* (FJCD, 5; Neukirchen-Vluyn: Neukirchener Verlag, 1983), pp. 131–63; K.-W. Niebuhr, *Gesetz und Paränese; Katechismusartige Weisungsreihen in der frühjüdischen Literatur* (WUNT, 2.28; Tübingen: J. C. B. Mohr, 1987), pp. 63–6; and G. Alon, 'The Halacha in the Teaching of the Twelve Apostles', in J. A. Draper (ed.), *The Didache in Modern Research* (AGJU, 37; Leiden: Brill, 1996), pp. 165–94 (170–1).

Pseudo-Phocylides 3–7 which includes injunctions against murder, adultery, theft, covetousness, and speaking falsely.[17] Another example comes from Paul in the Epistle to the Romans (13.8-10); 'for he who loves his neighbour has fulfilled the Law. The commandments, "you shall not commit adultery, you shall not kill, you shall not steal, you shall not covet", and any other commandment, are summed up in this sentence, "You shall love your neighbour as yourself"... therefore love is the fulfilling of the Law'.

Love of one's neighbour is perceived here as a general rule which is spelt out in the second half of the Decalogue. The same holds true for Mt. 19.16-22. Matthew, unlike the parallel accounts in Mark and Luke, lists the love command along with the 'social' commands of the second half of the Decalogue as commands which must be kept to enter eternal life. And again, Mt. 5.17-48, a section which concludes with an elaboration upon a quotation from Lev. 19.18 ('you shall love your neighbour as yourself'), also evidences parallels to the second half of the Decalogue (cf. murder, adultery and lying/false swearing in 5.21-37).

Does the *Didache* also include a list of Decalogue commandments which are considered to cover the essentials of the Torah? It is not difficult to answer the question positively. An inventory of prohibitions revolving around the second table of the Ten Commandments is a main feature of the Two Ways section (chs 1–6). A cursory glance at the text immediately reveals similarities in 2.2-7; 3.2-6 and 5.1.

Didache 2.2-7 contains a list of precepts clearly meant to illustrate, expand and expound upon the second half of the Decalogue. The section lists murder, adultery, theft, covetousness and bearing false witness. Although expanded with specific additional elements, including pederasty, magic, sorcery, abortion and infanticide, the paraenetic catalogue in 2.2-7 is in fact a development of the more general theme within the Decalogue's second table. The authority of the second half of the Decalogue is evident to the extent that the text applies these traditional commandments to practices in Gentile society.[18] A similar catalogue of Decalogue materials is found in the vices listed in *Did.* 3.1-

---

17. P. W. van der Horst, *The Sentences of Pseudo-Phocylides with Introduction and Commentary* (SVTP, 4; Leiden: Brill, 1978), p. 112, and W. T. Wilson, *The Mysteries of Righteousness. The Literary Composition and Genre of the Sentences of Pseudo-Phocylides* (TSAJ, 40; Tübingen: Mohr Siebeck, 1994), pp. 66–74.

18.   The extension was probably introduced with the purpose of providing a more thorough outline of the moral standards against what were the common accusations made in Jewish literature against Gentile society. See Audet, *La Didache*, pp. 286–9; Rordorf and Tuilier, *La Doctrine*, pp. 149–51; W. Rordorf, 'Un chapitre d'éthique Judéo-Chrétienne: les deux voies', *RSR* 60 (1972), pp. 109–28 (118); M. Slee, *The Church in Antioch in the First Century C.E.: Communion and Conflict* (JSNTSup, 244; London: T&T Clark International, 2003), pp. 78–9; and A. Milavec, *The Didache: Faith, Hope, and Life of the Earliest Christian Communities, 50–70 C.E.* (New York: Newman Press, 2003), pp. 131–42.

6 and 5.1. Although the trespasses do not match their parallels in the *Tenach* or LXX perfectly and are expanded by additional elements, the Jewish reader would have almost certainly recognized their source.

Interestingly, the Two Ways in the *Didache* also relates the second half of the Decalogue to the single, all-inclusive principle of loving one's neighbour. This phenomenon becomes all the more evident when one realizes that the Evangelical Section 1.3b–2.1 is a later insertion right after 1.3a ('Here is the teaching [that flows] from these words').[19] The addition caused the explanation of the double love command and the Golden Rule (1.2) to be Christianized, while the traditional Jewish interpretation in *Did.* 2.2-7 accordingly became the 'second commandment' (2.1). Yet even in the present Two Ways form of the *Didache*, the section in *Did.* 2.2-7 still spells out the general standard of the Golden Rule and the double love commandment in *Did.* 1.2.

b. *Observance of the Torah: the Path of Perfection*
In Mt. 5.20 Matthew has Jesus demand that the disciples' righteousness must exceed (περισσεύσῃ) that of the scribes and Pharisees.[20] This expression that their 'righteousness' must be 'greater' (πλεῖον) than that of the scribes and Pharisees is echoed in 5.48, 'You, therefore, must be perfect (τέλειοι), as your heavenly Father is perfect (τέλειος)'. The Lukan parallel (6.36) advocates mercy instead of perfection. Perfection in Mt. 5.48 is understood in a quantitative sense because it is directly linked with the preceding verse, 'And if you salute only your brethren, what more (περισσὸν) are you doing than others? Do not even the Gentiles do the same?' (5.47). Being perfect involves doing more than others. Interestingly, the term περισσόν reflects the verb περισσεύσῃ in v. 20. This inclusion denotes a righteousness measurable in terms of magnitude and a rigorous

19. This section undoubtedly derives from more recent sources. It clearly interrupts the connection between *Did.* 2.1 and 2.2 and it stands out from the immediate context in chs 1–6 with respect to its specific themes reminding us of sayings in the synoptic tradition. Moreover, the omission of this section in *Barnabas* 18–20, the *Doctrina Apostolorum* and other early Two Ways renderings clearly indicates that *Did.* 1.3b–2.1 is a later addition to the basic tradition of the Jewish Two Ways. See van de Sandt and Flusser, *The Didache*, pp. 57–8, 70. Thus a Jewish tradition, in which *Did.* 1.3a was linked with 2.2, stands behind the present form of the Two Ways in the *Didache*.

20. Because it is characteristic of Matthean terms that constitute its content, the relevant verse in Mt. 5.20 is likely to be redactional; cf. Guelich, *Sermon*, pp. 135, 156; U. Luz, *Matthew 1-7* (Hermeneia; Minneapolis: Fortress Press, rev. edn, 2007), p. 213; J. P. Meier, *Law and History in Matthew's Gospel. A Redactional Study of Mt. 5:17-48* (AnBib, 71; Rome: Biblical Institute Press, 1976), pp. 116–19; and W. D. Davies and D. C. Allison, *A Critical and Exegetical Commentary on the Gospel according to Saint Matthew* (ICC; 3 vols; Edinburgh: T&T Clark, 1988, 1991, 1997), I, p. 501.

observance of all commandments.[21] It refers to doing more Torah than the minimum level of morality laid down in the Torah.

The term τέλειος is used to conclude Mt. 5.21-48, a pericope which presents examples of what it means to abide by a 'greater righteousness'. Unfortunately the traditional designation of this section's contents as 'antitheses' implies that Jesus contradicts the Law of Moses here.[22] It is unlikely, however, that the antithetical formulation would suggest that Jesus intended to overturn Torah, since it is hard to find any indication of Jesus abrogating, let alone rejecting, parts of the Torah in Matthew. In these paragraphs, the counter-statement radicalizes, intensifies and transcends the premise rather than revoking or changing it.[23] The sayings concern anger and murder, lust and adultery, divorce, and teachings about oaths, retaliation and love of one's enemy. Their meaning boils down to the following. Not only must you not kill, you must not even reach that level of anger (5.21-22). Not only must you not commit adultery, you must not even look desirously at another man's wife (5.27-28). Rather than making use of the permission to divorce, you must not divorce at all or marry a divorced person (5.31-32). Not only must you keep the oaths

---

21. Cf. B. Przybylski, *Righteousness in Matthew and his World of Thought* (SNTSMS, 41; Cambridge: Cambridge University Press, 1980), pp. 85–7. See also Luz, *Matthew 1-7*, pp. 289–90; and Davies and Allison, *Matthew*, I, p. 500.

22. The second member of the repeated antithesis, 'but I say to you', is introduced by δέ instead of ἀλλά. The translation 'but' heightens the contrast too much and gives the impression that Jesus deliberately sets himself over against the Law; cf. D. Flusser, "'Den Alten ist gesagt". Zur Interpretation der sog. Antithesen der Bergpredigt', *Judaica* 48 (1992), pp. 35–9 (38); and R. H. Gundry, *Matthew: A Commentary on His Handbook for a Mixed Church under Persecution* (Grand Rapids: Eerdmans, 2nd edn, 1994), p. 83. See also Davies and Allison, *Matthew*, I, p. 507, who would translate the antitheses this way; 'You have heard that it was said (to the ancients)... but I (in addition) say to you'.

23. Most commonly, the specific antithetical formulations of the first, second, and fourth antitheses (Mt. 5.21-22, 27-28, 33-34a) are considered pre-Matthaean while the antithetical pattern in the remainder of the series is assumed to be a secondary arrangement on the basis of the earlier three. This means that those antitheses, showing a radicalization of the commandments rather than a direct opposite character, are generally considered to have been received by Matthew in antithetical form. In short, the first, second and fourth antitheses are traditional (pre-Matthaean) while the other three (with Lukan parallels) are assigned to Matthew's redaction; cf. R. Bultmann, *Die Geschichte der synoptischen Tradition* (FRLANT, 29; Göttingen: Vandenhoeck & Ruprecht, 8th edn, 1970), pp. 143–4; Luz, *Matthew 1-7*, pp. 227–8; (though he is inclined to believe that the fourth antithesis is redactional too); G. Strecker, *Die Bergpredigt. Ein exegetischer Kommentar* (Göttingen: Vandenhoeck & Ruprecht, 1984), pp. 64–7; E. Lohse, "'Ich aber sage euch'", in E. Lohse (ed.), *Die Einheit des Neuen Testaments. Exegetische Studien zur Theologie des Neuen Testaments* (ESTNT, 1; Göttingen: Vandenhoeck & Ruprecht, 1973), pp. 73–87; J. Lambrecht, *The Sermon on the Mount. Proclamation and Exhortation* (GNS, 14; Wilmington: Glazier, 1985), pp. 94–5; and Davies and Allison, *Matthew*, I, pp. 504–5.

sworn in God's name, you must not swear oaths at all (5.33-37). Rather than profiting by the clause that one may recompense violence with equal retribution, you must not retaliate at all (5.38-42). Rather than merely loving your neighbour, you must surpass this ruling and love your enemy as well (5.43-47). We can thus draw the conclusion that in these antitheses Jesus' demands transcend or exceed the requirements of the Law rather than opposing them.[24]

The writer presents Jesus as an authoritative teacher in order to establish a binding interpretation of the Torah against the views of a contending party. At the time Matthew wrote his Gospel, the Matthaean community was largely a Jewish Christian sect that was encountering severe opposition from the Pharisees and those belonging to emerging Rabbinic Judaism. This tension, conflict, and struggle probably concerned the interpretation and practice of Jewish Law.[25] It is undeniable that Mt. 5.20 presumes a high degree of concern about fulfilment of the Law on the part of the 'Pharisees and scribes'. They are righteous insofar as they live according to the demands of the Law. The suggestion that emerges from the verse, however, is that Matthew's community pursues a greater right-eousness. This moral standard implies a lifestyle based on a different interpretation of the Law. It involves exceeding the legal requirements of the Torah to the extent that additional norms not explicitly mentioned in the Biblical commandments are also stringently applied.

The only occurrence other than Mt. 5.48 where Matthew posits 'perfection' as an obtainable goal, that is, to do more than the minimum required by the Torah, is found in 19.21.[26] As seen above, Jesus tells the rich young man that he must keep the Decalogue's second table and the commandment to love his neighbour as himself in order to achieve salvation. When the man asserts that he has kept all these commandments and asks for a more elaborate explanation, Jesus replies, 'If you wish to be perfect (τέλειος), then go, sell all your possessions and give to the poor'. This is a charge which corresponds to the greater righteousness announced

24. See also Sim, *Matthew and Christian Judaism*, pp. 130–1; Davies and Allison, *Matthew*, I, pp. 504–5; Bultmann, *Geschichte*, pp. 143–4, and H. Merklein, *Die Gottesherrschaft als Handlungsprinzip. Untersuchung zur Ethik Jesu* (FzB, 34; Würzburg: Echter Verlag, 2nd edn, 1981), p. 260.

25. See, for example, A. J. Saldarini, *Matthew's Christian-Jewish Community* (CSHJ; Chicago: University of Chicago Press, 1994), pp. 7–9 and *passim*; J. A. Overman, *Matthew's Gospel and Formative Judaism. The Social World of the Matthean Community* (Minneapolis: Fortress Press, 1990), pp. 86–90; A. F. Segal, 'Matthew's Jewish Voice', in D. L. Balch (ed.), *Social History of the Matthean Community: Cross-Disciplinary Approaches* (Minneapolis: Fortress Press, 1991), pp. 3–37 (32–7), and Stanton, *Gospel for a New People*, pp. 113–45.

26. Apart from the occurrences in Mt. 5.48 and 19.21, the term 'perfect' is not found in the Gospels at all.

in Mt. 5.20, implying that more Torah must be done than the legal minimum. The righteousness demanded of the members of Matthew's community is identical to 'perfection' (5.48). This higher ethical standard, the call to renounce possessions and give to the poor, should be understood as the concrete enactment of the command to love one's neighbour.

The word 'perfect' (τέλειος) is found in the *Didache* twice. In 1.4 the phrase 'and you will be perfect' occurs in a non-retaliation context. The section deals with turning the other cheek, going an extra mile and not reclaiming one's own property from someone who has taken your possessions. These various elements are closely connected to the teachings assigned to Jesus in the synoptic tradition, particularly in Mt. 5.38-42.[27] It is true that the *Didache* section lacks the scriptural quotations and antithetical formulations of Mt. 5.17-48 of which the second part surpasses the Decalogue commandment in the first part. On the other hand, since the instructions in this verse exceed the literal interpretation of the commandments with respect to retribution, they present a case for more than the Law requires.

In *Did.* 6.2a those who are able to carry the 'whole yoke of the Lord' are called 'perfect'; 'If you can bear the entire yoke of the Lord, you will be perfect'. Two things may be noted about this statement. First, it makes clear that someone observing the entire Torah is in a position to attain perfection. The reference to Jewish Law as a yoke is well attested in Rabbinic Literature.[28] Second, the close correspondence between the clause 'you will be perfect' (τέλειος ἔσῃ) in *Did.* 6.2 and the wording of '(and) you will be perfect' ([καί] ἔσῃ τέλειος) in 1.4b suggests the same redactional hand. In any case, by repeating the clause of 1.4b in 6.2, the composer of the *Didache* might be reminding his readers of the specific Torah approach in the former verse.[29]

This view is corroborated by the argumentative strategy found in *Did.* 3.1-6. This passage bears important similarities to Matthew's antitheses section in Mt. 5.21-48.[30] The preoccupation of *Did.* 3.1-6 is expressed in the introductory sentence ('my child, flee from all evil and from anything

27. The compiler of this inserted *Sectio Evangelica* may have known the parallel verses in Lk. 6.29-30; cf. Kloppenborg, 'The Use of the Synoptics or Q in *Did.* 1:3b–2:1', pp. 105–29.

28. Rabbinic texts which speak of the 'yoke of the Law', 'yoke of the Kingdom' and so on are conveniently gathered by H. L. Strack and P. Billerbeck, *Kommentar zum neuen Testament aus Talmud und Midrasch. Vol. 1* (Munich: Beck, 1922), pp. 176–7, 608–10. See also P. Luomanen, *Entering the Kingdom of Heaven. A Study on the Structure of Matthew's View of Salvation* (WUNT, 2.101; Tübingen: Mohr Siebeck, 1998), p. 117.

29. Rordorf and Tuilier, *La Doctrine*, pp. 32–3, and Draper, 'Do the Didache and Matthew Reflect?', pp. 225–7.

30. van de Sandt and Flusser, *The Didache*, pp. 193–237.

resembling it'), and one can hardly doubt that the antitheses in Matthew presuppose the same idea. *Didache* 3.1 is intended to highlight the avoidance of anything resembling evil because it leads to evil itself. The intent is to warn against minor sins (being angry, quarrelsome, hot tempered, passionate, and so on) in order to prevent slipping into trespassing one or more 'major laws'. The major transgressions or sins occurring in this section are murder (3.2), fornication and adultery (3.3), idolatry (3.4), theft (3.5) and blasphemy (3.6). The connection with the Decalogue commandments is clear enough as the tresspasses of murder, adultery and theft are easily associated with the second table of the Ten Commandments.

The τέλειος in *Did.* 6.2, referring to the bearing of the entire 'yoke of the Lord', involves the fulfilment of the radical ethical demands as summarized in *Did.* 1.3-6 and 3.1-6. In both Matthew and the *Didache* striving for perfection involves a 'higher righteousness' with respect to current observations of the Torah. In sum, there is a great difference between the ethos of the communities behind Matthew and the *Didache* on the one hand, and that of the 'the scribes and Pharisees' (Mt. 5.20) on the other.

2. *Divergent Tendencies with Regard to the Torah at a Practical Level*

The treatment of the Torah in both Matthew and the *Didache* fits comfortably within the context of first-century Palestinian Judaism. The core values of the Law they single out are love of the neighbour and the second half of the Decalogue. At variance with many contemporaries, both Matthew and the *Didache* perceive perfection as the goal of the Christian life. Yet the two writings differ with regard to carrying out the Law fully in one's actions. Matthew emphasizes rigorous performance and stringent observation. In 5.17-19 he cautions that not only must the literal meaning of a commandment be kept but its broad intention also, surpassing the scope of widely accepted precepts. The *Didache*, however, shows a divergent tendency. This text is at odds with Matthew in displaying a tension between high ideals (i.e. perfection) and unpretentious practical requirements.

a. *Matthew*
As I have put forward above, in the context of the antitheses it is clear that nothing in the narrative of the first Gospel would suggest that Jesus intended to overturn the Torah. Jesus does not take issue with the Law. He much more assumes the validity of private sacrifice (Mt. 5.23-24), almsgiving, prayer and fasting (6.1-18), provided their practice is not induced by hypocritical incentives. The same position applies to sabbath observance and purity rites. In fact, Mt. 23.2-3 and other statements such as 23.23 and 24.20 suggest a concern for a detailed observance of the Law.

In Mt. 5.17-19/20,[31] Matthew offers the assurance that the antitheses are not intended to abolish but carry forward the tendencies already implicit in them. The first clause, 'Think not that I have come to abolish the Law or the prophets; I have come not to abolish them but to fulfil them' (5.17), does not mean replacement of the Law by Jesus. Jesus does not complete the Law by establishing a new one which transcends the old, or by abrogating the details of the Law through the love commandment.[32] These explanations would come too close to meaning the opposite of 5.17. Moreover, if v. 17 is understood as a statement to oppose the Law (i.e. that fulfilling the Law means opposing it), then continuity with 5.18-19 would be awkward, leaving us with the question what the 'jot' and 'tittle' (v. 18) and 'the least of these commandments' (v. 19) would signify. Fulfilment of the Law appears to be determined by one's interpretation of it. This 'implies that Jesus modifies in some ways contemporary understandings of the Law'.[33]

Emphasis remains on the continuing obedience to the commandments as long as the conditions of this transitory world persist (5.18); 'For truly, I say to you, till Heaven and earth pass away, not a jot or tittle will pass from the Law until all is accomplished'. The Torah is considered perpetually binding down to its tiniest jot and tittle, i.e. to the details of its wording. Interestingly, these minutiae, underscoring the immutability of the Torah thus far, come to serve as a metaphorical designation for the least important commands in 5.19; 'Whoever then relaxes one of the least of these commandments and teaches men so, shall be called least in the kingdom of Heaven, but he who does them and teaches them shall be called great in the kingdom of Heaven.' The reference 'one of the least of these commandments' or, better, 'one of these least commandments' (μίαν τῶν ἐντολῶν τούτων τῶν ἐλαχίστων) recalls the 'jot or tittle' in 5.18. The adjective 'least' makes it clear that the demonstrative pronoun 'these' adverts back to 5.18 and identifies the commandments in v. 19 with the jot and tittle mentioned in v. 18.[34] The jot and tittle represent both the smallest graphic elements of the Law in a literal (v. 18) and figurative (v. 19) sense.

---

31. Verse 20 has been dealt with in the main text above. See also n. 20.

32. For the possible interpretations of the fulfilment of the Law, see Davies and Allison, *Matthew*, I, pp. 485–6, and Luz, *Matthew 1-7*, pp. 214–5.

33. G. N. Stanton, 'The Origin and Purpose of Matthew's Gospel: Matthean Scholarship from 1945 to 1980', in H. Temporini and W. Haase (eds), *ANRW*, II, 25, 3 (Berlin: de Gruyter, 1985), pp. 1889–1951 (1937). This does not solve all problems, however, since, as Stanton makes clear, some scholars have unconvincingly attempted to explain Jesus' attitude towards the Law in Matthew by appealing to the latter's christology or eschatology; cf. Stanton, 'Origin and Purpose', pp. 1934–7.

34. Cf. H. Schürmann, '"Wer daher eines dieser geringsten Gebote auflöst...". Wo fand Matthäus das Logion Mt 5,19?', *BZ* 4 (1960), pp. 238–50 (241); Luz, *Matthew 1-7*, p. 219; Davies and Allison, *Matthew*, I, p. 496; Guelich, *Sermon*, pp. 151–2, and Meier, *Law and History*, pp. 91–2.

It is generally held by scholars that the phrase 'the least of these commandments' in Mt. 5.19 reflects the discussion in Jewish sources about 'light' and 'weighty' commandments of the Law. Such a differentiation has been dealt with above, where Mt. 5.20-48; 19.21; *Did.* 1.4; 3.1-6 and 6.2a were discussed. This can be variously documented in post-Biblical Jewish thought,[35] not least in Rabbinic discussion.[36] The main point in Mt. 5.19 is the importance of the light commandment. Matthew fights moral laxity. While one might expect that failing to teach the weighty commandments would result in being designated least in the kingdom (in Mt. 23.23 the weighty [major] things in the Law must be given precedence), in fact this title belongs to those who discard the light (minor) ones. Matthew 5.17-19 has the programmatic significance of supplying the reader with the value of the minor commandments as resulting in more obedience to the Law.[37] The observance of *all* Laws is explicitly demanded.

b. *Didache*

The important text in *Did.* 6.2a ('If you can bear the entire yoke of the Lord, you will be perfect') was discussed earlier. In view of the theme dealt with here, our interest will now centre upon its sequel; 'but if you cannot, do what you can. As for food, bear what you can, but be very much on your guard against food offered to idols, for it is (related to the) worship of dead gods' (6.2b-3). After rigorously teaching a comprehensive ethical blueprint and the imposition of a high standard for the Way of Life, the

---

35.   Cf. 4 Macc. 5.19-21, dismissing the suggestion that less weighty sins are less serious; 'Accordingly, you must not regard it as a minor sin (μὴ μικρὰν οὖν εἶναι... ἁμαρτίαν) for us to eat unclean food; minor sins are just as weighty as great sins (τὸ γὰρ ἐπὶ μικροῖς καὶ μεγάλοις παρανομεῖν ἰσοδύναμόν ἐστιν), for in each case the law is despised'. See H. Anderson, '4 Maccabees', in J. H. Charlesworth (ed.), *The Old Testament Pseudepigrapha. Vol. 2* (London: Darton, Longman & Todd, 1985), pp. 544–64 (550). In Philo's view the observance of the light commandments is as essential as having no basic part removed or destroyed from a building (*Leg. Gai.*, 117). Also, compare I. Heinemann, *Philo's griechische und jüdische Bildung. Kulturvergleichende Untersuchungen zu Philons Darstellung der jüdischen Gesetze* (Hildesheim: Georg Olms, 1962), pp. 478–80.

36.   About this concept, see already J. Wettstein, *Novum Testamentum Graecum. Vol. 1* (Amsterdam: Officina Dommeriana, 1751), pp. 295–6; cf. also Strack and Billerbeck, *Kommentar zum neuen Testament*, pp. 901–2; I. Abrahams, *Studies in Pharisaism and the Gospels. Vol. 1* (Cambridge: Ktav Publishing House, 1917), pp. 18–29; and E. E. Urbach, *The Sages – Their Concepts and Beliefs* (PPFBR; Jerusalem: Magnes Press, 1975), pp. 345–50.

37.   'Grosse und kleine Gebote sind vielmehr nicht voneinander zu trennen. Ein Tun der Gebote ohne Liebe ist für Matthäus ebenso unvorstellbar wie ein Ausserachtlassen der kleine Gebote. Beides ist nötig, damit die Gerechtigkeit der Jünger Jesu die der Schriftgelehrten und Pharisäer weit übersteigt'; so W. Reinbold, 'Das Matthäusevangelium, die Pharisäer und die Tora', *BZ* 50 (2006), pp. 51–73 (57–8).

Didache ultimately relaxes the rules and appears to suggest that partial compliance with the commandments of the Torah suffices (6.2b). Furthermore, with respect to food, everyone is allowed to determine what is to be eaten and only a minimum requirement is laid down (6.3).

Before moving on, it is noteworthy that one would expect the preceding exhortation in 6.1 to conclude the Two Ways section of the *Didache* in its entirety; 'See to it that no one leads you astray from this way of the doctrine, since (the person who would do so) teaches apart from God'. Both formulation and content suggest this statement to be the final verse. This impression is strengthened by the predominant concessive tenor in the next verses (6.2-3), which appear to strike out a new course. The ethical treatise of the Two Ways ends with the statement that the reader is not required to measure up to the earlier-mentioned guidelines. Accordingly, there is a strong possibility that these two verses did not belong to the original Jewish teaching of the Two Ways.

Whereas the prohibitions in *Did.* 6.1 suggest a morality applied to a community within the boundaries of Judaism proper, *Did.* 6.2-3 has all the markings of an address to non-Jewish Christians. An observant Jew does not have the choice mentioned here. Because the Torah was given to Israel, Jews were strictly charged to keep the Law at all costs. The passage thus represents an adjustment to Gentile believers who are not capable of bearing the entire 'yoke of the Lord' and may have difficulties in observing Jewish dietary laws. This assumption that the Two Ways as presented in the *Didache* provides an instruction for Gentiles is corroborated by two additional observations. The text's long title ('Doctrine of the Lord [brought] to the Nations by the Twelve Apostles') prefacing the *Didache* after its short title ('Doctrine of the Twelve Apostles') shows that this catechesis envisages converts to Christianity from paganism. Moreover, the phrase 'Having said all this beforehand, baptise in the name of...' in *Did.* 7.1b indicates that the preceding Two Ways teaching served in some form as pre-baptismal instructional within the community behind the *Didache*. The Jewish Two Ways was modified into a pre-baptismal catechesis for Gentiles entering the community.

3. Conclusions

Three conclusions can be drawn from this examination. First, Matthew and the *Didache* show remarkable similarities and correspondences which probably imply social proximity and perhaps geographical nearness. The validity of the Law is not argued, but simply assumed. Matthew and the *Didache* share the view that the followers of Jesus belong to Law-abiding Israel. This implies that both writings were edited and employed in a milieu in which the authority of the Torah was taken for granted. In stressing the triad of the second table of the Decalogue commandments, the principle of neighbourly love, and perfection, the two documents resemble one another.

Second, Matthew and the *Didache* speak about the Law as the way to perfection. The ideal of 'perfection' involves the difference between the ethos of the communities of Matthew and the *Didache* on one hand, and the behaviour of outsiders on the other. The aim was not to specify exactly what each commandment required in precise circumstances, but to instil the spirit of the Law, that is, to illustrate its ethical demands. The moral instructions in Matthew and the *Didache* are more radical than those in the Torah as conventionally interpreted in contemporary Judaism.

There is also an important difference between Matthew and the *Didache*. Both writings require full observation of the Torah from Jews and Jewish Christians. As far as the *Didache* is concerned, however, Gentile believers are not expected to take on full Torah-observance. For Gentiles 'who cannot bear the entire yoke of the Torah', a partial commitment to and observance of the prohibition on idol food was sufficient. The *Didache* expected full and strict observance of the Law by Jewish Christians without requiring the same of Gentile Christians.

The orientation toward Gentiles brings us to a third observation. We cannot interpret Matthew and the *Didache* in the light of Paul's letters. The implication of perfection in the Gospel of Matthew as well as in the *Didache* appears to imply that 'perfect' Christians will attempt to bear the burden of the yoke as they are able. In both documents, even in *Did.* 6.2-3, Gentile Christians are advised to fully observe the Torah. In Pauline circles, however, the Torah had been problematized. Paul consistently warned Gentiles not to keep Jewish commandments and strongly opposed those fellow Christians who advised Gentile believers to observe sacred days, circumcision or other Jewish commandments (Gal. 3–5; Phil. 3.2-21; Col. 2.16-23).[38] He urged every one to 'lead the life which the Lord has assigned to him, and in which God has called him' (1 Cor. 7.17), and inculcated every Christian to 'remain in the state in which he was called' (1 Cor. 7.20). He warned Gentile Christians about observing the Torah. Paul's conception of the Gentile mission entailed the incorporation of non-Jews into the people of God without requiring their submission to the Torah. Whereas for Paul righteousness is bestowed by God, Matthew and the *Didache* emphasize that it is not *in spite of* one's actions that one is justified but precisely *through* human action.

---

38. In van de Sandt and Flusser, *The Didache*, pp. 265–9, these two opinions are examined in the light of various trends within (later) Rabbinic sources.

8. MATTHEW AND IGNATIUS OF ANTIOCH

David C. Sim

1. Introduction

The question of the relationship between the author of Matthew's Gospel and Ignatius of Antioch arises because of their proximity in location and date. Both can be situated in Syrian Antioch within two decades or so of one another, the Gospel in the late first century and the epistles of Ignatius in the early second century. As will be shown in this study, the contrast between these two Christian authors could not be more striking. Matthew belonged to the Law-observant stream of the Christian tradition that had not broken with Judaism and which opposed the Law-free Pauline tradition, while Ignatius represented the Pauline version of the Christian message and saw no compatibility whatsoever between the Christian tradition and the practice of Judaism. The sharp theological differences between these authors, however, are not just evident at the ideological level. There is good evidence in the letters of Ignatius that the later Matthaean community and the Pauline church of Ignatius came into conflict in Antioch in the early years of the second century.

2. Matthew and Ignatius

What do we know about Matthew the evangelist and Ignatius the Bishop of Antioch? In the case of Matthew, our knowledge is rather limited. While R. H. Gundry has continued to support the traditional view that the evangelist was the disciple of Jesus,[1] his arguments are far from convincing.[2] Most

---

1. R. H. Gundry, *Matthew: A Commentary on His Handbook for a Mixed Church under Persecution* (Grand Rapids: Eerdmans, 2nd edn, 1994), pp. 609–22; and more recently *idem.*, 'The Apostolically Johannine Pre-Papian Tradition Concerning the Gospels of Mark and Matthew', in R. H. Gundry, *The Old is Better: New Testament Essays in Support of Traditional Interpretations* (WUNT, 178; Tübingen: Mohr Siebeck, 2005), pp. 49–73.

2. See the response to Gundry's arguments in D. C. Sim, 'The Gospel of Matthew, John the Elder and the Papias Tradition: A Response to R. H. Gundry', *HTS* 63 (2007), 283–99.

scholars are happy to concede that the author of this Gospel is unknown. It is possible though to infer some things about him from the Gospel he wrote. That he was certainly a Jew and perhaps a scribe are two such things,[3] but about his precise identity and the circumstances surrounding his composition of the Gospel we are very much in the dark.

The situation is rather different in the case of Ignatius, at least with regard to the last part of his life and the events that led to the writing of his epistles. Ignatius was the Bishop of Antioch who, for reasons not entirely clear, was arrested and transported to Rome where he eventually met a martyr's death. During his final journey, he wrote letters to six churches he either visited or intended to visit (Ephesus, Magnesia, Philadelphia, Tralles, Smyrna and Rome) and a personal letter to Polycarp, the Bishop of Smyrna. While these epistles provide much information about these particular churches and the problems they faced, they also convey a good deal about Ignatius' own church in Antioch. The theological orientation of the bishop and by extension his home church is manifestly clear from these writings. Further, the problems that Ignatius addressed in the Asian churches were probably similar to those that he had encountered in the Antiochene community. The wealth of advice he offered is so detailed and developed that it can only be assumed that he had met and responded to similar problems earlier.[4]

3. The Location and Date of Matthew and Ignatius

The first point to consider in any comparison of these two Christians is that of their respective locations and dates. While there is general agreement concerning the date of the Gospel of Matthew, there is some dispute over its location. In the case of Ignatius the situation is reversed. The location of this bishop is certain, but there is a major debate over the dating of his epistles.

3.   The view that the evangelist was a Gentile and not a Jew enjoyed some support from the 1940s to the 1980s. See the list of scholars holding this position compiled by W. D. Davies and D. C. Allison, *A Critical and Exegetical Commentary on the Gospel according to Saint Matthew* (ICC; 3 vols; Edinburgh: T&T Clark, 1988, 1991, 1997), I, pp. 10–11. Davies and Allison argue that Matthew was ethnically Jewish; see *Matthew*, I, pp. 7–58. In the last two decades no scholar has seriously proposed that the evangelist had Gentile origins. The most detailed discussion of Matthew as a Christian (Jewish) scribe is that of D. E. Orton, *The Understanding Scribe: Matthew and the Apocalyptic Ideal* (JSNTSup, 25; Sheffield: Sheffield Academic Press, 1989). For a more recent analysis, see A. M. Gale, *Redefining Ancient Borders: The Jewish Scribal Framework of Matthew's Gospel* (London: T&T Clark International, 2005), pp. 87–161.

4.   W. R. Schoedel, *Ignatius of Antioch: A Commentary on the Letters of Ignatius of Antioch* (Hermeneia; Philadelphia: Fortress Press, 1985), p. 11 n. 62.

With only a small handful of exceptions, most Matthaean scholars accept that the Gospel of Matthew was composed after the destruction of Jerusalem and its Temple (cf. Mt. 22.7), probably between 85 and 95 CE.[5] In terms of the Gospel's location, scholarly opinion is more diverse. The older hypothesis of B. H. Streeter that Matthew was written in Antioch still rules the day.[6] The most serious alternative hypothesis is that the Gospel had a Galilean provenance. The advocates of this position argue that the Matthaean community's conflict with Formative Judaism points to Galilee or somewhere nearby, since this region was the area where Formative Judaism first established itself in the immediate post-war period.[7]

This hypothesis appears sound at first glance, but it suffers from insurmountable problems upon closer inspection.[8] Despite the confidence of many scholars that there were Christians in Galilee in the late first century, there is very little evidence to support this view. And if there were, we would expect a Gospel for such Christians to have been written in Aramaic, the dominant language in the region. But even if we grant that there were Greek-speaking Christians in late-first-century Galilee, would these people have had the resources to underwrite a text such as the Gospel of Matthew? Galilee was decimated by the Roman reconquest of the Jewish homeland, and it is difficult to accept that this long and complex text was written amidst the social and economic turmoil of the post-war period. A further point is that Matthew does not focus much at all on the Jewish war. There is an oblique reference to the destruction of

---

5.   For detailed discussion, see D. C. Sim, *The Gospel of Matthew and Christian Judaism: The History and Social Setting of the Matthean Community* (SNTW; Edinburgh: T&T Clark, 1998), pp. 31–40. Recent scholars who argue for a date prior to 70 CE include Gundry, *Matthew*, pp. 599–609, and J. Nolland, *The Gospel of Matthew: A Commentary on the Greek Text* (NIGTC; Grand Rapids: Eerdmans, 2005), pp. 14–17.

6.   B. H. Streeter, *The Four Gospels: A Study of Origins* (London: Macmillan, 1924), pp. 500–23. See too Sim, *Matthew and Christian Judaism*, pp. 53–62, and literature cited there. Later studies that support the Antiochene hypothesis include W. Carter, *Matthew and the Margins: A Sociopolitical and Religious Reading* (Maryknoll: Orbis, 2000), pp. 15–16; M. Slee, *The Church in Antioch in the First Century C.E.: Communion and Conflict* (JSNTSup, 244; London: T&T Clark International, 2003), pp. 118–22; and A. O. Ewherido, *Matthew's Gospel and Judaism in the Late First Century C.E.: The Evidence from Matthew's Chapter on Parables (Matthew 13:1-52)* (SBL, 91; New York: Peter Lang, 2006), pp. 10–11.

7.   See J. A. Overman, *Matthew's Gospel and Formative Judaism: The Social World of the Matthean Community* (Minneapolis: Fortress Press, 1990), pp. 158–9; A. J. Saldarini, 'The Gospel of Matthew and Jewish-Christian Conflict in Galilee', in L. I. Levine (ed.), *Studies on Galilee in Late Antiquity* (New York: Jewish Theological Seminary, 1992), pp. 23–8, and most recently, Gale, *Redefining Ancient Borders*, pp. 41–63.

8.   For further detail, see Sim, *Matthew and Christian Judaism*, pp. 40–1; Davies and Allison, *Matthew*, I, pp. 139–41, and J. P. Meier, 'Antioch', in R. E. Brown and J. P. Meier, *Antioch and Rome* (New York: Paulist Press, 1983), pp. 12–86 (18–19).

Jerusalem in the parable of the wedding feast (Mt. 22.7), but the general nature of this allusion suggests that the evangelist and his community were not directly caught up in the horrors of this conflict.

While the Antiochene location for the Gospel of Matthew remains a hypothesis, albeit one that is much more probable than any alternative, there is no dispute concerning the provenance of Ignatius. He identifies himself as the Bishop of Syria (*Rom.* 2.2) but it is clear that his city of residence was Antioch.[9] It was there that he was first made a prisoner (*Smyrn.* 11.1-2), and he shows great interest in developments of the Antiochene community since his departure (*Phld.* 10.1; *Pol.* 7.1). Where there is scholarly dispute resides in the dating of the Ignatian corpus. The traditional view, based upon the chronology of Eusebius (*H. E.* 3.36.2-4), is that Ignatius was arrested and transported to Rome during the reign of the emperor Trajan (98–117). There is some division over a more precise time-frame, some scholars opting for the middle period (*c.* 107) and others for a period towards the end of Trajan's reign (*c.* 115–117).[10] This view has, however, been challenged in a number of recent studies. R. M. Hübner has argued that the epistles were written pseudonymously by a follower of Noetus of Smyrna around the years 165–175 CE in order to combat the growing threat of Gnosticism.[11] In similar vein T. Lechner has claimed that the Ignatian corpus was composed in this period as a direct response to the heretical notions of Valentinus.[12] Responses to these challenges were quick to appear, and all of them criticized the claim of pseudonymity and/or the late dating of the Ignatian letters.[13]

---

9.   That Ignatius hailed from Antioch has never been challenged by the early church writers or modern scholars. See C. N. Jefford, 'The Milieu of Matthew, the *Didache*, and Ignatius of Antioch: Agreements and Differences', in H. van de Sandt (ed.), *Matthew and the Didache: Two Documents from the Same Jewish-Christian Milieu?* (Assen: Royal van Gorcum, 2005), pp. 35–47 (35–6).

10.   See the discussion in C. Trevett, *A Study of Ignatius of Antioch in Syria and Asia* (SBEC, 29; Lewiston: Edwin Mellen Press, 1992), pp. 3–9. Trevett prefers the earlier of the two dates.

11.   R. M. Hübner, 'Thesen zur Echtheit und Datierung der sieben Briefe des Ignatius von Antiochien', *ZAC* 1 (1997), pp. 44–72.

12.   T. Lechner, *Ignatius Adversus Valentinianos? Chronologische und theologiegeschichtliche Studien zu den Briefen des Ignatius von Antiochen* (VCSup, 47; Leiden: Brill, 1999).

13.   For responses to Hübner, see A. Lindemann, 'Antwort auf die Thesen zur Echtheit und Datierung der sieben Briefe des Ignatius von Antiochien', *ZAC* 1 (1997), pp. 185–94; G. Schöllgen, 'Die Ignatianen als pseudepigraphisches Briefcorpus: Anmerkung zu den Thesen von Reinhard M. Hübner', *ZAC* 2 (1998), pp. 16–25; M. J. Edwards, 'Ignatius and the Second Century: An Answer to R. Hübner', *ZAC* 2 (1998), pp. 214–26, and H. J. Vogt, 'Bemerkungen zur Echtheit der Ignatiusbriefe', *ZAC* 3 (1999), pp. 50–63. For a rejoinder to Lechner, see the review of his book by A. Lindemann, *ZAC* 6 (2002), pp. 157–61.

It is not possible in this study to engage this complex d̶͟
detail, but it appears to me that neither Hübner nor Lechner ha͟
fully refuted the prevailing view. The connections between the la͟
and themes of the epistles and Gnostic writings can more easily be vie͟
as Gnostic dependence upon Ignatius than vice versa. Moreover, much o͟
the theology and ecclesiology of the Ignatian corpus finds its closest
parallels in the Christian literature of the late first century, the Pastorals
in particular, than in the Christian writings of two generations later.
There is then no need to abandon the traditional dating of the epistles of
Ignatius to the time of the emperor Trajan. This means that Matthew and
Ignatius were very near contemporaries in the Syrian capital.

4. *The Theology of Matthew and Ignatius*

The theological tradition of the evangelist and his community can be
accurately called 'Christian Judaism'.[14] In simple terms Christian Judaism
can be defined as a tradition whose members accepted the messiahship of
Jesus of Nazareth within the traditional parameters of Judaism. The
coming of the Christ in no way involved any rupture with traditional
Jewish beliefs and practices; on the contrary, the revelation imparted by
the life, death and resurrection of Jesus was consistent and continuous with
the earlier covenant between the God of Israel and the people of Israel,
which was mediated through Moses at Mount Sinai. In accordance with
this belief, Christian Judaism maintained that the followers of the Christ
were to observe the terms of that covenant, including faithful obedience
to the Mosaic Law. In this respect Christian Jews were no different from
their Jewish contemporaries. However, they differed from other Jews in
so far as they believed that the revelation of the Christ necessitated a whole
range of additional beliefs and practices. They accepted that Jesus was the
long-awaited messiah, that in his life and death he fulfilled the Jewish
scriptures, that God had raised him from the dead, that Jesus now resides
in heaven, that he would soon return to oversee the final judgement, and
that Jesus the Christ is the key to salvation. These people practised
baptism in the name of Jesus as the initiation rite into their sectarian Jewish
movement, and they held specifically Christian meetings based upon a
common meal.

---

14. For discussion of the meaning of this term, see Sim, *Matthew and Christian Judaism*,
pp. 19–21, and *idem.*, 'Christian Judaism: A Reconstruction and Evaluation of the Original
Christian Tradition', in E. Kessler and M. J. Wright (eds), *Themes in Jewish-Christian
Relations* (Cambridge: Orchard Academic, 2005), pp. 39–58.

ıal allegiance of these people; they were both
ght of the supplementation (not replacement)
newer revelation of the Christ, they argued
Jewish and Christian to enjoy the salvation
e hand, simply being Jewish and obeying the
the ancient covenant was no longer sufficient;
messiahship of Jesus and all that this entailed.
e a Christian as well as a Jew. Non-Christian
ted Jesus as an integral figure in the divine plan,
would be exc._____ salvation (cf. Acts 4.12). On the other hand,
simply professing Jesus as Christ and saviour was not sufficient for
salvation unless this was done within the terms of the Sinai covenant. Thus
one needed to be a Jew as well as a Christian. Non-Jewish followers of
Jesus would also be excluded from salvation. It was on account of this
belief that Christian Jews attempted to convince Gentile Christians in
Antioch, Galatia and elsewhere to join the covenant people of Israel and
obey the Torah as a necessary component of their Christian commitment
(cf. Acts 15.1).

That the evangelist belonged to this particular early Christian tradition
is evident from the Gospel. His Christian credentials are obvious and need
little comment. Jesus is given a whole gamut of christological titles –
messiah, Son of God, Son of Man, Son of David, Lord, and others in
addition to these. He is conceived of the Holy Spirit (1.20), and his definitive role in the divine plan is to save his people from their sins (1.21),
which he accomplishes with his sacrificial death on the cross (26.28). Prior
to his death Jesus performs miracles and conveys fundamental teachings
to his followers. Many of the events in his life fulfil the Jewish scriptures
and thereby testify to his status within and his importance to the divine
plan. After his death God raised him from the dead and delivered to him
all authority in Heaven and on earth (28.18). It is clear that Matthew's
community practised the specifically Christian rituals of eucharistic
celebration (26.26-29) and the initiatory rite of baptism in the name of
the Father, the Son and the Holy Spirit (28.19).

While the Christian component of Matthew's theology is obvious, his
overt Jewishness is no less in evidence. Scholars have long noted that
Matthew's presentation of Jesus is the most Jewish of any of the canonical
Gospels. Perhaps the most striking element in this respect is the evangelist's
understanding of the Torah in the light of the messiah's appearance. The
question of the role of the Mosaic Law and its application in the
Matthaean community is a complex issue, but all that is necessary here
are a few important points.[15] Towards the beginning of the Sermon on the

---

15. See Sim, *Matthew and Christian Judaism*, pp. 123–39 for a more comprehensive
analysis. Further important treatments of this issue, which present a variety of arguments

Mount the Matthaean Jesus delivers his programmatic statement with regard to the Torah (5.17-19). This material stipulates with crystal clarity that Jesus has not come to abolish the Law and the prophets, and that each and every part of the Torah is to be obeyed until at least the time of the *parousia*. There is no option but to conclude from this tradition that observance of all the Torah was a fundamental requirement for the Matthaean community. The next issue that arises is the precise manner in which the demands of the Torah are to be interpreted and applied, and Matthew devotes considerable attention to the definitive interpretation that Jesus the messiah delivers to his followers.

In 22.34-40 Jesus affirms that all the Law and the prophets hang upon the two greatest commandments, which are described as love of God (Deut. 6.5) and love of neighbour as oneself (Lev. 19.18). Here the Matthaean Jesus presents the view that the double love command is both the central element of the Torah and the hermeneutical key for interpreting its demands. Another way of expressing the love of neighbour is found in the Golden Rule of 7.12. In this tradition Jesus specifies that the Torah and the prophets also find their fulfilment by doing to others what you wish they would do to you. An integral component of this theme is the concept of mercy (cf. 5.7; 9.13; 12.7; 18.23-35), which is defined along with justice and faithfulness as comprising the weightier matters of the Law (23.23). The so-called antitheses of 5.21-48 illustrate how the principle of love of neighbour works in concrete situations. Despite the view of some scholars that there seem to be some annulments of the Mosaic code in this material, this cannot be the case in the light of the clear statement just a few verses previously that Jesus affirms and ratifies all aspects of the Torah. What we find in this material is rather an intensification of the Law's demands which is more in line with the original intention of God.

On the basis of 5.17-19 we would also expect that the Matthaean community faithfully observed the ritual requirements of the Torah, and the Gospel evidence confirms this expectation. Matthew 23.23 reveals that

---

and perspectives, include Overman, *Matthew's Gospel*, pp. 73–90; R. Mohrlang, *Matthew and Paul: A Comparison of Ethical Perspectives* (SNTSMS, 48; Cambridge: Cambridge University Press, 1984), pp. 8–26; A. J. Saldarini, *Matthew's Christian-Jewish Community* (CSHJ; Chicago: University of Chicago Press, 1994), pp. 124–64; D. Senior, *What Are They Saying About Matthew?* (New York: Paulist Press, rev. edn, 1996) pp. 62–73; K. Snodgrass, 'Matthew and the Law', in D. R. Bauer and M. A. Powell (eds), *Treasures New and Old: Recent Contributions to Matthean Studies* (SBLSS, 1; Atlanta: Scholars Press, 1996), pp. 99–127; W. R. G. Loader, *Jesus' Attitude Towards the Law: A Study of the Gospels* (WUNT, 2.97; Tübingen: Mohr Siebeck, 1997), pp. 137–272; P. Foster, *Community, Law and Mission in Matthew's Gospel* (WUNT, 2.177; Tübingen: Mohr Siebeck, 2004), pp. 80–217; and R. Deines, *Die Gerechtigkeit der Tora im Reich des Messias: Mt 5,13-20 als Schlüsseltext der matthäischen Theologie* (WUNT, 177; Tübingen: Mohr Siebeck, 2004), pp. 95–654.

tithing was practised. Moreover, the evangelist's redaction of Mark 7.1-23 in 15.1-20, especially his omission of Mark 7.19b, turns the Markan dispute over the validity of the Jewish purity and dietary laws into a debate over the purely Pharisaic practice of ritual handwashing. There is no question that the Matthaean community continued to keep the Mosaic rules concerning purity and diet.[16] The same applies to sabbath obser-vance. Once again Matthew carefully edits Mk 2.23–3.6, which arguably depicts Jesus overriding the sabbath, and focuses on the correct interpre-tation of this demand (Mt. 12.1-14). Matthew's view is that the sabbath should be observed (cf. 24.20), but it can be overturned if doing so leads to the fulfilment of an even weightier law. In these sabbath controversies the demand for mercy (Hos. 6.6), defined in 23.23 as one of the most important parts of the Torah, outweighs the sabbath rest.[17] These are, however, special cases and it must be assumed that the norm in Matthew's community was to keep the sabbath as diligently as any other Jew.

The discussion of the place of the Torah in the Christian life of the Matthaean community leads to a further important question. Were Gentile converts to the evangelist's group also expected to follow the Torah in its entirety? While it must be conceded that Matthew does not provide a straightforward answer in his Gospel, it may be inferred from the evidence that does exist that such converts would have been expected to join the people of Israel and follow the Law according to the messianic interpre-tation of Jesus. For men this would have entailed undergoing the ritual of circumcision. The requirements for conversion are spelt out in the Great Commission of the risen Christ at the very end of the Gospel (28.16-20). Jesus commands the disciples to make disciples of all nations, baptizing them as the initiation rite into the community and teaching them to observe all that Jesus has taught them. It is a common scholarly view that the mention of baptism here and not circumcision as the rite of initiation indicates that Gentile converts need not have been circumcised.[18] The major problem with this position, however, is that it overlooks the further commandment of the risen Christ, which is to convey all that he has taught the disciples. What must be meant is the extensive teaching of Jesus as recorded in Matthew's Gospel, and this includes, as we have seen, the explicit directive to observe all of the Torah; no distinction is made

---

16. See B. Repschinski, *The Controversy Stories in the Gospel of Matthew: Their Redaction, Form and Relevance for the Relationship between the Matthean Community and Formative Judaism* (FRLANT, 189; Göttingen: Vandenhoeck & Ruprecht, 2000), pp. 154–66.

17. Repschinski, *Controversy Stories*, pp. 94–116.

18. See, for example, Saldarini, *Matthew's Christian-Jewish Community*, pp. 156–60; and J. K. Riches, *Conflicting Mythologies: Identity Formation in the Gospels of Mark and Matthew* (SNTW; Edinburgh: T&T Clark, 2000), pp. 216–22.

anywhere in the Gospel between the requirements for Jewish converts and those for Gentile converts. In fact 5.19, which condemns followers who relax any of the Torah's rules and teach others to do so, precludes the possibility that Matthew's community expected less Law-observance for Gentile members than for their Jewish counterparts. The reason circumcision is not mentioned in the Great Commission is because it is assumed for Gentile converts on the basis of Mt. 5.17-19. The emphasis falls on Christian baptism, which is required for both Jewish and Gentile converts, because it was a new revelation of the Christ and had received no prior mention in the Gospel.[19]

The Matthaean community's continuing attachment to the Torah, though now interpreted through the lens of messianic revelation, provides firm evidence that this Christian group still identified itself within the parameters of first-century Judaism. Not all scholars of course would agree with this conclusion, and it is probably true to say that the most prominent debate in Matthaean studies in the past two decades or so has been over this very issue. The context for this debate has largely been the conflict between the evangelist's community and Formative Judaism, which emerged in the period following the first Jewish revolt against Rome. Was this a conflict between two different Jewish groups within the boundaries of Judaism,[20] or does this conflict reveal that the Matthaean community had broken away from its parent religion?[21]

If it is true that Matthew's theological tradition was Christian Judaism, and that he expected Gentile Christian converts to become members of the people of Israel by submitting to circumcision (if male) and full Law-observance, then an obvious question arises. What would have been Matthew's attitude towards Paul? After all, Paul stood in a totally different Christian stream that did not demand observance of the ritual laws even for Jews and which explicitly denied their validity for Gentile converts. While recent Markan studies have addressed the possible connections between

---

19.   Sim, *Matthew and Christian Judaism*, pp. 251–4. In agreement, see Slee, *The Church in Antioch*, pp. 140–5.

20.   The most important contributions to this view are Overman, *Matthew's Gospel*; and Saldarini, *Matthew's Christian-Jewish Community*. See also Sim, *Matthew and Christian Judaism*, pp. 109–63; and Repschinski, *Controversy Stories*, pp. 14–61, 343–9.

21.   Perhaps the most prominent defender of this position is G. N. Stanton, *A Gospel for a New People: Studies in Matthew* (Edinburgh: T&T Clark, 1992). In agreement with this general view are Riches, *Conflicting Mythologies*, pp. 202–28; Foster, *Community*, pp. 22–79; Ewherido, *Matthew's Gospel*, pp. 20–27; D. R. A. Hare, 'How Jewish is the Gospel of Matthew?', *CBQ* 62 (2000), pp. 264–77; D. A. Hagner, 'Matthew: Apostate, Reformer, Revolutionary?', *NTS* 49 (2003), pp. 193–209; and *idem.*, 'Matthew: Christian Judaism or Jewish Christianity?', in S. McKnight and G. R. Osborne (eds), *The Face of the New Testament: A Survey of Recent Research* (Grand Rapids: Baker Academic, 2004), pp. 263–82.

Mark and Paul,[22] Matthaean scholarship has all but neglected the question of Matthew's view of the apostle.[23] None the less, most scholars would concede that Matthew stood in a different Christian tradition from Paul and can therefore be described as non-Pauline. This safe and rather bland assessment does not go far enough. There is good evidence in Matthew's Gospel, both in his editing of Mark and in his introduction of new material, that suggests that Matthew was more than simply non-Pauline; he was vehemently anti-Pauline. I have discussed this issue elsewhere,[24] and will not rehearse the arguments again here. It is, however, important to bear in mind this aspect of Matthew's thought as we turn our attention to his near contemporary, Ignatius of Antioch.

Recent Ignatian scholarship has correctly argued that the Bishop of Antioch and his church were heavily influenced by the Pauline version of the Christian tradition.[25] Ignatius himself was an avid follower of Paul who modelled himself on the apostle in many ways. The first point to note in this connection is that Ignatius was familiar with at least some of the Pauline epistles, including a few of the Deutero-Pauline letters.[26] This is clear from his own letter to the Ephesians, where he writes in 12.2 that Paul mentioned those in the Ephesian church in every epistle (ἐν πάσῃ ἐπιστολῇ). The reference here to 'every epistle' establishes that he was familiar with a number of Paul's writings. There is, however, a difficulty in determining precisely how many of these letters he knew. The problem is that Ignatius never acknowledges the apostle as his source and he never quotes his letters word for word. Instead, we find

22. Cf. W. R. Telford, *The Theology of the Gospel of Mark* (NTT; Cambridge: Cambridge University Press, 1999), pp. 164–9; J. Painter, *Mark's Gospel: Worlds in Conflict* (NTR; London: Routledge, 1997), pp. 4–6; J. Marcus, *Mark 1-8: A New Translation with Introduction and Commentary* (AB, 27; New York: Doubleday, 1999), pp. 73–5; *idem.*, 'Mark – Interpreter of Paul', *NTS* 46 (2000), pp. 473–87; J. Svartvik, *Mark and Mission: Mk 7:1-23 in its Narrative and Historical Contexts* (CBNTS, 32; Stockholm: Almqvist & Wiksell, 2000), pp. 344–7; and J. R. Donahue and D. J. Harrington, *The Gospel of Mark* (SP, 2; Collegeville: Liturgical Press, 2002), pp. 39–40. See too the contribution by J. Svartvik in this volume.

23. See the survey of Matthaean scholarship on this issue in D. C. Sim, 'Matthew's Anti-Paulinism: A Neglected Feature of Matthean Studies', *HTS* 58 (2002), pp. 767–83 (769–81). See too the contribution by D. J. Harrington in this volume.

24. See Sim, *Matthew and Christian Judaism*, pp. 188–211; and *idem.*, 'Matthew 7.21-3: Further Evidence of its Anti-Pauline Perspective', *NTS* 53 (2007), pp. 325–43.

25. So Jefford, 'Milieu', pp. 43–4; D. M. Reis, 'Following in Paul's Footsteps: *Mimēsis* and Power in Ignatius of Antioch', in A. F. Gregory and C. M. Tuckett (eds), *Trajectories Through the New Testament and the Apostolic Fathers* (Oxford: Oxford University Press, 2005), pp. 288–305 (288, 293). For the opposite and much less likely view that Ignatius had little interest in Paul or his theology, see A. Lindemann, 'Paul's Influence on "Clement" and Ignatius', in Gregory and Tuckett, *Trajectories*, pp. 9–24 (16–24).

26. A more detailed discussion of Ignatius and the Pauline corpus can be found in Sim, *Matthew and Christian Judaism*, pp. 60–2.

countless allusions to and echoes of Pauline texts in the Ignatian corpus. Two reasons may be proposed for this phenomenon.

First of all, there is no reason why Ignatius should be expected to quote any Pauline text accurately or word for word. At this stage Paul was not considered scriptural, and the tendency of the early Christians at this time was to paraphrase, adapt and rewrite their sources to suit their own immediate needs. The free use of Mark by both Matthew and Luke is evidence enough of this practice. But in the case of Ignatius there is an even more simple explanation of his preference for allusion rather than direct quotation. Ignatius wrote his epistles as a prisoner being transported under guard to the Imperial capital. Under these trying conditions, he would not have had access to copies of the Pauline documents. Unlike Matthew and Luke, who each had a copy of Mark in front of them when they wrote, Ignatius did not have the luxury of having readily available his corpus of Pauline texts. Because of his special circumstances, he was therefore forced to rely on memory when wishing to recall a Pauline passage that he believed was appropriate to the point he was making.[27] We may assume that on some occasions his memory served him well, and not so well in other cases. So the question remains; how many Pauline epistles did Ignatius know?

Almost all scholars concur that he knew 1 Corinthians very well. There are five explicit references to this epistle (*Eph.* 16.1 and *Phld.* 3.3//1 Cor. 6.9-10; *Eph.* 18.1//1 Cor. 1.20, 23; *Rom.* 5.1//1 Cor. 4.4; *Rom.* 9.2//1 Cor. 15.8-9) and there are many distant echoes in addition to these. W. R. Schoedel contends that we can be certain only that Ignatius knew this Pauline letter; he believes that many of the other parallels between the Ignatian and Pauline writings are independent use of traditional materials.[28] But this view is far too sceptical. P. Foster has recently argued that, in addition to 1 Corinthians, Ignatius was also familiar with Ephesians and the two epistles to Timothy.[29] This more generous hypothesis, however, is still too cautious. Given the heavy influence of Paul on Ignatius, which we shall consider shortly, we should perhaps adopt a maximalist position regarding the letters of Paul available to the bishop. A much more likely view is that of R. M. Grant, who contends that Ignatius had read Romans, 1 and 2 Corinthians, Galatians, Ephesians, Philippians, Colossians, 1 Thessalonians, and 1 and 2 Timothy.[30]

27. So correctly P. Foster, 'The Epistles of Ignatius of Antioch and the Writings that later formed the New Testament', in A. F. Gregory and C. M. Tuckett (eds), *The Reception of the New Testament in the Apostolic Fathers* (Oxford: Oxford University Press, 2005), pp. 159–86 (161).

28. Schoedel, *Ignatius of Antioch*, pp. 9–10.

29. Foster, 'Epistles of Ignatius of Antioch', pp. 164–72.

30. R. M Grant, *The Apostolic Fathers, Vol. I: An Introduction* (London: Thomas Nelson & Sons, 1964), p. 57. For detailed analysis of the Pauline allusions in the Ignatian epistles, see Grant's commentary, R. M. Grant, *The Apostolic Fathers, Vol. IV: Ignatius of Antioch* (London: Thomas Nelson & Sons, 1966).

It is not surprising then to find that, although Ignatius was exposed to a number of different Christian theological traditions and had access to a good many Christian texts in addition to the Pauline corpus, he was most influenced by the example of Paul and the apostle's theology. The Ignatian literature testifies that the bishop was an ardent admirer of Paul. In *Eph.* 12.12 he states that Paul was sanctified, approved and worthy of blessing, and he expresses his desire to follow in Paul's footsteps. The inclination of Ignatius to imitate Paul was partly motivated by the similarities of their respective fates. Just as the apostle was taken to Rome as a prisoner where he met a martyr's death, so too was Ignatius on his way to the imperial capital where a similar fate awaited him. This unfortunate parallel between the two led Ignatius to model himself on Paul in other ways. Like his apostolic hero, he wrote letters to Christian churches offering instruction, advice, comfort, and warnings of 'heretical' views that might compromise the true gospel. In addition, Ignatius adopted Paul's self-effacing attitude. While Paul had referred to himself as an abortion (1 Cor. 15.8) and the least of all the apostles (1 Cor. 15.9), Ignatius described himself as an abortion (*Rom.* 9.2) and the last of the Antiochene church (*Eph.* 21.2; *Trall.* 13.1; *Smyrn.* 11.1).[31]

The theology of Ignatius was unashamedly Pauline. A detailed comparison of the two cannot be undertaken here,[32] but it is permissible to focus on the topic of the role of the Torah in Christian existence. There is no question that Ignatius embraced the Pauline contrast between Law and grace (e.g. Rom. 6.14; 11.6; Gal. 5.4), and between justification by faith alone and by works of the Torah (e.g. Rom. 3.20-26; Gal. 2.15-16), though he expresses these concepts with different terminology. This is most clearly articulated in the epistle to the Magnesians. In *Mag.* 8.1 he stipulates that those who are living according to Judaism (κατὰ Ἰουδαϊσμὸν ζῶμεν) must confess that they have not received grace. Ignatius expands upon this in 10.1-3. In the initial verse he encourages his readers to live according to Christianity (κατὰ Χριστιανισμὸν ζῆν), and this is followed in v. 3 with the rather harsh statement that it is monstrous to speak of Jesus Christ and to practise Judaism (ἰουδαΐζειν). While Ignatius does not spell out concretely what is meant by 'living according to Judaism' or by 'practising Judaism', his intended meaning is clear. It involves embracing strange doctrines and old fables (*Mag.* 8.1; cf. 1 Tim. 1.4; 4.7; 2 Tim. 4.4; Tit. 1.14; 3.9), but in addition it also means the adoption of the Jewish lifestyle, which was characterized by observance of the Torah.[33]

---

31. For further evidence of Ignatius' conscious imitation of Paul, see Reis, 'Following in Paul's Footsteps', pp. 293–300.

32. See Sim, *Matthew and Christian Judaism*, pp. 262–9 for a more detailed comparison of Ignatius' theological debt to Paul.

33. See P. J. Donahue, 'Jewish Christianity in the Letters of Ignatius of Antioch', *VC* 32 (1978), pp. 81–93 (84).

In justifying his view the Gentile Ignatius embarks upon a path that the Jewish Paul would never have trodden. He uses the Old Testament prophets in a surprising way to demonstrate his point. In *Mag.* 8.2 he states that the prophets were actually Christians who lived according to Jesus Christ; they were inspired by his grace and received persecution on account of their belief in him. In the following chapter Ignatius expands upon this. The prophets formerly walked in ancient (Jewish) customs, but then came to new hope by giving up the sabbath and observing instead the Lord's day (9.1). The Christians of Ignatius' day should follow suit. They need to put aside the old leaven which has grown old and sour (Judaism) and turn to the new leaven which is called Jesus Christ (*Mag.* 10.2). On the basis of his innovative view that the prophets were in reality Christians (in an Ignatian sense), Ignatius draws the rather startling conclusion that Christianity did not base its faith on Judaism, but Judaism on Christianity (*Mag.* 10.3).

It is clear from the above discussion that Ignatius believed he was continuing the fight against Law-observance that so dominated the life and work of Paul. Like the apostle, Ignatius contrasts the life of Law according to Judaism with the new life in Christ characterized by faith and grace. The major difference between them is that Paul contrasts faith and grace with Law and works, while the bishop draws the simpler distinction between Judaism and Christianity. The change of terminology can be explained by the fact that 'Christianity' (Χριστιανισμός) had become by the time of Ignatius the accepted technical term for the Gentile Christian tradition in which the Torah played no role whatsoever. The usage of Ignatius indicates that it was coined for the very purpose of distinguishing this Christian tradition from the religion of Judaism itself.[34]

5. *The Matthaean Community and Ignatius*

The above discussion has revealed that Matthew and Ignatius stood at opposite ends of the Christian theological spectrum. While the former argued that being a follower of Jesus was only legitimate within the boundaries of Judaism, the latter was just as adamant that the Christian tradition and the practice of Judaism were fundamentally incompatible. Given that Antioch on the Orontes was the probable location for both authors, is there any evidence of contact between the very different communities they represented? It is certainly conceivable that the anti-Paulinism of the Matthaean group was directed towards Ignatius' Pauline church some decades prior to the bishop's journey to Rome, but there is

34. Schoedel, *Ignatius of Antioch*, p. 126 n. 1.

more concrete evidence that Ignatius was involved in a polemical battle with the evangelist's community in the decades after the composition of the Gospel.

This brings us to the topic of the opponents of Ignatius. A reading of the Ignatian corpus indicates that the Bishop of Antioch warned his readers against the false views of certain Christian opponents, though scholars are still undecided whether there were two distinct groups or only one. Scholars who perceive two groups identify one as having a 'judaizing' tendency and the other as a form of docetism that denied the suffering of Jesus and the physical nature of his resurrected body; the former is attacked in the epistles to the Philadelphians and the Magnesians, and the latter in the letters to the Trallians and Smyrnaeans. Other scholars argue that there was in fact a single 'heresy', a Judaeo-Docetic position, that combined elements from both Judaism (or Christian Judaism) and docetism.[35] This debate cannot be discussed in any detail here. It is sufficient to state that I follow the position that in his letters Ignatius wrote about two sets of opponents, Christian 'judaizing' adversaries and a separate group of Christian docetists.[36] It is the first of these groups that is of significance in this study.

Where were these 'judaizers' located? There is no doubt that they were active in the churches of Magnesia and Philadelphia, but were they also found in the bishop's hometown of Antioch? Once again there is scholarly dispute over this issue. While some hold the view that Ignatius encountered such people only in Asia Minor,[37] others infer that his response to this 'heresy' was so detailed and so well integrated into his own theological perspective that he must have met and confronted Christians of similar persuasion earlier in Antioch.[38] If this is a reasonable assumption, then what can be said of these Antiochene opponents?

---

35.   For a recent and detailed history of this debate, see M. Myllykoski, 'Wild Beasts and Rabid Dogs: The Riddle of the Heretics in the Letters of Ignatius', in J. Ådna (ed.), *The Formation of the Early Church* (WUNT, 183; Tübingen: Mohr Siebeck, 2005), pp. 341–77 (345–50).

36.   In basic agreement with Myllykoski, 'Wild Beasts and Rabid Dogs', pp. 351–74. For a recent defence of the view that Ignatius stood in opposition to a single group of opponents, see J. W. Marshall, 'The Objects of Ignatius' Wrath and Jewish Angelic Mediators', *JEH* 56 (2005), pp. 1–23. According to Marshall, these adversaries were Jewish Christians who understood Jesus to be an angel.

37.   So C. K. Barrett, 'Jews and Judaizers in the Epistles of Ignatius', in R. Hamerton-Kelly and R. Scroggs (eds), *Jews, Greeks and Christians: Religious Cultures in Late Antiquity. Essays in Honor of William David Davies* (Leiden: Brill, 1976), pp. 220–44 (240); and H. O. Maier, *The Social Setting of the Ministry as Reflected in the Writings of Hermas, Clement and Ignatius* (Waterloo: Wilfrid Laurier University Press, 1991), p. 147.

38.   See V. Corwin, *St. Ignatius and Christianity in Antioch* (New Haven: Yale University Press, 1960), pp. 24–30. In agreement, see Donahue, 'Jewish Christianity', pp. 81–2; Trevett, *Ignatius of Antioch*, p. 76; and J. T. Sanders, 'Jewish Christianity in Antioch before the Time of Hadrian', in E. H. Lovering (ed.), *Society of Biblical Literature 1992 Seminar Papers* (Atlanta: Scholars Press, 1992), pp. 346–61 (359).

On the basis of the above discussion, we may infer that these Christians were similar to Paul's 'judaizing' opponents some generations earlier. They lived according to Judaism and therefore followed the Torah as a fundamental component of their Christian commitment. They also understood the relationship between the Christ and the Hebrew scriptures in a distinctive way. This is clear from *Phld.* 8.2 where Ignatius reports a conversation he shared with these opponents. These people had told him that they could not believe certain parts of the Christian message unless they were also found in the archives (ἐν τοῖς ἀρχείοις), a clear reference to the Jewish scriptures.[39] What this means is that these Christian Jews based their version of the gospel on the sacred texts; they accepted about Jesus what was compatible with the Hebrew Bible and rejected what in their opinion was not. Ignatius records his response to this argument. He contends that the archives are in fact the cross, death and resurrection of Christ and the faith which is through him. It is clear that the Gentile Ignatius could not match the exegetical expertise of these opponents, so he attempts to undercut their argument by another method. He simply denies the independent authority of the Jewish scriptures, and affirms that the true authority is Jesus himself. His 'christianization' of the prophets that we noted above reveals that Ignatius completely reversed the argument of his opponents. The Old Testament was to be interpreted through the life, death and resurrection of the Christ and not vice versa as his opponents maintained.

It is more likely than not that these Christian Jewish opponents of Ignatius in Antioch were members of the Matthaean community some two decades or so after the composition of the Gospel.[40] Both groups were located in Antioch, both upheld the requirements of the Torah, and both placed great emphasis on the interpretation of the Hebrew scriptures and especially the prophets. What strengthens the link is a peculiar phenomenon in the writings of Ignatius. It is well accepted that Ignatius knew the written Gospel of Matthew,[41] but was not influenced at all by its theology. Yet when he is disputing with his Christian Jewish opponents, he sometimes uses Matthaean language and concepts drawn from the evangelist's critique of the scribes and Pharisees. Matthew 15.13 describes the Pharisees as plants not planted by the Father, while Ignatius (*Phld.* 3.1) refers to his Christian Jewish adversaries as evil growths that are not the planting of the Father. Whereas the Gospel likens the scribes and Pharisees to whitewashed tombs that are unclean inside (Mt. 23.27), the bishop

---

39. See the discussion of W. R. Schoedel, 'Ignatius and the Archives', *HTR* 71 (1978), pp. 97–106.

40. For full treatment of the evidence, see Trevett, *Ignatius of Antioch*, pp. 180–3, and Sim, *Matthew and Christian Judaism*, pp. 282–5.

41. See the discussion in Sim, *Matthew and Christian Judaism*, pp. 31–3.

declares that his 'judaizing' opponents are tombstones and sepulchres of the dead (*Phld.* 6:1). The Matthaean statement that the scribes and Pharisees would have persecuted the prophets (Mt. 23.29-34) finds a ready parallel in *Mag.* 8.2 where Ignatius claims that the prophets were persecuted for embracing Christ and abandoning Judaism. What these examples demonstrate is a particular strategy by Ignatius in dealing with these remnants of the Matthaean community. He attempts to condemn them with words that derive from their very own Gospel. All the criticisms that the Gospel makes against its Jewish opponents can be redirected to the Christian Jewish Matthaean community itself.

6. *Conclusions*

The comparison undertaken here between Matthew the evangelist and Ignatius of Antioch reveals that these two Christian authors stood very much at different ends of the primitive Christian theological spectrum. The evangelist was firmly entrenched within Christian Judaism and saw no incompatibility whatsoever between the traditional beliefs and practices of Judaism and full commitment to Jesus the Christ. Salvation in fact was dependent upon one being both a Jew and a Christian. This view necessitated the adoption of Torah-observance by Gentile converts, and it directly contributed to Matthew's implacable opposition to Paul's alternative gospel free from the requirements of the Law. By contrast, the theological position of the Gentile Ignatius was unambiguously Pauline. Well versed as he was in the Pauline literature, he accepted the Pauline contrast between Law and grace and between faith and works, but he expressed this view in the terminology of his day. The contrast was now between Judaism and Christianity, and these two traditions were completely incompatible with one another. In a severe departure from the position of Matthew, the view of Ignatius was that a true Christian cannot embrace the traditional practices of the Jewish faith. Since both the Matthaean and Ignatian traditions were found in Antioch, it is only to be expected that they would inevitably come into contact and into conflict, and the epistles of Ignatius testify that this was indeed the case.

9. MATTHEW AND JESUS OF NAZARETH

DAVID C. SIM

1. *Introduction*

In this study I wish to offer a comparison between Matthew and the historical Jesus. The subject of discussion is not so much the respective theological views of the evangelist and Jesus, although that topic is itself worthwhile and would doubtless yield interesting results, but more a comparison of Mathew's portrayal of Jesus with the real Jesus of history. How well does Matthew's narrative depict the mission and teaching of Jesus of Nazareth? Such an enterprise may be judged by some to be an exercise in futility because of the late date and the derivative nature of Matthew's Gospel.

Most scholars date the Gospel of Matthew in the 80s or 90s of the first century, some 60–70 years after the mission of Jesus. Furthermore, many scholars would argue that the evangelist has little to offer in terms of independent Jesus material. Much of his Gospel derives from two earlier sources, Mark and Q, which he has edited in a distinctive way. The remaining material in the Gospel, the traditions unique to Matthew, is often not considered to be historical to any large extent. A good percentage of this material can be safely traced back to the editorial hand of Matthew himself, and what is based upon sources, the Matthaean infancy narrative for example, is generally treated as creations of the early church rather than genuine historical material. In short, it is a widespread view that the Gospel of Matthew is not a reliable quarry from which we can extract quality materials for a reconstruction of the historical Jesus. Matthew's primary sources, Mark and Q, are much more reliable alternatives.[1]

There is, however, a need for caution at this point. A later and even a derivative source may not in every respect be less historical than the material upon which it is based. In a recent study of the historical Jesus, D. C. Allison contends that scholars must allow for the possibility that the earlier source may be tendentious and unhistorical, while the later and

---

1.   For detailed discussion of these criteria, see J. P. Meier, *A Marginal Jew: Rethinking the Historical Jesus. Vol. 1, The Roots of the Problem and the Person* (ABRL; New York: Doubleday, 1991), pp. 43–5.

dependent writing may improve or correct the spurious elements in the original text.[2] C. S. Keener has articulated the same point in the specific case of Matthew. In the Introduction to his commentary, Keener expresses his surprise to find how much the evangelist rejudaizes his sources, which he then attributes to Matthew's access to early and reliable Palestinian traditions. Keener suggests that 'Matthew remains closer to the earliest strata of tradition than has often been supposed'.[3] This is an important insight.

While it would exceed the evidence to claim that Matthew's redaction of Mark always improves the historicity of that source, it can be argued that in some important ways Matthew dismisses some of the more tendentious aspects of Mark's portrayal of Jesus and provides a more reliable depiction of his ministry. In this brief study I wish to consider two such themes which are very differently represented in these two Gospels. The first is Jesus' involvement in a Gentile mission, and the second is the attitude of Jesus towards the Torah. In both cases it will be argued that the Matthaean portrayal of these issues stands much closer to the position of the historical Jesus than does the Markan account.

2. Jesus and the Gentile Mission in Mark and Matthew

A comparison of Mark and Matthew on the question of Jesus and the Gentile mission reveals a startling contrast. In the Markan narrative it is clear that Jesus conducts simultaneously two quite distinct and separate missions, one to Jews and the other to Gentiles. This theme has been highlighted in the excellent study of E. K. Wefald,[4] and the following general discussion draws significantly from his analysis.

Wefald identifies four journeys by the Markan Jesus into Gentile territory. The first is recounted in 4.35–5.21. Here Jesus crosses the Sea of Galilee to the land of the Gerasenes, performs a successful exorcism, and the grateful Gentile demoniac then proclaims in the Decapolis what Jesus has done for him (5.14-20). The second journey is described in 6.45-

---

2.   D. C. Allison, *Jesus of Nazareth: Millenarian Prophet* (Minneapolis: Fortress Press, 1998), pp. 18–19.

3.   C. S. Keener, *A Commentary on the Gospel of Matthew* (Grand Rapids: Eerdmans, 1999), p. 3.

4.   E. K. Wefald, 'The Separate Gentile Mission in Mark: A Narrative Explanation of Markan Geography, The Two Feeding Accounts and Exorcisms', *JSNT* 60 (1995), pp. 3–26 (9–13). See too the earlier important analysis of E. S. Malbon, *Narrative Space and Mythic Meaning in Mark* (TBS, 13; Sheffield: JSOT Press, 1991), pp. 40–3. Cf. also the recent affirmation of Malbon's work in K. R. Iverson, *Gentiles in the Gospel of Mark: 'Even the Dogs Under the Table Eat the Children's Crumbs'* (LNTS, 339; London: T&T Clark International, 2007), pp. 15–19.

53, though in this case the disciples fail to arrive at their destination in Bethsaida and return by boat to Jewish territory.[5] The next visit to Gentile regions in 7.24–8.10 is perhaps the most significant. On this occasion Jesus and the disciples travel northwards by foot to the Gentile area of Tyre and Sidon, where Jesus heals the daughter of a Syrophoenician woman. Mark then relates in 7.31 a very confusing itinerary, but it is best read as Jesus travelling from Tyre to Sidon and making his way to the Sea of Galilee by journeying through the Decapolis. In other words, Mark makes the point that Jesus remains in Gentile territory and eventually finds himself on the eastern or Gentile side of the Sea.[6] Jesus then heals a deaf man and feeds in miraculous fashion four thousand people (7.32–8.9) before sailing to Dalmanutha in Jewish territory (8.10). The fourth and final journey is described in 8.13–9.30. Jesus and his companions depart by boat back to the other side of the Sea of Galilee (8.13) where they land at Bethsaida (8.22) before ending up in Caesarea Philippi (8.27). Following the confession of Peter, the transfiguration of Jesus and an exorcism (8.28–9.29), Jesus returns in an unspecified manner back to Jewish Galilee (9.30). This completes the missions of Jesus in Gentile areas, and the narrative from this point focuses on Jesus' journey to Jerusalem where his execution and resurrection will take place.

What is the significance of this motif for Mark? It is clear that the evangelist intends to convey the point that Gentiles, as well as the Jews, were the intended targets of Jesus' missionary activity; there are in fact two separate but parallel missions. Perhaps the most important element within this theme are the two feedings of the crowds, the first of which occurs in Jewish territory and involves only Jews (6.30-44) and the second of which takes place on Gentile ground and applies only to Gentiles (8.1-10).[7] If, as is generally acknowledged, these two miraculous feedings have eucharistic overtones,[8] then Mark is making the point that each group on its own terms can share the eucharist and participate equally in the life of the Christian community.

When we turn to the Gospel of Matthew, a rather different picture emerges. The evangelist takes great care to restrict the mission of Jesus and the disciples to Jewish territory and to the Jewish people alone. This is

---

5.   Since this intended visit fails to materialize, it is questionable whether Wefald is correct to identify it as a second journey.

6.   Wefald, 'Separate Gentile Mission in Mark', p. 12 n. 17, and Iverson, *Gentiles*, pp. 57–60.

7.   See the detailed discussion concerning the identities of the two recipient groups in Wefald, 'Separate Gentile Mission in Mark', pp. 16–25. Cf. too Iverson, *Gentiles*, pp. 67–9, and J. Svartvik, *Mark and Mission: Mk 7:1-23 in its Narrative and Historical Contexts* (CBNTS, 32; Stockholm: Almqvist & Wiksell, 2000), pp. 295–301.

8.   J. Marcus, *Mark 1-8: A New Translation with Introduction and Commentary* (AB, 27; New York; Doubleday, 1999), pp. 403, 409–10, 419–20, 434–5, 488, 497, 509–10.

nowhere more clearly stated than in his redaction of the healing of the Gentile woman's daughter in Mk 7.24-30 (Mt. 15.21-28) when Jesus tells the woman that he was sent only to the lost sheep of the house of Israel (15.24). This editorial statement from Matthew strictly confines the mission of Jesus to the Jews and it precludes any possibility of a mission by Jesus himself to the Gentiles. The evangelist's redaction here is consistent with his earlier insertion into the mission charge (10.5b-6), whereby Jesus explicitly instructs the disciples to avoid the Gentiles and the Samaritans and to restrict their activities only to the lost sheep of the house of Israel. These redactional insertions by Matthew clearly signal his intention to overturn Mark's portrayal of Jesus' Gentile mission. For Matthew the historical ministry of Jesus involves only the Jews. The Gentile mission is deferred until the post-resurrection period, when it is enjoined by the risen Christ himself (28.16-20).

It comes as no surprise therefore to find that Matthew significantly edits his Markan source in terms of Jesus' forays into Gentile territories. He does retain the first visit of Jesus to a Gentile region on the other side of the Sea of Galilee, and describes the performance of a successful exorcism (8.28-34). Yet the pericope ends not with the demoniacs proclaiming Jesus in the Decapolis but with the Gentiles from the local city begging Jesus to leave their neighbourhood (8.34). Matthew also retains the general thrust of the aborted (second) journey to the Gentile side of the Galilean Sea (14.22-34). It is, however, the third journey, the most important journey in Mark's scheme, that Matthew has cause to edit most dramatically.

Whereas Mk 7.24-30 depicts Jesus venturing by foot to the Gentile region of Tyre, entering a house and healing the daughter of the Syrophoenician woman, the Matthaean parallel in 15.21-28 is much more ambiguous on the issue whether Jesus leaves Jewish territory and enters a Gentile region for the second time. The initial verse speaks of Jesus withdrawing from where he was εἰς τὰ μέρη Τύρου καὶ Σιδῶνας, which could mean either that he withdrew into the actual region of Tyre and Sidon or that he withdrew towards that area but did not enter it. Some scholars note the ambiguity of the text and refuse to choose between the options,[9] while others argue that the first alternative is the correct one.[10]

---

9.   So W. D. Davies and D. C. Allison, *A Critical and Exegetical Commentary on the Gospel according Saint Matthew* (ICC; 3 vols; Edinburgh: T&T Clark, 1988, 1991, 1997), II, pp. 546, 548. Cf. too D. A. Hagner, *Matthew 14-28* (WBC, 33B; Dallas: Word Books, 1996), pp. 440–1.

10.   R. H. Gundry, *Matthew: A Commentary on His Handbook for a Mixed Church under Persecution* (Grand Rapids: Eerdmans, 2nd edn, 1994), p. 310; U. Luz, *Matthew 8-20* (Hermeneia: Minneapolis: Fortress Press, 2001), pp. 338–9, and J. Nolland, *The Gospel of Matthew: A Commentary on the Greek Text* (NIGTC; Grand Rapids: Eerdmans, 2005), pp. 631–2.

But the second possibility seems more logical in terms of the immediate context.[11] First, Matthew rewrites Mark's introduction of the woman, stating that a Canaanite woman *from that region, came out* (ἐξελθοῦσα) to engage Jesus on behalf of her daughter. These additions to Mark's text would be entirely unnecessary were Matthew simply following the Markan story at this point. They suggest in fact that Jesus has ventured near to the Gentile region and the woman came out from that area to meet him. Secondly, the redactional comment by Jesus to the woman that he was sent only to the lost sheep of the house of Israel (15.24) makes no sense at all had Jesus entered Gentile territory. We have to conclude that Matthew at this point in the narrative presents Jesus being consistent with his restriction of the disciples' mission in 10.5-6.

As noted earlier, Mk 7.31 keeps Jesus in Gentile territory until his return to Jewish land in 8.10; it is during this journey that he feeds the Gentile four thousand. The Matthaean parallel is very different. After healing the Canaanite woman's daughter in Jewish territory, Jesus simply travels to the Sea of Galilee (15.29). Since there is no mention at all of Sidon or the Decapolis, the implication is that Jesus reaches the Sea on the western or Jewish side. This is important because it means that the healings in 15.30-31 and the second miraculous feeding in 15.32-39 occur in Jewish territory and pertain only to Jews. Matthew has therefore altered the Markan account of the feeding of a Gentile crowd into a second miraculous feeding of a Jewish crowd.[12]

In recounting the next visit of Jesus to a Gentile region, Matthew largely follows Mark. Jesus and the disciples again cross the Sea of Galilee (16.5) and make their way to the district of Caesarea Philippi (16.13). Here a number of significant events take place – the confession of Peter and Jesus' teaching on discipleship (16.13-28), the transfiguration of Jesus and the teaching about John the Baptist and Elijah (17.1-13) and the cure of an epileptic boy (17.14-21) – before Jesus returns to Galilee in 17.22. Since almost all of these events deal with interactions between Jesus and the disciples, there is no suggestion of a Gentile mission. Not even the healing of the boy, who is seemingly but not definitively Gentile, can be construed as such. The cases of the centurion of Capernaum and the Canaanite woman testify that the Matthaean Jesus was prepared to assist individual Gentiles in need without compromising his singular mission to Israel.

---

11. In agreement with A.-J. Levine, *The Social and Ethnic Dimensions of Matthean Salvation History: 'Go Nowhere among the Gentiles...' (Matt. 10:5b)* (SBEC, 14; Lewiston: Edwin Mellen Press, 1988), pp. 133–7. Cf. too D. J. Harrington, *The Gospel of Matthew* (SP, 1; Collegeville: Liturgical Press, 1991), p. 235.

12. See the excellent discussion of this subject by J. R. C. Cousland, 'The Feeding of the Four Thousand *Gentiles* in Matthew? Matthew 15:29-39 as a Test Case', *NovT* 41 (1999), pp. 1–23. Cousland convincingly dispels the thesis, widely held by Matthaean scholars, that Matthew has followed the Markan schema that the second feeding concerns Gentiles.

3. *Jesus and the Torah in Mark and Matthew*

The subject of Jesus' attitude towards the Torah in these Gospels is a highly complex one that cannot be treated in any detail. However, all that is required here is a general statement of how each evangelist positions Jesus with regard to the Mosaic Law. There is a fair degree of consensus that the Markan Jesus embraces a rather liberal stance on Torah-observance, especially with regard to the ritual or ceremonial requirements, while the Matthaean Jesus adopts a much more conservative position.

In Mark a case can be made that Jesus affirms the moral commandments of the Law and in particular those that appear in the Decalogue (i.e. 7.10; 10.19; cf. 7.21b-22). This emphasis on the ethical component of the Torah is highlighted in the teaching on the two greatest commandments, the love of God and the love of neighbour (12.28-34). But this positive attitude does not extend to the ritual requirements of the Law or at least to some parts of it. This is most clearly articulated in the dispute with the Pharisees over the issue of purity (7.1-23). In this pericope Jesus explains that impurity and defilement do not come from external sources but come from within the person (v. 15). True impurity in this passage is equated with evil thoughts and actions (vv. 22-23). Mark the narrator makes perfectly clear his understanding of this tradition when he appends in v. 19b 'thus he declared all foods clean'. The Markan Jesus therefore in one fell swoop renders obsolete and invalid the whole dietary and purity system as enjoined in the Mosaic Law.[13] It is arguable as well that the Markan Jesus critiques and overrides sabbath observance (Mk 2.23–3.6) and the law concerning divorce (10.2-12), but there is no need for our purposes to demonstrate this point. The case of the invalidation of the dietary and purity system of Judaism is sufficient to demonstrate that in Mark Jesus does not demand obedience to the Torah *in toto*.

The view of the Matthaean Jesus on the Torah is, as is widely recognized, fundamentally different. The triad of sayings in 5.17-19 provides unambiguous testimony that Jesus did not come to abolish the Torah, and that all of its components, including the least important commandments, are to be obeyed in full until the *parousia*. These verses introduce the teaching of Matthew's Jesus on the Law, and they set the standard by which other teachings on this subject in the Gospel must be measured. While the Matthaean Jesus has his own interpretation of the Torah, which is based upon the double love command as the interpretative key

---

13.   So most scholars; see Marcus, *Mark 1-8*, pp. 457–8, and W. R. G. Loader, *Jesus' Attitude Towards the Law: A Study of the Gospels* (WUNT, 2.97; Tübingen: Mohr Siebeck, 1997), pp. 77–9. Svartvik, *Mark and Mission*, pp. 354–75 argues that in this pericope the Markan Jesus renders invalid only the food laws and not the purity laws of Judaism, but this distinction, even if correct, does not affect the overall point.

(22.34-40; cf. 7.12; 19.18-19) and which distinguishes between greater and lesser demands (23.23), he never, unlike his Markan counterpart, invalidates any of its ritual or ceremonial components.[14] It is for this reason that Matthew is careful to omit Mark's narrative addition at 7:19b. For Matthew, in stark contrast to Mark, all of the Torah remains valid.

4. *The Historical Jesus*

Let us now turn to the historical Jesus. What are the scholarly views concerning his attitude to Gentiles and the Gentile mission, and his position with respect to the Torah? As we might expect on such complex issues, the opinions of scholars cover a wide variety of views. There is no necessity, however, to examine all of these. For our purposes it is sufficient to give a few examples of scholars at either end of the spectrum, who either reconstruct a liberal historical Jesus similar to the Markan Jesus or a more conservative historical Jesus along the lines of the Matthaean Jesus.

With regard to the question of the Gentiles,[15] the view that it was Jesus himself who initiated the Gentile mission, the depiction we find in Mark, is well supported. The most recent advocate of this position is E. J. Schnabel who has argued his case in a number of studies.[16] Schnabel builds his argument more upon the Gospel accounts of the interactions between

---

14. For this general understanding of the Torah in Matthew, see Loader, *Jesus' Attitude*, pp. 137–272; J. A Overman, *Matthew's Gospel and Formative Judaism: The Social World of the Matthean Community* (Minneapolis: Fortress Press, 1990), pp. 72–90; K. Snodgrass, 'Matthew and the Law', in D. R. Bauer and M. A. Powell (eds), *Treasures New and Old: Contributions to Matthean Studies* (SBLSS, 1; Atlanta: Scholars Press, 1996), pp. 99–127, and D. C. Sim, *The Gospel of Matthew and Christian Judaism: The History and Social Setting of the Matthean Community* (SNTW; Edinburgh: T&T Clark, 1998), pp. 123–39. In Matthew the controversies with the scribes and Pharisees are never set within the context of whether the Torah is still valid – that is a given – but are set within the context of the correct interpretation of the Law. On this specific issue, see the definitive study of B. Repschinski, *The Controversy Stories in the Gospel of Matthew: Their Redaction, Form and Relevance for the Relationship between the Matthean Community and Formative Judaism* (FRLANT, 189; Göttingen: Vandenhoeck & Ruprecht, 2000).

15. For a survey of all the competing theories on this topic, see M. F. Bird, 'Jesus and the Gentiles Since Jeremias: Problems and Prospects', *CBR* 4 (2005), pp. 83–108; and *idem., Jesus and the Origins of the Gentile Mission* (LNTS, 331; London; T&T Clark International, 2007), pp. 11–23.

16. E. J. Schnabel, 'Jesus and the Beginnings of the Mission to the Gentiles', in J. B. Green and M. Turner (eds), *Jesus of Nazareth: Lord and Christ. Essays on the Historical Jesus and New Testament Christology* (Grand Rapids: Eerdmans, 1994), pp. 37–58. More recently, Schnabel has articulated his views in greater detail; E. J. Schnabel, *Early Christian Mission. Vol. I. Jesus and the Twelve* (Downers Grove: InterVarsity Press, 2004), pp. 327–86.

Jesus and Gentiles (e.g. Mk 3.7-8; 5.1-20; 7.24-30, 32-7; 8.1-10; Mt. 8.5-13//Lk. 7.1-10) than the teaching of Jesus, though he does contend that Jesus predicted the future universal mission of his disciples (cf. Mk 10.18; 14.9) which he ratified after his resurrection (Mt. 28.18-20; Lk. 24.46-49; Jn 20.21; Acts 1.8; cf. Mk 13.10; 14.9). The work of M. F. Bird can be categorized here as well, though his discussion is more critical and nuanced than Schnabel's. Bird argues that the proclamation of Jesus was concerned with the restoration of Israel and that, in accord with Jewish restoration eschatology, this inevitably raised the issue of the salvation of the Gentiles.[17] According to Bird, 'Jesus linked the salvation of the Gentiles with the restoration of Israel, and probably envisaged a continuing preaching mission that would include the Gentiles... the origin of the various Gentile missions in the early church ultimately derives from the effective history of the historical Jesus'.[18]

The alternative view is also well attested. According to this thesis, Jesus may have had intermittent contact with Gentiles but he never entertained a Gentile mission for himself or for his disciples. This view largely supports the Matthaean presentation of this aspect of Jesus' mission. Once again there are different nuances in this general position. E. P. Sanders maintains that the Gentiles simply did not feature in the teaching or example of Jesus. He contends that 'We need not think that Jesus imparted to his disciples any view at all about the Gentiles and the kingdom'.[19] A modified and more popular version of this view is that Jesus, despite never initiating a Gentile mission, may have envisaged the salvation of the Gentiles at the eschaton (cf. Mt. 8.11-12).[20]

With respect to the Torah we find a similar division in scholarship. Some give weight to Mark's portrayal of Jesus, while others give primacy to Matthew's. One representative of the first category is J. Jeremias whose uncompromising stance contends that Jesus criticized the Mosaic Law and even abolished certain aspects of it.[21] A similar thesis is presented by

17.   Bird, *Jesus*, pp. 26–177.
18.   Bird, *Jesus*, p. 177
19.   E. P. Sanders, *Jesus and Judaism* (London: SCM, 1985), pp. 212–21. The quote appears on p. 221.
20.   This is the view of J. Jeremias, *Jesus' Promise to the Nations* (Philadelphia: Fortress Press, 1958). See too C. H. H. Scobie, 'Jesus or Paul? The Origin of the Universal Mission of the Christian Church', in P. Richardson and J. C. Hurd (eds), *From Jesus to Paul: Studies in Honour of Francis Wright Beare* (Ontario: Wilfrid Laurier University Press, 1984), pp. 47–60; J. P. Meier, *A Marginal Jew: Rethinking the Historical Jesus. Vol. 2, Mentor, Message and Miracles* (ABRL; New York: Doubleday, 1994), pp. 315, 374–5; and J. D. G. Dunn, *Christianity in the Making. Vol. 1. Jesus Remembered* (Grand Rapids: Eerdmans, 2003), pp. 537–59.
21.   J. Jeremias, *New Testament Theology. Vol. 1. The Proclamation of Jesus* (London: SCM, 1971), pp. 204–14.

J. Riches who also maintains that Jesus was critical of the Torah to the point that he rejected the whole purity system of Judaism (cf. Mk 7.15).[22] Those who see things rather differently and generally support the Matthaean version include E. P. Sanders, who argues that Jesus may not have viewed the Law as final and absolute but he none the less believed that it could not be freely transgressed.[23] A similar conclusion is reached by D. C. Allison in a recent monograph. After a detailed sifting of all the relevant Gospel materials, Allison concludes that, while Jesus demanded obedience to the Torah, he himself had an imaginative interpretation of it and may have relaxed (but not abolished) some its imperatives.[24]

Which of these alternative views is correct? Is Mark or Matthew closer to the positions of the historical Jesus? In attempting to answer these questions, I do not wish to go over old ground by assessing the common methods used in historical Jesus scholarship, the so-called criteria of authenticity.[25] Many of these criteria are dubious and simply do not provide the concrete results that are often attributed to them.[26] A much better approach for the subjects under discussion here is to utilize an underused and unnamed historical method that delivers much more accurate results. This method involves a reconstruction of the practices of the original Christian community in Jerusalem, and uses that information to decide what the position of the historical Jesus was on a given issue. While this approach to historical Jesus reconstruction has been appealed to in previous studies, I would argue that it has not been employed in the most productive way. In the course of the following discussion, I will spell out just how effective the proper use of this method can be when determining Jesus' attitude to the Gentile mission and to the Torah.

5. *The Practice of the Earliest Jerusalem Church*

In reconstructing the practice of the earliest Jerusalem church, I am interested only in its initial stage, the time immediately following the resur-

22.   J. Riches, *Jesus and the Transformation of Judaism* (London: Darton, Longman and Todd, 1980), pp. 130–44.

23.   Sanders, *Jesus and Judaism*, pp. 245–69.

24.   D.C. Allison, *Resurrecting Jesus: The Earliest Christian Tradition and Its Interpreters* (London: T&T Clark International, 2005), pp. 149–97.

25.   See the detailed discussion of these criteria – embarrassment, dissimilarity, multiple attestation, coherence, rejection and execution, and others as well in Meier, *A Marginal Jew*, *Vol. I*, pp. 167–95.

26.   Many scholars have correctly expressed concerns over the validity of some or all of these criteria. For a recent critique, see A.-J. Levine, 'Introduction', in A.-J. Levine, D. C. Allison and J. D. Crossan (eds), *The Historical Jesus in Context* (PRR; Princeton: Princeton University Press, 2006), pp. 1–39 (9–11).

rection of Jesus and the assembly of his followers in Jerusalem. Our major source for this period of the Jerusalem church is Acts 1–5, though the Pauline epistles provide a secondary and often corroborating witness. The composition of the original Jerusalem church is crucial. Acts informs us that at the very beginning there were approximately 120 members (1.15), including the eleven remaining disciples, the mother and brothers of Jesus and some unspecified women who perhaps are to be identified with the females who followed Jesus in Galilee (cf. Lk. 8.1-3; Mk 15.40-41). The other members of the church must have included the wives and children of the disciples and the families of the brothers of Jesus (Mk 10.29; Lk. 14.26; 1 Cor. 9.5). The remaining members were presumably other Galilean followers or supporters of Jesus who also accepted the reality of his resurrection (cf. Acts 1.21-26).[27] The membership of the original Jerusalem church thus comprised Galileans who knew the historical Jesus intimately, his disciples, other followers and his own kinship group. It hardly needs saying that this group was in a unique position to know through personal experience the teachings of the historical Jesus and his perspective on almost every issue. What were the positions of this Christian community with regard to the Gentiles and with respect to the Torah?

In response to the first question, the evidence of Acts is clear that the Jerusalem church in its initial phase had no interest at all in Gentiles and certainly never considered conducting a Gentile mission. Luke relates two interesting points about the missionary practice of the original Christian community. First, they preached their message about Jesus only to Jews and proselytes (cf. 2.5, 10, 22; 3.12-13). This is confirmed by Paul's account of the apostolic council where Peter is acknowledged as the one entrusted with the mission to the Jews, and it is agreed that Peter, James and John would continue to conduct the Jewish mission (Gal. 2.7-9). Secondly, in pursuing this mission the original Jerusalem church confined itself to the city of Jerusalem itself (cf. Acts 3.16, 28). There is no hint in Acts 1–5 that any of these early Christians saw the need to take their gospel to Jews beyond the walls of Jerusalem, let alone to Gentiles in the wider world.[28] The mission of the initial Jerusalem church was therefore a restricted one, confined certainly to the Jews and probably to Jerusalem. Luke of course has tried to cover the reality of the situation by having the risen Christ tell the disciples that they will be witnesses beyond Jerusalem to the ends of the earth (Acts 1.8), but the original church he

---

27. See D. C. Sim, 'How Many Jews Became Christians in the First Century? The Failure of the Christian Mission to the Jews', *HTS* 61 (2005), pp. 417–40 (419–20).

28. See Sim, 'How Many Jews?', pp. 426–9.

depicts shows no inclination to expand either its ethnic or geographical outreach.[29]

With regard to the Torah, there is overwhelming evidence that this community continued to obey its regulations. Acts does not spell out this point directly, but it is assumed throughout the narrative. First, the text does specify that the members of the earliest Jerusalem community continued to participate in the Temple cult (Acts 2.46; 3.1), and it would have been rather odd for them to have done this if they had criticized or renounced the Torah. The fact that Luke states that the Jerusalem church attracted both priests and Pharisees to its cause (Acts 6.7; 15.5) presumes not just participation in the Temple cult but also continued obedience to the Mosaic Law. Secondly, the Hellenist Stephen is charged with subverting both the Temple and the laws of Moses (Acts 6.13-14), which ultimately leads to his martyrdom and to the persecution of the other Hellenists. The fact that the disciples were not charged with these offences (Acts 8.1) suggests that they were not guilty of undermining the Temple or the Torah. Thirdly, when Peter experiences his visions which inform him that there are no unclean animals (10.9-16; 11.4-10), the implication is that prior to these events he followed the traditional Jewish view detailed in the Law that there were such unclean foodstuffs. The whole episode of Peter's conversion of the Gentile Cornelius (Acts 10.1–11.18) is almost certainly legendary,[30] but the point remains that even in the schema of Acts Peter observes the Torah up to this point in the narrative. Finally, Luke suggests that the apostolic council was convened because the Jerusalem church sent agents to Antioch in an attempt to convince the Gentile converts to observe the Torah (Acts 15.1). This makes sense only if the Jerusalem church itself followed the Mosaic Law. The picture we reconstruct of the earliest Jerusalem church in Acts is confirmed by the Pauline epistles. In all of his descriptions of this church and its leaders, Paul never even hints that they were anything but Law-observant. Had they relaxed or abandoned any aspect of the Torah, Paul would surely have appealed to their example when defending his own Law-free gospel amongst the Gentiles.

We may therefore draw the important conclusion that the original Jerusalem church, comprising people who knew intimately the historical Jesus, his family and especially his disciples, continued to observe the

29. Schnabel, *Early Christian Mission, Vol. I*, pp. 519–36 disputes this conclusion. While he concedes that the initial material in Acts restricts the mission to the Jews in the Jewish capital, he counters that the disciples must have been involved in a universal mission, even if only in planning and strategy, because they had been called to evangelize the world by the risen Christ. The argument is as circular as it is uncritical.

30. See E. Haenchen, *The Acts of the Apostles* (Philadelphia: Westminster Press, 1971), pp. 357–63.

Mosaic Law and restricted their missionary endeavours to other Jews. At some point, however, there were important developments in the primitive Christian movement. The original Jewish mission expanded to include the Gentiles and the gospel preached to these people appears to have been a version that did not necessitate obedience to the Law. It is crucial to note that neither of these developments can be attributed to the original Galilean members of the Christian community in Jerusalem. Both were almost certainly initiatives of a group of early Greek-speaking Jewish converts in Jerusalem, whom Luke designates 'the Hellenists' (Acts 6.1–8.3).[31]

For reasons that are difficult to reconstruct from our sources, the Hellenist Christians adopted a critical view of both the Torah and the Temple. As noted above, one of their leaders, Stephen, was accused of speaking against both of these fundamental Jewish institutions. Stephen was martyred and the remaining Hellenists were persecuted and forced to flee Jerusalem (8.1). They returned to their former residences in the Diaspora and continued the original practice of preaching only to Jews, but those who fled to Antioch began to preach their distinctive message about Jesus to Gentiles (11.19-20). There is no reason to doubt the veracity of this tradition preserved in Acts, and most scholars accept that the Gentile mission began in Antioch at the instigation of the Hellenists who fled Jerusalem. It is also highly probable that the gospel preached by the Hellenists did not demand observance of the Mosaic Law. This would have been consistent with their critique of the Torah in Jerusalem, and it is supported by other evidence as well. Luke relates in Acts 15.1 that the Jerusalem church later sent agents to Antioch with the message that salvation was impossible for Gentile Christians unless they were circumcised, an event that led to the apostolic council, and this assumes that the laws of Moses had no place at all in the Antiochene community. Further, the fact that Paul travelled to Jerusalem to defend the Law-free gospel he preached in Antioch (Gal. 2.1-10) leads to the same conclusion.

Of course Paul has a different account of the origin of the Gentile mission and its Law-free orientation. He claims in his epistles that he was appointed by the risen Christ to be the apostle to the Gentiles (Gal. 1.16-17; 2.7-9; cf. Rom. 1.5, 13-14; 11.13; 15.16; 16.4), and that his gospel free from the requirements of the Torah was revealed to him at the time of his commission (Gal. 1.11-12). Luke knew traditions about Paul's conversion and may have tried to credit him with these innovations by placing his meeting with the risen Christ prior to the Hellenist mission in

31. Much of the following discussion is based upon my more detailed analysis of the Hebrews and the Hellenists. See Sim, *Matthew and Christian Judaism*, pp. 64–77, and literature cited there.

Antioch (Acts 9.3-22). For our purposes there is no need to decide between the Hellenists and Paul for the ultimate responsibility of the Gentile mission and its Law-free orientation. What is important to note is that on either view these significant developments in the Christian movement were instigated by later converts to the Christian tradition. These people had not followed Jesus in Galilee nor had they ever heard him speak.

6. *Matthew, Mark and the Historical Jesus*

Some scholars have argued that the practices of the original Jeruslaem church should have an important impact on the reconstruction of the historical Jesus. For example, E. P. Sanders contends that if Jesus did renounce the dietary and purity laws as Mk 7.1-23 attests, then the later position of the Jerusalem church becomes impossible to understand.[32] He makes the same point with regard to the issue of the Gentile mission, maintaining that the disinterest of the Jerusalem church has its basis in the prior lack of interest by Jesus himself.[33] The issue for Sanders is one of historical continuity. We can easily explain a Law-observant Jewish mission on the part of the Jerusalem church if we posit a Law-observant Jesus who focused only on the Jews. By contrast, it is difficult to explain a Law-observant Jewish mission on the part of the Jerusalem church if Jesus had criticized or renounced the Torah and preached openly to Gentiles. Even given the new understanding of Jesus in the light of the resurrection experience, it stands to reason, as A.-J. Levine comments, 'that Jesus and the early church founded in his name were substantially continuous rather than distinct'.[34]

The contention that there was considerable continuity between Jesus and the earliest Jerusalem church usually stops at that point, and in doing so it leaves itself open to a possible objection. It could well be argued that the Galilean followers of Jesus simply misunderstood him on these fundamental issues. Such a possibility must be given some credence in the light of Mark's very unflattering depictions of these followers. He depicts the mother and brothers of Jesus as unbelievers and blasphemers (Mk 3.21-35; 6.1-4) and the disciples as failing constantly to understand the teaching and mission of Jesus (cf. 4.13; 6.51-2; 8.14-21; 8.31-33; 9.9-10, 31-2, 38-41; 10.32-34). If Mark is correct, then the practices of the Jerusalem church should not be given such a primary role in determining the prior actions of Jesus. It could even be argued that people like the Hellenists and

---

32. Sanders, *Jesus and Judaism*, p. 266. See too I. M. Zeitlin, *Jesus and the Judaism of His Time* (Cambridge: Polity Press, 1988), pp. 52–60.
33. Sanders, *Jesus and Judaism*, p. 220.
34. Levine, 'Introduction', p. 10.

Paul understood the radical nature of Jesus' mission better than his Galilean followers. In implementing their policy of a Law-free Gospel to the Gentiles, they may have actually stood closer to the position of the historical Jesus. This view is widely attested in the scholarly literature. One example is C. H. H. Scobie, who argues that, in terms of the Gentile mission, there is substantial continuity between Jesus and Paul with the Hellenists bridging the gap between the two.[35] M. Hengel suggests much the same with respect to the Torah. The Hellenists' critique of the Law and the Temple were grounded in Jesus' own criticisms of these Jewish institutions.[36] J. D. G. Dunn argues along similar lines in his suggestion that the Law-critical material in Mk 2.15–3.6 is a pre-Pauline unit collected by the Hellenists that provides a bridge between Jesus and the apostle.[37]

While this general argument appears reasonable on the surface, it suffers from a serious, perhaps even an insurmountable, problem. I have mentioned this difficulty before in another context,[38] but it deserves to be spelled out clearly and carefully. The views of Scobie, Hengel and Dunn (and many others) assume to a large extent the veracity of the Markan portrayal of Jesus, at least with regard to the Gentile mission and the Law. If we put the historical scenario they propose in tabular form, we get the following results:

1. The historical Jesus (a Gentile mission and critical of the Torah)
2. The earliest Jerusalem church (no Gentile mission and faithful to the Torah)
3. The Hellenists and Paul (a Gentile mission and critical of the Torah)

According to this view, the earliest Christian community in Jerusalem did not follow the example of Jesus on these fundamental issues. They either misunderstood Jesus (so Mark) or they deliberately reversed his policy. By contrast with the original Christians, the Hellenists and Paul did follow the example set by Jesus.

The first step in this argument, that the Jerusalem community misunderstood or disobeyed the teachings of Jesus, is of course a historical possibility. Followers and disciples of religious teachers do not always comprehend or emulate their masters. The Markan depiction of the disciples and the family of Jesus cannot therefore be excluded out of hand. But the problem comes to the fore in the next step, the contention that the Hellenists and Paul understood and imitated the example of Jesus on the issues of the Law and the Gentiles. We need to remind ourselves that these people were not followers of the historical Jesus; they

35. Scobie, 'Jesus or Paul?', pp. 59–60.
36. M. Hengel, *Between Jesus and Paul: Studies in the Earliest History of Christianity* (London: SCM, 1983), pp. 22–9.
37. J. D. G. Dunn, 'Mark 2.1–3.6: A Bridge Between Jesus and Paul on the Question of the Law', in J. D. G. Dunn, *Jesus, Paul and the Law* (London: SPCK, 1990), pp. 10–36.
38. See Sim, *Matthew and Christian Judaism*, pp. 69–70.

were converts after the Easter events. If they never knew the historical Jesus, then how did they learn about his life and message? The only reasonable answer is that they were instructed about him by those in the Christian community who followed Jesus in Galilee and who knew him intimately. In short, Paul and the Hellenists were taught about the historical Jesus by the original Christians, especially, we may assume, the disciples who had greater exposure to Jesus' teaching than anyone else. The Hellenists lived in Jerusalem and would have been instructed on the mission of Jesus by his Galilean followers after their conversion, while Paul, years after his encounter with the risen Christ, spent two weeks with Peter in Jerusalem (Gal. 1.18). But once we realize that their source for the historical Jesus tradition was the disciples (and perhaps other Galilean followers of Jesus), then a further difficult question emerges.

How could the disciples, if they themselves failed to understand the position of Jesus on the Gentiles or the Torah, have conveyed accurate information to these converts on these subjects? How could they possibly have imparted the true import of Jesus' teachings when their own grasp of it was so faulty? Both logic and honesty compel us to conclude that such a scenario is not even remotely plausible. Nor is it any more likely on the assumption that the disciples understood the teachings and actions of Jesus but decided for reasons unknown not to implement them. Apart from the unevidenced attack on the disciples' integrity, the problem of the communication of Jesus' true teaching remains. If the disciples were intent on presenting a distorted version of Jesus' message that supported their own position, then why would they undermine their own policy by conveying accurate teachings of Jesus that contradicted that stance? In these initial years they controlled the Jesus tradition and it was entirely their decision as to what new converts would be taught.

Nor can the problem be overcome by postulating, as does D. C. Allison, that the different points of view in the church can be traced back to Jesus himself. Allison suggests that there was much in Jesus' teaching to satisfy the conservatives who continued to obey the Law, but also less stringent elements that would have appealed to the liberals or Law-free Christians in the church.[39] But again it is necessary to ask whether this is realistic. Why would the disciples, who obviously held the more conservative position, have conveyed to their converts the more liberal elements of Jesus' teaching which they themselves chose not to follow? And how would they have done so? Is it really conceivable that they could have managed to provide such an accurate presentation of Jesus' liberalism through the filter of their own conservatism?

---

39. Allison, *Resurrecting Jesus*, pp. 195-6.

However it is expressed, any attempt to establish a fundamental agreement between the historical Jesus and Paul (or the Hellenists) when the Jerusalem church held a different view is beset by this singular difficulty. Since the conduits of the Jesus tradition were the members of the original Jerusalem church, the historical progression of ideas it proposes is utterly implausible.[40] Historical Jesus scholarship has to face the facts and begin to question seriously all versions of the thesis that Paul and/or the Hellenists understood the life and teaching of the historical Jesus better than did the disciples (and the family) of Jesus. The only way to overcome this problem would be to argue that these converts were given information about Jesus from another source, but there is no evidence whatsoever that this was the case.

The upshot of this is that we have good reason to question the Markan portrayal of Jesus both in terms of the Mosaic Law and the Gentile mission. It does not make any sense in terms of historical continuity. If we consider why Mark would paint Jesus in these terms, then a ready explanation presents itself. Mark stood either within or close to the Pauline school.[41] It was therefore in his theological and political interests to paint Jesus with very Pauline colours. He does this in many ways, but the two that are of interest to us are his depiction of Jesus as a critic of the Torah and as the initiator of the Gentile mission. Moreover, it was in Mark's interests to portray Paul's opponents in Jerusalem, notably the family and disciples of Jesus, as unbelievers or incompetents.[42]

Let us now consider the historical progression from the viewpoint of the Matthaean portrait of Jesus. Does this pose any major problems in terms of historical continuity?

1. The historical Jesus (no Gentile mission and faithful to the Torah)
2. The earliest Jerusalem church (no Gentile mission and faithful to the Torah)
3. The Hellenists and Paul (a Gentile mission and critical of the Torah)

On this scenario the people in the Jerusalem church who knew well Jesus and his teaching simply followed his example by continuing to observe the Mosaic Law and by engaging in a mission strictly to the Jews. There is historical continuity where we would expect it. The Gentile mission and the Law-free gospel that so characterized Paul and the Hellenists were not

---

40. It is somewhat surprising that H. Räisänen's otherwise excellent critique of the thesis that the Hellenists provided a bridge between Jesus and Paul does not mention this argument. See his 'The "Hellenists": A Bridge Between Jesus and Paul?', in H. Räisänen, *Jesus, Paul and Torah: Collected Essays* (JSNTSup, 43; Sheffield: JSOT Press, 1992), pp. 149–202.

41. So many scholars, but see the recent study by J. Marcus, 'Mark – Interpreter of Paul', *NTS* 46 (2000), pp. 473–87.

42. See E. Trocmé, *The Formation of the Gospel according to Mark* (London: SPCK, 1975), pp. 120–37. Cf. too Sim, *Matthew and Christian Judaism*, pp. 188–90, 192–4.

inherited from the practice of Jesus, but were innovations introduced by these later Christian converts, perhaps on the basis of their experiences of the risen Christ. Acts in fact supports this reading of the historical progression by crediting the Hellenists with the origin of the Gentile mission and its Law-free gospel.

Paul too confirms this point, though he traces the origin of both back to his own encounter with the risen Jesus. This is most clearly articulated in Gal. 1.1, 11-19, where Paul is adamant that neither his Law-free gospel nor his commission to preach it was given to him by the disciples. And Paul is entirely consistent about this throughout his epistles. Nowhere in his writings does he ever suggest that he was imitating the practices of the historical Jesus. When defending his own Law-free position, Paul comes up with all sorts of reasons why the Law is now obsolete and need no longer be observed, but he never once justifies his stance by referring to the example of the historical Jesus. Nor does he seek to justify his mission to the Gentiles by pointing to a previous Gentile mission on the part of Jesus. On the contrary, his statement in Gal. 4.4-5 that Jesus was born under the Law to redeem those who were under the Law (cf. Rom. 6.14-15; 1 Cor. 9.20; Gal. 3.23; 4.21; 5.18) suggests that Paul was well aware that the historical Jesus was fully Law-observant and that he restricted his mission to the Jews.[43] Consequently, Paul testifies that the resurrection event triggered significant developments in the divine plan. While the historical Jesus was obedient to the Torah and preached only to Jews, the risen Christ had lifted the restriction in both cases. The witness of Paul therefore confirms Matthew's portrait of the pre-Easter Jesus as a Law-observant Jew who conducted only a Jewish mission.

7. Conclusions

It has been argued in this study that the Gospel of Matthew, despite its late date and its reliance on Mark and Q, cannot be dismissed as a reliable source for the historical Jesus. In terms of Jesus' involvement in a Gentile mission and his attitude to the Torah, it actually stands closer to the positions of the historical Jesus than does Mark. The major evidence in favour of this conclusion is the issue of historical continuity. The Markan portrait of Jesus, which envisages substantial discontinuity between Jesus and his followers who knew him and substantial continuity between him and later converts who did not, is inherently implausible. The alternative Matthaean depiction of Jesus presents a much more plausible historical progression that involves considerable agreement between Jesus and his

---

43. J. D. G. Dunn, *The Epistle to the Galatians* (BNTC; London: A&C Black, 1993), p. 216.

Galilean followers and the introduction of new and different ideas and practices by converts in the post-Easter period. Matthew's description of Jesus as a Law-observant Jew interested only in a Jewish mission is to a large extent supported by Acts and the Pauline epistles.

It is hoped that this short study paves the way for a reconsideration of Matthew as an important source for historical Jesus research. The evangelist's often drastic revision of Mark should not be seen just as a 're-judaizing' of that source, but as a conscious and determined effort to correct some aspects of the Markan Jesus that were theologically suspect and simply unhistorical.

10. Conclusions

Boris Repschinski SJ

Even after two thousand years it is intriguing to think of a small band of Jewish believers in Jesus facing opposition in Jerusalem and, as a consequence, spreading out over Judaea, Samaria, and the whole world as it was known at the time. Even if the account of Christianity's spread as reported by the Acts of the Apostles contains legendary traits, the fact remains that by the time Matthew recounted the story of Jesus as teacher of the Law and saviour of his people Israel, Matthew's was only one voice among a great and diverse chorus of early Christian authors. The explorations of the preceding chapters have shown how distinctive Matthew's voice is within that chorus.

One of the issues that kept coming up in the comparisons between Matthew and his Christian contemporaries is that of Torah. There is good reason for returning to consideration of Matthew's approach to the Jewish Law. It is perhaps the one feature that separates Matthew from other Christian writings. Even other Christian writings with close ties to Judaism, like Hebrews or James or the *Didache*, do not exhibit such a strong adherence to the Law. Matthew's 'not one iota or stroke of a letter' (5.18) is not mitigated by a 'until John' (Lk. 16.16) or a 'do what you can' (*Did.* 6.2). Matthew would not have had any sympathy for John's opposition to the Law, nor for the way Paul interpreted the consequences of faith in the resurrection of Jesus as liberation from Law. He probably saw a number of deficiencies in Mark's Gospel as a story of a Jesus for Gentiles, and would have shaken his head at the *Didache*'s *laissez-faire* approach to purity and dietary laws.

One result of this initial exploration of Matthew from the perspective of his Christian contemporaries is certainly an illumination of just how diverse early Christianity was. But there were also some very surprising convergences. To name but one, the theology of the death of Jesus as a sacrificial act of salvation sealing a new covenant in his blood revealed a common theme between Matthew and Hebrews. It is particularly startling to see a shared theme between just two early Christian writings, particularly since they obviously share an interest in things Jewish, but not in Torah.

If Torah is one of the touchstones for interpreting Matthew, the comparisons of this volume have raised a number of questions that bear further study. One area where Matthew's Gospel distinguishes itself is the high regard in which it holds the Jewish Torah. It is not just a fond memory of ancient traditions, but it is a live issue that not only comes to the fore in discussions with opposing Pharisees and scribes, but also has a firm place in the instruction of the community represented by the disciples and, to a lesser degree, by the crowds. As some of the studies collected in this volume have shown, Matthew's approach to the Law is distinctive within early Christian literature. Even arguably Jewish Christian writings like the Epistle of James or Hebrews do not advocate such a central role for the Law. Yet in the discussion of the Torah Matthew does not just take it as a fixed entity but puts his own spin on it by making it subject to the teaching of Jesus. This becomes obvious not only in the typically Matthaean phrase connecting the Law with the prophets in the teaching of Jesus, but also in the striking reformulations of certain commandments in the antitheses of the Sermon on the Mount or the prominence of the quotation from Hos. 6.6 in the discussion of legal material. Furthermore, if the scene of the eschatological judgement makes salvation solely dependent on a moral conduct that is formulated in terms of love for 'the least of my brothers' and not in terms of the Law, Matthaean regard for the Torah ought to be reconsidered. It is possible that a strong emphasis on an ethical interpretation of the Law under the influence of prophetic traditions is much closer to at least some of Matthew's Christian contemporaries than is generally assumed.

But there is a further implication of Matthew's approach to the Law. In the present volume little attention has been paid to the hermeneutics of Matthew's interpretation of Torah. Yet the way Jesus is presented as the teacher of Torah in the mould of Moses[1] also goes far beyond the figure of Moses as mediator between God and his people. Thus the issue of christology has a direct bearing on the interpretation of Torah in Matthew. If this is so, then more attention needs to be focused on the hermeneutics of legal interpretation on the authority of Jesus put forth by Matthew. Here a further comparison would probably reveal many points of contact between Matthew and his Christian contemporaries.

Going on from the issue of Torah a related problem arises. When Matthew talks of judgement, he does so in the stock language of Jewish apocalyptic.[2] Nevertheless, the criteria for judgement as laid out in Matthew 25 concern a form of ethics that on the surface has little to do with Torah. The final judgement scene contains no allusions to the Law

---

1.   For such typological approaches in Jewish and Christian literature, see D. C. Allison, *The New Moses: A Matthean Typology* (Edinburgh: T&T Clark, 1993); and J. Lierman, *The New Testament Moses* (WUNT 2.173; Tübingen: Mohr Siebeck, 2004).

2.   See D. C. Sim, *Apocalyptic Eschatology in the Gospel of Matthew* (SNTSMS, 88; Cambridge: Cambridge University Press, 1996).

but only to the good works done to one's neighbour. Of course, even this
language can be related to certain forms of Jewish apocalyptic and may
also be related to Matthew's prophetic hermeneutics of the Law. However,
this turn to ethics as a deciding factor for judgement also places Matthew
quite squarely within the Christian traditions evident from contemporary
texts. The preceding studies have shown how much the ethics of neighbourly love is a common feature of many of the early Christian writings.
If this is so even for Matthew, more questions arise concerning the specific
role of the Torah in Matthew's scheme of salvation. Does Matthew really
believe that without keeping the Torah there is no salvation? Or does he
view the Torah as a specification of the larger and more commonly shared
Christian ethics? The second answer finds some support in the discussion
of the Golden Rule and the Great Commandment, and the recurring
emphasis on Jesus as the righteous teacher of Law and justice as opposed
to others who try to interpret the Law. If this is so, then Torah is a valid
formulation of Christian ethics, but it is not the only one possible.

This leads to a further area of remaining questions. Matthew's Gospel
is an adaptation of a Gentile gospel. Occasionally Matthew takes a critical
attitude towards Gentile groups who did away with some of the Jewish
traditions like the Torah. He enjoins full Torah observance even for
Gentiles. His ecclesiology occasionally defines a Jewish group identity
against Gentiles (5.47; 6.7, 32; 10.5-6; 15.24; 18.17). There is little doubt
that Matthew's group not only knew of Gentiles believing in Jesus but
pursued them in an active mission.[3] So far this might not be surprising.
However, the question remains; why would the Matthaean group be
attractive to Gentiles? This concerns first of all Gentiles with the wish to
join the Matthaean community. These Gentiles had, as seems obvious from
Matthaean allusions and implications, a whole range of possibilities to
choose from. There are certainly no simple answers to this question. But
it ought to be considered whether the way Matthew taught the Law as
interpreted by Jesus did in fact ease the way for Gentiles. The sabbath
controversies and the instruction over purity issues might be examples of
an interpretation of Torah that emphasises ethics over legalism or cult. In
this context even circumcision could be considered expendable.

The question of Gentiles has implications beyond the actual mission of
the Matthaean community at the time of the writing of the Gospel when
one considers Matthew's history of reception. While many Jewish
Christian groups eschewed the appropriation of Matthew, or at least

---

3.   There is little point in trying to assign these traditions to 'a later stage in the history
of the text', as does P. J. Tomson, *"If this be from heaven..." Jesus and the New Testament
Authors in their Relationship to Judaism* (TBS, 76; Sheffield: Sheffield Academic Press, 2001),
p. 281. Would such a later redaction not try to take the edge off some of the more Jewish
features?

found the need to edit and comment extensively, the Gospel became popular in Gentile circles.[4] This draws attention to the specifically Christian features of the Gospel rather than its Jewish ones. Here a further area for continued research opens itself. Christians in the generations after Matthew obviously saw that the call to Law-observance was not as central to the Gospel as today's students of Matthew make it out to be. They found enough evidence in the Gospel to claim that adherence to the ethics of neighbourly love was in fact the kind of Law-observance enjoined by Matthew and could thus claim that indeed it was the Christian groups that were the true successors to the people of God and, therefore, to the promises of old.[5] Matthew's sharp antagonism to Pharisees and scribes provided just the kind of material such groups claimed as evidence.

The studies presented in this volume only claim to be initial voices in the dialogue between Matthew and his Christian contemporaries. As such they provide some intriguing answers and observations, but even more they provide students of early Christianity with a range of questions not only with regard to Matthew's Gospel, but also for the development of early Christianity.

4.   For the discussion of Matthew's weak influence on Jewish Christian groups, see A. F. J. Klijn, *Jewish-Christian Gospel Tradition* (VCSup, 17; Leiden: Brill, 1992); A. F. J. Klijn and G. J. Reinink, *Patristic Evidence for Jewish-Christian Sects* (NovTSup, 36; Leiden: Brill, 1973); and P. Vielhauer, *Geschichte der urchristlichen Literatur. Einleitung in das Neue Testament, die Apokryphen und die Apostolischen Vätern* (Berlin: de Gruyter, 1985).

5.   Justin Martyr was the first to make these claims explicit (*Dial.* 111-42). For a brief discussion, see S. G. Wilson, *Related Strangers: Jews and Christians 70-170 C.E.* (Minneapolis: Fortress Press, 1995).

BIBLIOGRAPHY

Abrahams, I., *Studies in Pharisaism and the Gospels. Vol. 1* (Cambridge: Ktav Publishing House, 1917).

Allison, D. C., *The New Moses: A Matthean Typology* (Edinburgh: T&T Clark, 1993).

———, *Jesus of Nazareth: Millenarian Prophet* (Minneapolis: Fortress Press, 1998).

———, *Resurrecting Jesus: The Earliest Christian Tradition and Its Interpreters* (London: T&T Clark International, 2005).

Alon, G., 'The Halacha in the Teaching of the Twelve Apostles', in J. A. Draper (ed.), *The Didache in Modern Research* (AGJU, 37; Leiden: Brill, 1996), pp. 165–94.

Amir, Y., 'Die Zehn Gebote bei Philon von Alexandrien', in Y. Amir (ed.), *Die Hellenistische Gestalt des Judentums bei Philon von Alexandrien* (FJCD, 5; Neukirchen-Vluyn: Neukirchener Verlag, 1983), pp. 131–63.

Anderson, H., '4 Maccabees', in J. H. Charlesworth (ed.), *The Old Testament Pseudepigrapha. Vol. 2* (London: Darton, Longman & Todd, 1985), pp. 544–64.

Audet, J. P., *La Didache: Instructions des apôtres* (Paris: Gabalda, 1958).

Avemarie, F., 'Die Werke des Gesetzes im Spiegel des Jakobusbriefs: A Very Old Perspective on Paul', *ZTK* 98 (2001), 282–309.

Bacher, W., *Die Agada der Tannaiten. Vol. 1* (Strassburg: Trübner, 1884).

Barrett, C. K., 'Jews and Judaizers in the Epistles of Ignatius', in R. Hamerton-Kelly and R. Scroggs (eds), *Jews, Greeks and Christians: Religious Cultures in Late Antiquity. Essays in Honor of William David Davies* (Leiden: Brill, 1976), pp. 220–44.

Bartel, R., J. S. Ackerman and T. S. Warshaw (eds), *Biblical Images in Literature* (Nashville: Abingdon, 1975).

Bauckham, R., *James: Wisdom of James, Disciple of Jesus the Sage* (NTR; London: Routledge, 1999).

Becker, A. H. and A. Y. Reed (eds), *The Ways That Never Parted: Jews and Christians in Late Antiquity and the Early Middle Ages* (TSAJ, 95; Tübingen: Mohr Siebeck, 2003).

Berger, K., *Die Gesetzesauslegung Jesu. Ihr historischer Hintergrund im Judentum und im Alten Testament* (WMANT, 40; Neukirchen-Vluyn: Neukirchener Verlag, 1972).

————, *Theologie des Urchristentums: Theologie des Neuen Testaments* (Tübingen: Francke, 2nd edn, 1995).

Betz, H. D., *Essays on the Sermon on the Mount* (Philadelphia: Fortress Press, 1985).

————, *The Sermon on the Mount* (Hermeneia; Minneapolis: Fortress Press, 1995).

Bieringer, R., D. Pollefeyt and E. Vandecasteele-Vanneuville (eds), *Anti-Judaism and the Fourth Gospel* (Louisville: Westminster John Knox, 2001).

Bird, M. F., 'Jesus and the Gentiles Since Jeremias: Problems and Prospects', *CBR* 4 (2005), 83–108.

————, *Jesus and the Origins of the Gentile Mission* (LNTS, 331; London; T&T Clark International, 2007).

Böhm, M., *Samarien und die Samaritai. Eine Studie zum religionshistorischen und traditionsgeschichtlichen Hintergrund der lukanischen Samarientexte und zu deren topographischer Verhaftung* (WUNT, 2.111; Tübingen: Mohr Siebeck, 1999).

Borgen, P., 'The Golden Rule. With Emphasis on Its Usage in the Gospels', in P. Borgen (ed.), *Paul Preaches Circumcision and Pleases Men. And Other Essays on Christian Origins* (Relieff, 8; Trondheim: Tapir, 1983), pp. 99–114.

Bornkamm, G., 'The Authority to "Bind" and "Loose" in the Church in Matthew's Gospel: The Problem of Sources in Matthew's Gospel', in G. N. Stanton (ed.), *The Interpretation of Matthew* (IRT, 3; London: SPCK, 1983), pp. 85–97.

Bovon, F., *Das Evangelium nach Lukas* (EKKNT, 3; 3 vols; Zürich: Benziger Verlag, 1989, 1996, 2001).

Brodie, T. L., *The Birthing of the New Testament: The Intertextual Development of the New Testament Writings* (NTMon, 1: Sheffield: Sheffield Phoenix, 2004).

Brown, R. E., *The Community of the Beloved Disciple* (New York: Paulist Press, 1979).

Brown, S., 'The Matthean Community and the Gentile Mission', *NovT* 22 (1980), pp. 193–221.

Bultmann, R., *Theology of the New Testament. Vol. 2* (London: SCM, 1955).

————, *Die Geschichte der synoptischen Tradition* (FRLANT, 29; Göttingen: Vandenhoeck & Ruprecht, 8th edn, 1970).

Byrne, B., 'The Messiah in Whose Name "The Gentiles Will Hope" (Matt 12:21): Gentile Inclusion as an Essential Element of Matthew's Christology', *ABR* 50 (2002), 55–73.

Byrskog, S., *Jesus the Only Teacher: Didactic Authority and Transmission in Ancient Israel, Ancient Judaism and the Matthean Community* (CBNTS, 24; Stockholm: Almqvist & Wiksell, 1994).

Cadbury, H. J., *The Making of Luke-Acts* (London: Macmillan, 1927).
Callahan, A. D., *A Love Supreme: A History of the Johannine Tradition* (Minneapolis: Fortress Press, 2005).
Carter, W., *Matthew and the Margins: A Sociopolitical and Religious Reading* (Maryknoll: Orbis, 2000).
——, *Matthew and Empire: Initial Explorations* (Harrisburg: Trinity Press International, 2001).
Chilton, B., and C. A. Evans (eds), *James the Just and Christian Origins* (NovTSup, 98; Leiden: Brill, 1999).
Clark, K. W., 'The Gentile Bias in Matthew', *JBL* 66 (1947), pp. 165–72.
Collins, J. J., 'A Symbol of Otherness: Circumcision and Salvation in the First Century', in J. Neusner and E. S. Frerichs (eds), *'To See Ourselves as Others See Us': Christians, Jews, 'Others' in Late Antiquity* (SPSH; Chico: Scholars Press, 1985), pp. 163–86.
Collins, R. F., *First Corinthians* (SP, 7; Collegeville: Liturgical Press, 1999).
Connolly, R. H., 'Canon Streeter on the Didache', *JTS* 38 (1937), 364–79.
Conzelmann, H., *Die Mitte der Zeit. Studien zur Theologie des Lukas* (BHT; Tübingen: J. C. B. Mohr [Paul Siebeck], 4th edn, 1962).
Corwin, V., *St. Ignatius and Christianity in Antioch* (New Haven: Yale University Press, 1960).
Cousland, J. R. C., 'The Feeding of the Four Thousand *Gentiles* in Matthew? Matthew 15:29-39 as a Test Case', *NovT* 41 (1999), 1–23.
Cullmann, O., *Der johanneische Kreis: Sein Platz im Spätjudentum, in der Jüngerschaft Jesu und im Urchristentum* (Tübingen: J. C. B. Mohr [Paul Siebeck], 1975).

Davies, W. D., *The Setting of the Sermon on the Mount* (Cambridge: Cambridge University Press, 1964).
Davies, W. D., and D. C. Allison, *A Critical and Exegetical Commentary on the Gospel according to Saint Matthew* (ICC; 3 vols; Edinburgh: T&T Clark, 1988, 1991, 1997).
Deines, R., *Die Gerechtigkeit der Tora im Reich des Messias: Mt 5,13-20 als Schlüsseltext der matthäischen Theologie* (WUNT, 177; Tübingen: Mohr Siebeck, 2004).
Dibelius, M., *Der Brief des Jakobus* (ed. and suppl. H. Greeven; KEK, 15; Göttingen: Vandenhoeck & Ruprecht, 11th edn, 1964).
Dobschütz, E. von, 'Matthew as Rabbi and Catechist', in G. N. Stanton (ed.), *The Interpretation of Matthew* (IRT, 3; London: SPCK, 1983), pp. 27–38.
Dodd, C. H., 'Matthew and Paul', in C. H. Dodd, *New Testament Studies* (Manchester: Manchester University Press, 1953), pp. 53–66.

————, *The Interpretation of the Fourth Gospel* (Cambridge: Cambridge University Press, 1953).

Donahue, J. R. and D. J. Harrington, *The Gospel of Mark* (SP, 2; Collegeville: Liturgical Press, 2002).

Donahue, P. J., 'Jewish Christianity in the Letters of Ignatius of Antioch', *VC* 32 (1978), 81–93.

Draper, J. A., 'Do the *Didache* and Matthew Reflect an "Irrevocable Parting of the Ways" with Judaism?', in H. van de Sandt (ed.), *Matthew and the Didache. Two Documents From the Same Jewish-Christian Milieu?* (Assen: Royal van Gorcum, 2005), pp. 217–41.

Drews, P., 'Untersuchungen zur Didache', *ZNW* 5 (1904), 53–79.

Dunn, J. D. G., 'Mark 2.1–3.6: A Bridge Between Jesus and Paul on the Question of the Law', in J. D. G. Dunn, *Jesus, Paul and the Law* (London: SPCK, 1990), pp. 10–36.

————, *The Partings of the Ways Between Christianity and Judaism and their Significance for the Character of Christianity* (London: SCM, 1991).

————, *The Epistle to the Galatians* (BNTC; London: A&C Black, 1993).

————, *Christianity in the Making. Vol. 1. Jesus Remembered* (Grand Rapids: Eerdmans, 2003).

————, *The New Perspective on Paul: Collected Essays* (WUNT, 185; Tübingen: Mohr Siebeck, 2005).

Edwards, M. J., 'Ignatius and the Second Century: An Answer to R. Hübner', *ZAC* 2 (1998), 214–26.

Enslin, M. S., 'Luke and the Samaritans', *HTR* 36 (1943), 274–97.

Ewherido, A. O., *Matthew's Gospel and Judaism in the Late First Century C.E.: The Evidence from Matthew's Chapter on Parables (Matthew 13:1-52)* (SBL, 91; New York: Peter Lang, 2006).

Fitzmyer, J. A., *The Gospel According to Luke: Introduction, Translation, and Notes* (AB, 28-28A; 2 vols; New York: Doubleday, 1983).

Flusser, D., 'The Ten Commandments and the New Testament', in B.-Z. Segal and G. Levi (eds), *The Ten Commandments in History and Tradition* (PPFBR; Jerusalem: Magnes Press, 1990), pp. 219–46.

————, '"Den Alten ist gesagt". Zur Interpretation der sog. Antithesen der Bergpredigt', *Judaica* 48 (1992), 35–9.

Forster, E. M., *Aspects of the Novel* (London: Penguin, 1990).

Foster, P., *Community, Law and Mission in Matthew's Gospel* (WUNT, 2.177; Tübingen: Mohr Siebeck, 2004).

————, 'The Epistles of Ignatius of Antioch and the Writings that later formed the New Testament', in A. F. Gregory and C. M. Tuckett (eds), *The Reception of the New Testament in the Apostolic Fathers* (Oxford: Oxford University Press, 2005), pp. 159–86.

Frankemölle, H., *Der Brief des Jakobus. Vol. 1* (Gütersloh: Gütersloher Verlagshaus, 1994).

Franklin, E., *Luke: Interpreter of Paul, Critic of Matthew* (JSNTSup, 92; Sheffield: JSOT Press, 1994).

Gale, A. M., *Redefining Ancient Borders: The Jewish Scribal Framework of Matthew's Gospel* (London: T&T Clark International, 2005).

Garland, D. E., *1 Corinthians* (BECNT; Grand Rapids: Baker Academic, 2003).

Garrow, A. J. P., *The Gospel of Matthew's Dependence on the Didache* (JSNTSup, 254; London: T&T Clark International, 2004).

Goulder, M. D., *Midrash and Lection in Matthew* (London: SPCK, 1974).

Grant, R. M., *The Apostolic Fathers, Vol. I: An Introduction* (London: Thomas Nelson & Sons, 1964).

———, *The Apostolic Fathers, Vol. IV: Ignatius of Antioch* (London: Thomas Nelson & Sons, 1966).

Grässer, E., *An die Hebräer* (EKKNT, 17; 2 vols; Zürich: Benziger Verlag, 1990, 1993).

Guelich, R. A., *The Sermon on the Mount. A Foundation for Understanding* (Waco: Word Books, 1982).

Gundry, R. H., 'A Responsive Evaluation of the Social History of the Matthean Community in Roman Syria', in D. L. Balch (ed.), *Social History of the Matthean Community: Cross-Disciplinary Approaches* (Minneapolis: Fortress Press, 1991), pp. 62–7.

———, *Matthew: A Commentary on His Handbook for a Mixed Church under Persecution* (Grand Rapids: Eerdmans, 2nd edn, 1994).

———, 'The Apostolically Johannine Pre-Papian Tradition Concerning the Gospels of Mark and Matthew', in R. H. Gundry, *The Old is Better: New Testament Essays in Support of Traditional Interpretations* (WUNT, 178; Tübingen: Mohr Siebeck, 2005), pp. 49–73.

Haenchen, E., *The Acts of the Apostles* (Philadelphia: Westminster Press, 1971).

Hagner, D. A., *Matthew 1-13* (WBC, 33A; Dallas: Word Books, 1993).

———, *Matthew 14-28* (WBC, 33B; Dallas: Word Books, 1996).

———, 'Matthew: Apostate, Reformer, Revolutionary?', *NTS* 49 (2003), 193–209.

———, 'Matthew: Christian Judaism or Jewish Christianity?', in S. McKnight and G. R. Osborne (eds), *The Face of the New Testament: A Survey of Recent Research* (Grand Rapids: Baker Academic, 2004), pp. 263–82.

Hare, D. R. A., 'How Jewish is the Gospel of Matthew?', *CBQ* 62 (2000), 264–77.

Hare, D. R. A. and D. J. Harrington, '"Make Disciples of All the Gentiles" (Mt 28:19)', *CBQ* 37 (1975), 359–69.

Harrington, D. J., *The Gospel of Matthew* (SP, 1; Collegeville: Liturgical Press, 1991).

———, *Paul on the Mystery of Israel* (Collegeville: Liturgical Press, 1992).

Hartin, P. J., *James and the Q Sayings of Jesus* (JSNTSup, 47; Sheffield: Sheffield Academic Press, 1991).

———, *A Spirituality of Perfection: Faith in Action in the Letter of James* (Collegeville: Liturgical Press, 1999).

———, 'Ethics in the Letter of James, the Gospel of Matthew and the *Didache*: Their Place in Early Christian Literature', forthcoming in H. van de Sandt and J. Zangenberg (eds), *Matthew, James and the Didache: Three Related Documents in their Jewish and Christian Contexts* (SBLSS; Atlanta: Scholars Press).

Heinemann, I., *Philo's griechische und jüdische Bildung. Kulturvergleichende Untersuchungen zu Philons Darstellung der jüdischen Gesetze* (Hildesheim: Georg Olms, 1962).

Hengel, M., *Between Jesus and Paul: Studies in the Earliest History of Christianity* (London: SCM, 1983).

———, 'Der Jakobusbrief als antipaulinische Polemik', in M. Hengel, *Paulus und Jakobus: Kleine Schriften III* (WUNT, 141; Tübingen: Mohr Siebeck, 2002), pp. 511–48.

———, 'Jakobus der Herrenbruder – der erste "Papst"?', in M. Hengel, *Paulus und Jakobus: Kleine Schriften III* (WUNT, 141; Tübingen: Mohr Siebeck, 2002), pp. 549–82.

Horst, P. W. van der, *The Sentences of Pseudo-Phocylides with Introduction and Commentary* (SVTP, 4; Leiden: Brill, 1978).

———, 'Pseudo-Phocylides and the New Testament', *ZNW* 69 (1978), 187–202.

Hübner, R. M., 'Thesen zur Echtheit und Datierung der sieben Briefe des Ignatius von Antiochien', *ZAC* 1 (1997), 44–72.

Hurtado, L. W., *Lord Jesus Christ: Devotion to Jesus in Earliest Christianity* (Grand Rapids: Eerdmans, 2003).

Iverson, K. R., *Gentiles in the Gospel of Mark: 'Even the Dogs Under the Table Eat the Children's Crumbs'* (LNTS, 339; London: T&T Clark International, 2007).

Jefford, C. N., 'The Milieu of Matthew, the *Didache*, and Ignatius of Antioch: Agreements and Differences', in H. van de Sandt (ed.), *Matthew and the Didache: Two Documents from the Same Jewish-Christian Milieu?* (Assen: Royal van Gorcum, 2005), pp. 35–47.

Jeremias, J., *Jesus' Promise to the Nations* (Philadelphia: Fortress Press, 1958).

————, *New Testament Theology. Vol. 1. The Proclamation of Jesus* (London: SCM, 1971).

Jervell, J., 'The Lost Sheep of the House of Israel: The Understanding of the Samaritans in Luke-Acts', in J. Jervell, *Luke and the Divided People of God: A New Look at Luke-Acts* (Minneapolis: Fortress Press, 1979), pp. 113–32.

————, *Die Apostelgeschichte* (KEK, 3; Göttingen: Vandenhoeck & Ruprecht, 1998).

Johnson, L. T., *The Letter of James: A New Translation with Introduction and Commentary* (AB, 37A; New York: Doubleday, 1995).

Johnson, M. D., *The Purpose of the Biblical Genealogies with Special Reference to the Setting of the Genealogies of Jesus* (SNTSMS, 8; Cambridge: Cambridge University Press, 1969).

Keener, C. S., *A Commentary on the Gospel of Matthew* (Grand Rapids: Eerdmans, 1999).

Klijn, A. F. J., *Jewish-Christian Gospel Tradition* (VCSup, 17; Leiden: Brill, 1992).

Klijn, A. F. J. and G. J. Reinink, *Patristic Evidence for Jewish-Christian Sects* (NovTSup, 36; Leiden: Brill, 1973).

Kloppenborg, J. S., 'The Use of the Synoptics or Q in *Did*. 1:3b–2:1', in H. van de Sandt (ed.), *Matthew and the Didache. Two Documents From the Same Jewish-Christian Milieu?* (Assen: Royal van Gorcum, 2005), pp. 105–29.

————, 'Poverty and Piety in Matthew, James and the *Didache*', forthcoming in H. van de Sandt and J. Zangenberg (eds), *Matthew, James and the Didache: Three Related Documents in their Jewish and Christian Contexts* (SBLSS; Atlanta: Scholars Press).

Konradt, M., *Christliche Existenz nach dem Jakobusbrief. Eine Studie zu seiner soteriologischen und ethischen Konzeption* (SUNT, 22; Göttingen: Vandenhoeck & Ruprecht, 1998).

————, 'Theologie in der "strohernen Epistel": Ein Literaturbericht zu neueren Ansätzen in der Exegese des Jakobusbriefes', *VF* 44 (1999), 54–78.

————, 'Der Jakobusbrief als Brief des Jakobus. Erwägungen zum historischen Kontext des Jakobusbriefs im Lichte der traditionsgeschichtlichen Beziehungen zum 1. Petrusbrief und zum Hintergrund der Autorfiktion', in P. von Gemünden, M. Konradt and Gerd Theißen (eds), *Der Jakobusbrief. Beiträge zur Rehabilitierung der 'strohernen Epistel'* (BVB, 3; Münster: LIT, 2003), pp. 16–53.

Kugelman, R., *James and Jude* (NTM, 19; Dublin: Veritas, 1980).

Lambrecht, J., *The Sermon on the Mount. Proclamation and Exhortation* (GNS, 14; Wilmington: Glazier, 1985).

Lechner, T., *Ignatius Adversus Valentinianos? Chronologische und theolo-giegeschichtliche Studien zu den Briefen des Ignatius von Antiochen* (VCSup, 47; Leiden: Brill, 1999).

Levine, A.-J., *The Social and Ethnic Dimensions of Matthean Salvation History: 'Go Nowhere among the Gentiles...' (Matt. 10:5b)* (SBEC, 14; Lewiston: Edwin Mellen Press, 1988).

———, 'Introduction', in A.-J. Levine, D. C. Allison and J. D. Crossan (eds), *The Historical Jesus in Context* (PRR; Princeton: Princeton University Press, 2006), pp. 1–39.

Lierman, J., *The New Testament Moses* (WUNT, 2.173; Tübingen: Mohr Siebeck, 2004).

Lindemann, A., 'Antwort auf die Thesen zur Echtheit und Datierung der sieben Briefe des Ignatius von Antiochien', *ZAC* 1 (1997), 185–94.

———, Review of T. Lechner, *Ignatius Adversus Valentinianos? Chronologische und theologiegeschichtliche Studien zu den Briefen des Ignatius von Antiochen* (VCSup, 47; Leiden: Brill, 1999), *ZAC* 6 (2002), 157–61.

———, 'Der "äthiopische Eunuch" und die Anfänge der Mission', in C. Breytenbach and J. Schröter (eds), *Die Apostelgeschichte und die hellenistische Geschichtsschreibung. Festschrift für Eckhard Plümacher* (Leiden: Brill, 2004), pp. 109–33.

———, 'Paul's Influence on "Clement" and Ignatius', in A. F. Gregory and C. M. Tuckett (eds), *Trajectories Through the New Testament and the Apostolic Fathers* (Oxford: Oxford University Press, 2005), pp. 9–24.

Loader, W. R. G., *Jesus' Attitude Towards the Law: A Study of the Gospels* (WUNT, 2.97; Tübingen: Mohr Siebeck, 1997).

Lohse, E., '"Ich aber sage euch"', in E. Lohse (ed.), *Die Einheit des Neuen Testaments. Exegetische Studien zur Theologie des Neuen Testaments* (ESTNT, 1; Göttingen: Vandenhoeck & Ruprecht, 1973), pp. 73–87.

Luomanen, P., *Entering the Kingdom of Heaven. A Study on the Structure of Matthew's View of Salvation* (WUNT, 2.101; Tübingen: Mohr Siebeck, 1998).

Luther, M., 'Vorrede auf das Neue Testament', in *D. Martin Luthers Werke. Kritische Gesamtausgabe. Die Deutsche Bibel. 6 Band* (Weimar: Böhlaus, 1929 [1522]).

Luz, U., *Matthew 1-7* (Augsburg: Minneapolis, 1989; rev. edn Hermeneia; Minneapolis: Fortress Press, 2007).

———, *Matthew 8-20* (Hermeneia: Minneapolis: Fortress Press, 2001).

———, *Matthew 21-28* (Hermeneia: Minneapolis: Fortress Press, 2005).

———, *Studies in Matthew* (Grand Rapids: Eerdmans, 2005).

McNicol, A. J. (ed.), *Luke's Use of Matthew: Beyond the Q Impasse* (Valley Forge: Trinity Press International, 1996).

Maier, H. O., *The Social Setting of the Ministry as Reflected in the Writings of Hermas, Clement and Ignatius* (Waterloo: Wilfrid Laurier University Press, 1991).

Malbon, E. S., *Narrative Space and Mythic Meaning in Mark* (TBS, 13; Sheffield: JSOT Press, 1991).

Malherbe, A., *Moral Exhortation: A Greco-Roman Sourcebook* (Philadelphia: Westminster, 1986).

Mann, C. S., *Mark: A New Translation with Introduction and Commentary* (AB, 27; New York: Doubleday, 1986).

Manson, T. W., *The Teaching of Jesus: Studies of its Form and Content* (Cambridge: Cambridge University Press, 2nd edn, 1948).

Marcus, J., *Mark 1-8: A New Translation with Introduction and Commentary* (AB, 27; NewYork: Doubleday, 1999).

——, 'Mark – Interpreter of Paul', *NTS* 46 (2000), 473–87.

Marshall, J. W., 'The Objects of Ignatius' Wrath and Jewish Angelic Mediators', *JEH* 56 (2005), 1–23.

Martyn, J. L., *History and Theology in the Fourth Gospel* (New York: Harper & Row, 1968).

Meeks, W. A., 'Breaking Away: Three New Testament Pictures of Christianity's Separation from the Jewish Communities', in J. Neusner and E. S. Frerichs (eds), *'To See Ourselves as Others See Us': Christians, Jews, 'Others' in Late Antiquity* (SPSH; Chico: Scholars Press, 1985), pp. 93–116.

——, *The Origins of Christian Morality: The First Two Centuries* (New Haven: Yale University Press, 1993).

——, *Jesus is the Question* (Louisville: Westminster John Knox, 2006).

Meier, J. P., *Law and History in Matthew's Gospel. A Redactional Study of Mt. 5:17-48* (AnBib, 71; Rome: Biblical Institute Press, 1976).

——, *The Vision of Matthew: Christ, Church and Morality in the First Gospel* (New York: Paulist Press, 1979).

——, 'Antioch', in R. E. Brown and J. P. Meier, *Antioch and Rome* (New York: Paulist Press, 1983), pp. 12–86.

——, *A Marginal Jew: Rethinking the Historical Jesus. Vol. 1, The Roots of the Problem and the Person* (ABRL; New York: Doubleday, 1991).

——, *A Marginal Jew: Rethinking the Historical Jesus. Vol. 2, Mentor, Message and Miracles* (ABRL; New York: Doubleday, 1994).

Merklein, H., *Die Gottesherrschaft als Handlungsprinzip. Untersuchung zur Ethik Jesu* (FzB, 34; Würzburg: Echter Verlag, 2nd edn, 1981).

Michel, O., 'Der Abschluß des Matthäusevangeliums', *EvT* 10 (1950), 16–26.

Milavec, A., *The Didache: Faith, Hope, and Life of the Earliest Christian Communities, 50-70 C.E.* (New York: Newman Press, 2003).

Mohrlang, R., *Matthew and Paul: A Comparison of Ethical Perspectives* (SNTSMS, 48; Cambridge: Cambridge University Press, 1984).

Murphy-O'Connor, J., *Paul: A Critical Life* (Oxford: Clarendon Press, 1996).

———, *Paul: His Story* (Oxford: Oxford University Press, 2004).

Mussner, F., *Der Jakobusbrief* (Freiburg: Herder, 1964).

Myllykoski, M., 'Wild Beasts and Rabid Dogs: The Riddle of the Heretics in the Letters of Ignatius', in J. Ådna (ed.), *The Formation of the Early Church* (WUNT, 183; Tübingen: Mohr Siebeck, 2005), pp. 341–77.

Nepper-Christensen, P., *Das Matthäusevangelium: Ein judenchristliches Evangelium?* (ATDan, 1; Åarhus: Universitetsforlaget, 1958).

Niebuhr, K.-W., *Gesetz und Paränese; Katechismusartige Weisungsreihen in der frühjüdischen Literatur* (WUNT, 2.28; Tübingen: J. C. B. Mohr, 1987).

———, '"A New Perspective on James"? Neuere Forschungen zum Jakobusbrief', *TLZ* 129 (2004), 1019–44.

Niederwimmer, K., *Die Didache* (KAV, 1; Göttingen: Vandenhoeck & Ruprecht, 2nd edn, 1993).

Nolland, J., *Luke 1:1-9:20* (WBC, 35A; Dallas: Word Books, 1989).

———, *Luke 9:21-18:34* (WBC, 35B; Dallas: Word Books, 1993).

———, *The Gospel of Matthew: A Commentary on the Greek Text* (NIGTC; Grand Rapids: Eerdmans, 2005).

O'Leary, A. M., *Matthew's Judaization of Mark: Examined in the Context of the Use of Sources in Graeco-Roman Antiquity* (JSNTSup, 323; London: T&T Clark International, 2006).

Orton, D. E., *The Understanding Scribe: Matthew and the Apocalyptic Ideal* (JSNTSup, 25; Sheffield: Sheffield Academic Press, 1989).

Overman, J. A., *Matthew's Gospel and Formative Judaism: The Social World of the Matthean Community* (Minneapolis: Fortress Press, 1990).

———, *Church and Community in Crisis: The Gospel According to Matthew* (TNTIC; Valley Forge: Trinity Press International, 1996).

———, 'Problems with Pluralism in Second Temple Judaism: Matthew, James and the *Didache* in Their Jewish-Roman Milieu', forthcoming in H. van de Sandt and J. Zangenberg (eds), *Matthew, James and the Didache: Three Related Documents in their Jewish and Christian Contexts* (SBLSS; Atlanta: Scholars Press).

Painter, J., 'Christ and the Church in John 1.45-51', in M. de Jonge (ed.), *L' Évangile de Jean* (Leuven: Peeters, 1977), pp. 359–62.

———, 'The Church and Israel in the Gospel of John', *NTS* 25 (1978), 102–12.

———, 'Text and Context in John 5', *ABR* 35 (1987), 28–34.

———, *The Quest for the Messiah* (Edinburgh: T&T Clark, 2nd edn, 1993).

———, 'Theology and Eschatology in the Prologue of John', *SJT* 46 (1993), 27–42.

———, *Mark's Gospel: Worlds in Conflict* (NTR; London: Routledge, 1997).

———, *1, 2, and 3 John* (SP, 18; Collegeville: Liturgical Press, 2002).

———, 'Earth Made Whole: John's Rereading of Genesis', in J. Painter, R. A. Culpepper and F. F. Segovia (eds), *Word, Theology, and Community* (St Louis: Chalice, 2002), pp. 65–84.

———, *Just James: The Brother of Jesus in History and Tradition* (Colombia: University of South Carolina Press, 2nd edn, 2004).

———, 'Monotheism and Dualism: John and Qumran', in G. van Belle, J. G. van der Watt and P. Maritz (eds), *Theology and Christology in the Fourth Gospel* (Leuven: Peeters, 2005), pp. 225–43.

Parkes, J., *The Conflict of the Church and the Synagogue: A Study of the Origins of Anti-Semitism* (London: Soncino, 1934).

Patterson, S. J., *The Gospel of Thomas and Jesus* (Sonoma: Polebridge, 1993).

Popkes, W., *Adressaten, Situation und Form des Jakobusbriefes* (SBS, 125; Stuttgart: Katholisches Bibelwerk, 1986).

———, *Der Brief des Jakobus* (THKNT, 14; Leipzig: Evangelische Verlagsanstalt, 2001).

Pratscher, W., *Der Herrenbruder Jakobus und die Jakobustradition* (FRLANT, 139; Göttingen: Vandenhoeck & Ruprecht, 1987).

Przybylski, B., *Righteousness in Matthew and his World of Thought* (SNTSMS, 41; Cambridge: Cambridge University Press, 1980).

Räisänen, H., *Paul and the Law* (WUNT, 29; Tübingen: Mohr Siebeck, 1987).

———, 'The "Hellenists": A Bridge Between Jesus and Paul?', in H. Räisänen, *Jesus, Paul and Torah: Collected Essays* (JSNTSup, 43; Sheffield: JSOT Press, 1992), pp. 149–202.

Ravens, D., *Luke and the Restoration of Israel* (JSNTSup, 119; Sheffield: Sheffield Academic Press, 1995).

Reinbold, W., 'Das Matthäusevangelium, die Pharisäer und die Tora', *BZ* 50 (2006), 51–73.

Reis, D. M., 'Following in Paul's Footsteps: *Mimēsis* and Power in Ignatius of Antioch', in A. F. Gregory and C. M. Tuckett (eds), *Trajectories Through the New Testament and the Apostolic Fathers* (Oxford: Oxford University Press, 2005), pp. 288–305.

Repschinski, B., *The Controversy Stories in the Gospel of Matthew: Their Redaction, Form and Relevance for the Relationship between the Matthean Community and Formative Judaism* (FRLANT, 189; Göttingen: Vandenhoeck & Ruprecht, 2000).

———, 'Of Mice and Men and Matthew 2', in K. Pandikattu and A. Vonach (eds), *Religion, Society and Economics. Eastern and Western Perspectives in Dialogue* (Frankfurt: Peter Lang, 2003), pp. 75–94.

———, 'For He Will Save His People from Their Sins (Matthew 1:21): A Christology for Christian Jews', *CBQ* 68 (2006), 248–67.

———, 'Purity in Matthew, James and the Didache', forthcoming in H. van de Sandt and J. Zangenberg (eds), *Matthew, James and the Didache: Three Related Documents in their Jewish and Christian Contexts* (SBLSS; Atlanta: Scholars Press).

Riches, J., *Jesus and the Transformation of Judaism* (London: Darton, Longman and Todd, 1980).

———, *Conflicting Mythologies: Identity Formation in the Gospels of Mark and Matthew* (SNTW; Edinburgh: T&T Clark, 2000).

Riches, J. and D. C. Sim (eds), *The Gospel of Matthew in Its Roman Imperial Context* (JSNTSup, 276; London: T&T Clark International, 2005).

Robinson, J. M. and C. Heil, 'The Lilies of the Field: Saying 36 of the *Gospel of Thomas* and Secondary Accretions in Q 12.22b-31', *NTS* 47 (2001), 1–25.

Rordorf, W., 'Un chapitre d'éthique Judéo-Chrétienne: les deux voies', *RSR* 60 (1972), 109–28.

———, 'Does the Didache Contain Jesus Tradition Independently of the Synoptic Gospels?', in H. Wansbrough (ed.), *Jesus and the Oral Gospel Tradition* (JSOTSup, 64; Sheffield: JSOT Press, 1991), pp. 394–423.

Rordorf, W. and A. Tuilier, *La Doctrine des douze Apôtres (Didachè)* (SC, 248; Paris: Les Éditions du Cerf, 2nd edn, 1998).

Rosner, B. S. (ed.), *Understanding Paul's Ethics: Twentieth Century Approaches* (Grand Rapids: Eerdmans, 1995).

Rousmaniere, J., *A Bridge to Dialogue: The Story of Jewish-Christian Relations* (New York: Paulist Press, 1991).

Saldarini, A. J., 'The Gospel of Matthew and Jewish-Christian Conflict in Galilee', in L. I. Levine (ed.), *Studies on Galilee in Late Antiquity* (New York: Jewish Theological Seminary, 1992), pp. 23–8.

———, *Matthew's Christian-Jewish Community* (CSHJ; Chicago: University of Chicago Press, 1994).

Sanders, E. P., *Paul and Palestinian Judaism: A Comparison of Patterns of Religion* (Philadelphia: Fortress Press, 1977).

———, *Paul, the Law, and the Jewish People* (Philadelphia: Fortress Press, 1983).

———, *Jesus and Judaism* (London: SCM, 1985).

Sanders, J. T., *The Jews in Luke-Acts* (Philadelphia: Fortress Press, 1987).

————, 'Jewish Christianity in Antioch before the Time of Hadrian', in E. H. Lovering (ed.), *Society of Biblical Literature 1992 Seminar Papers* (Atlanta: Scholars Press, 1992), pp. 346–61.

Sandt, H. van de, 'Two Windows on a Developing Jewish-Christian Reproof Practice: Matt 18:15-17 and *Did* 15:3', in H. van de Sandt (ed.), *Matthew and the Didache. Two Documents From the Same Jewish-Christian Milieu?* (Assen: Royal van Gorcum, 2005), pp. 173–92.

Sandt, H. van de and D. Flusser, *The Didache: Its Jewish Sources and Its Place in Early Judaism and Early Christianity* (CRINT, 3.5; Assen: Royal van Gorcum, 2002).

Schaberg, J., *The Father, the Son, and the Holy Spirit. The Triadic Phrase in Matthew 28:19b* (SBLDS, 31; Chico: Scholars Press, 1982).

Schnabel, E. J., 'Jesus and the Beginnings of the Mission to the Gentiles', in J. B. Green and M. Turner (eds), *Jesus of Nazareth: Lord and Christ. Essays on the Historical Jesus and New Testament Christology* (Grand Rapids: Eerdmans, 1994), pp. 37–58.

————, *Early Christian Mission. Vol. I. Jesus and the Twelve* (Downers Grove: InterVarsity Press, 2004).

Schnelle, U., *Einleitung in das Neue Testament* (Göttingen: Vandenhoeck & Ruprecht,4th edn, 2002).

————, *Apostle Paul: His Life and Theology* (Grand Rapids: Baker Academic, 2005).

Schoedel, W. R., 'Ignatius and the Archives', *HTR* 71 (1978), 97–106.

————, *Ignatius of Antioch: A Commentary on the Letters of Ignatius of Antioch* (Hermeneia; Philadelphia: Fortress Press, 1985).

————, 'Ignatius and the Reception of Matthew in Antioch', in D. L. Balch (ed.), *Social History of the Matthean Community: Cross-Disciplinary Approaches* (Minneapolis: Fortress Press, 1991), pp. 129–77.

Schöllgen, G., 'Die Ignatianen als pseudepigraphisches Briefcorpus: Anmerkung zu den Thesen von Reinhard M. Hübner', *ZAC* 2 (1998), 16–25.

Schröter, J., 'Jesus Tradition in Matthew, James and the *Didache*: Searching for Characteristic Emphases', forthcoming in H. van de Sandt and J. Zangenberg (eds), *Matthew, James and the Didache: Three Related Documents in their Jewish and Christian Contexts* (SBLSS; Atlanta: Scholars Press).

Schürmann, H., '"Wer daher eines dieser geringsten Gebote auflöst...". Wo fand Matthäus das Logion Mt 5,19?', *BZ* 4 (1960), pp. 238–50.

Scobie, C. H. H., 'Jesus or Paul? The Origin of the Universal Mission of the Christian Church', in P. Richardson and J. C. Hurd (eds), *From Jesus to Paul: Studies in Honour of Francis Wright Beare* (Ontario: Wilfrid Laurier University Press, 1984), pp. 47–60.

Segal, A. F., 'Matthew's Jewish Voice', in D. L. Balch (ed.), *Social History of the Matthean Community: Cross-Disciplinary Approaches* (Minneapolis: Fortress Press, 1991), pp. 3–37.

Senior, D., *What Are They Saying About Matthew?* (New York: Paulist Press, rev. edn, 1996).

——, 'Between Two Worlds: Gentiles and Jewish Christians in Matthew's Gospel', *CBQ* 61 (1999), 1–23.

Shepherd, M. H., 'The Epistle of James and the Gospel of Matthew', *JBL* 75 (1956), 40–51.

Sim, D. C., 'The "Confession" of the Soldiers in Matthew 27:54', *HeyJ* 34 (1993), 401–24.

——, 'The Gospel of Matthew and the Gentiles', *JSNT* 57 (1995), 19–48.

——, *Apocalyptic Eschatology in the Gospel of Matthew* (SNTSMS, 88; Cambridge: Cambridge University Press, 1996).

——, *The Gospel of Matthew and Christian Judaism: The History and Social Setting of the Matthean Community* (SNTW; Edinburgh: T&T Clark, 1998).

——, 'Are the Least Included in the Kingdom of Heaven? The Meaning of Matthew 5:19', *HTS* 54 (1998), 573–87.

——, 'The Magi: Gentiles or Jews?', *HTS* 55 (1999), 980–1000.

——, 'The Social Setting of the Matthean Community: New Paths for an Old Journey', *HTS* 57 (2001), 268–80.

——, 'Matthew's Anti-Paulinism: A Neglected Feature of Matthean Studies', *HTS* 58 (2002), 767–83.

——, 'Christian Judaism: A Reconstruction and Evaluation of the Original Christian Tradition', in E. Kessler and M. J. Wright (eds), *Themes in Jewish-Christian Relations* (Cambridge: Orchard Academic, 2005), pp. 39–58.

——, 'How Many Jews Became Christians in the First Century? The Failure of the Christian Mission to the Jews', *HTS* 61 (2005), 417–40.

——, 'The Gospel of Matthew, John the Elder and the Papias Tradition: A Response to R. H. Gundry', *HTS* 63 (2007), 283–99.

——, 'Matthew 7.21-23: Further Evidence of Its Anti-Pauline Perspective', *NTS* 53 (2007), 325–43.

——, 'Matthew and the Pauline Corpus: A Preliminary Intertextual Study', forthcoming *JSNT*.

——, 'Reconstructing the Social and Religious Milieu of Matthew: Methods, Sources and Possible Results', forthcoming in H. van de Sandt and J. Zangenberg (eds), *Matthew, James and the Didache: Three Related Documents in their Jewish and Christian Contexts* (SBLSS; Atlanta: Scholars Press).

Slee, M., *The Church in Antioch in the First Century C.E.: Communion and Conflict* (JSNTSup, 244; London: T&T Clark International, 2003).

Snodgrass, K., 'Matthew and the Law', in D. J. Lull (ed.), *Society of Biblical Literature 1988 Seminar Papers* (Atlanta: Scholars Press, 1988), pp. 536–54.

———, 'Matthew and the Law', in D. R. Bauer and M. A. Powell (eds), *Treasures New and Old: Recent Contributions to Matthean Studies* (SBLSS, 1; Atlanta: Scholars Press, 1996), pp. 99–127.

Stanton, G. N., 'The Origin and Purpose of Matthew's Gospel: Matthean Scholarship from 1945 to 1980', in H. Temporini and W. Haase (eds), *ANRW*, II, 25, 3 (Berlin: de Gruyter, 1985), pp. 1889–951.

———, *A Gospel for a New People: Studies in Matthew* (Edinburgh: T&T Clark, 1992).

———, 'Matthew's Christology and the Parting of the Ways', in J. D. G. Dunn (ed.), *The Parting of the Ways A.D. 70 to 135* (WUNT, 66; Tübingen: Mohr Siebeck, 1992), pp. 99–116.

Stenschke, C., *Luke's Portrait of Gentiles Prior to Their Coming to Faith* (WUNT, 2.108; Tübingen: Mohr Siebeck, 1999).

Strack, H. L. and P. Billerbeck, *Kommentar zum Neuen Testament aus Talmud und Midrasch. Vol. 1* (Munich: Beck, 1922).

Strecker, G., *Der Weg der Gerechtigkeit* (FRLANT, 82; Göttingen: Vandenhoeck & Ruprecht, 3rd edn, 1971).

———, *Die Bergpredigt. Ein exegetischer Kommentar* (Göttingen: Vandenhoeck & Ruprecht, 1984).

Streeter, B. H., *The Four Gospels: A Study of Origins* (London: Macmillan, 1924).

Svartvik, J., *Mark and Mission: Mk 7:1-23 in its Narrative and Historical Contexts* (CBNTS, 32; Stockholm: Almqvist & Wiksell, 2000).

———, 'Forging an Incarnational Theology Two Score Years after *Nostra Aetate*', *SCJR* 1 (2005), 1–13.

———, 'How Noah, Jesus and Paul Became Captivating Figures: The Side Effects of the Canonization of Slavery Metaphors in Jewish and Christian Texts', *JGRCJ* 2 (2005), 168–227.

———, 'The Quest of the Unique Jesus and Its Implications for Global Interreligious Dialogue', in W. Jeanrond and A. Lande (eds), *The Concept of God in Global Dialogue* (Maryknoll: Orbis, 2005), pp. 126–44.

———, 'The Markan Interpretation of the Pentateuchal Food Laws', in T. R. Hatina (ed.), *Biblical Interpretation in Early Christian Gospels, Vol. 1: The Gospel of Mark* (JSNTSup, 304; London: T&T Clark International, 2006), pp. 169–81.

Swift, J., 'On Poetry', in P. Rogers (ed.), *The Complete Poems* (New Haven: Yale University Press, 1983), pp. 522–36.

Syreeni, K., *The Making of the Sermon on the Mount: A Procedural Analysis of Matthew's Redactoral Activity 1: Methodology and Compositional Analysis* (AASF, 44; Helsinki: Suomalainen Tiedeakatemia, 1987).

Tannehill, R. C., *The Narrative Unity of Luke-Acts: A Literary Interpretation* (2 vols; Minneapolis: Fortress Press, 1994).

Telford, W. R., *The Theology of the Gospel of Mark* (NTT; Cambridge: Cambridge University Press, 1999).

Thompson, W. G., *Matthew's Advice to a Divided Community: Mt 17,22–18,35* (AnBib, 44; Rome: Biblical Institute Press, 1970).

Tomson, P. J., *"If this be from heaven..." Jesus and the New Testament Authors in their Relationship to Judaism* (TBS, 76; Sheffield: Sheffield Academic Press, 2001).

———, 'The halakhic evidence of *Didache* 8 and Matthew 6 and the *Didache* community's relationship to Judaism', in H. van de Sandt (ed.), *Matthew and the Didache. Two Documents From the Same Jewish-Christian Milieu?* (Assen: Royal van Gorcum, 2005), pp. 131–141.

Trevett, C., *A Study of Ignatius of Antioch in Syria and Asia* (SBEC, 29; Lewiston: Edwin Mellen Press, 1992).

Trocmé, E., *The Formation of the Gospel according to Mark* (London: SPCK, 1975).

Tuilier, A., 'La Didachè et le problème synoptique', in C. N. Jefford (ed.), *The Didache in Context. Essays on Its Text, History and Transmission* (NovTSup, 77; Leiden: Brill, 1995), pp. 110–30.

———, 'Les charismatiques itinérants dans la Didachè et dans l'Évangile de Matthieu', in H. van de Sandt (ed.), *Matthew and the Didache. Two Documents From the Same Jewish-Christian Milieu?* (Assen: Royal van Gorcum, 2005), pp. 157–72.

Ucko, H., *Common Roots, New Horizons: Learning about Christian Faith from Dialogue with Jews* (Geneva: WCC, 1994).

Urbach, E. E., *The Sages – Their Concepts and Beliefs* (PPFBR; Jerusalem: Magnes Press, 1975).

Vahrenhorst, M., 'The Presence and Absence of a Prohibition of Oaths in James, Matthew and the *Didache* and its Significance for Contextualization', forthcoming in H. van de Sandt and J. Zangenberg (eds), *Matthew, James and the Didache: Three Related Documents in their Jewish and Christian Contexts* (SBLSS; Atlanta: Scholars Press).

Verheyden, J., 'Eschatology in the *Didache* and the Gospel of Matthew', in H. van de Sandt (ed.), *Matthew and the Didache. Two Documents From the Same Jewish-Christian Milieu?* (Assen: Royal van Gorcum, 2005), pp. 193–216.

Verseput, D. J., 'Genre and Story: The Community Setting of the Epistle of James', *CBQ* 62 (2000), 96–110.

Vielhauer, P., *Geschichte der urchristlichen Literatur. Einleitung in das Neue Testament, die Apokryphen und die Apostolischen Vätern* (Berlin: de Gruyter, 1985).

Vogt, H. J., 'Bemerkungen zur Echtheit der Ignatiusbriefe', *ZAC* 3 (1999), 50–63.

Vokes, F. E., *The Riddle of the Didache. Fact or Fiction, Heresy or Catholicism?* (TCHS, 32; London: SPCK, 1938).

———, 'The Ten Commandments in the New Testament and in First Century Judaism', *SE* 5 (1968), 146–54.

Weeden, T. J., *Mark – Traditions in Conflict* (Philadelphia: Fortress Press, 1971).

Wefald, E. K., 'The Separate Gentile Mission in Mark: A Narrative Explanation of Markan Geography, The Two Feeding Accounts and Exorcisms', *JSNT* 60 (1995), 3–26.

Weiss, H.-F., *Der Brief an die Hebräer* (KEK, 13; Göttingen: Vandenhoeck & Ruprecht, 1991).

Weren, W. J. C., 'Following Jesus: The "Ideal Community" According to Matthew, James and the *Didache*', forthcoming in H. van de Sandt and J. Zangenberg (eds), *Matthew, James and the Didache: Three Related Documents in their Jewish and Christian Contexts* (SBLSS; Atlanta: Scholars Press).

Westerholm, S., *Israel's Law and the Church's Faith: Paul and His Recent Interpreters* (Grand Rapids: Eerdmans, 1988).

Wettstein, J., *Novum Testamentum Graecum. Vol. 1* (Amsterdam: Officina Dommeriana, 1751).

Williams, R., *Why Study the Past? The Quest for the Historical Church* (London: Darton, Longman & Todd, 2005).

Wilson, S. G., *Luke and the Law* (SNTSMS, 50; Cambridge: Cambridge University Press, 1983).

———, *Related Strangers: Jews and Christians 70-170 C.E.* (Minneapolis: Fortress Press, 1995).

Wilson, W. T., *The Mysteries of Righteousness. The Literary Composition and Genre of the Sentences of Pseudo-Phocylides* (TSAJ, 40; Tübingen: Mohr Siebeck, 1994).

Zangenberg, J., 'A Conflict Among Brothers. Who were the *hypokritai* in Matthew?', forthcoming in M. D. Denton, B. McGing and Z. Rodgers (eds), *Festschrift S. Freyne* (Leiden: Brill).

Zeitlin, I. M., *Jesus and the Judaism of His Time* (Cambridge: Polity Press, 1988).

Zetterholm, M., 'The *Didache*, Matthew, and Paul: Reconstructing Historical Developments in Antioch', forthcoming in H. van de Sandt and J. Zangenberg (eds), *Matthew, James and the Didache: Three Related Documents in their Jewish and Christian Contexts* (SBLSS; Atlanta, Scholars Press).

Index of References

Index of Authors

Abrahams, I. 136
Ackerman, J. S. 44
Allison, D. C. 4, 156, 163, 169, 174
Alon, G. 128
Amir, Y. 128
Anderson, H. 136
Audet, J. P. 124, 129
Avemarie, F. 119

Bacher, W. 126
Barrett, C. K. 68, 152
Bartel, R. 44
Bauckham, R. 35, 36, 106, 114
Becker, A. H. and Reed, A. Y. 50
Berger, K. 106, 108, 109, 114, 115, 118, 119, 128
Betz, H. D. 74, 75, 126
Bieringer, R. 66
Bird, M. F. 161, 162
Böhm, M. 60, 62
Borgen, P. 126
Bornkamm, G. 70
Bovon, F. 61
Brodie, T. L. 5
Brown, R. E. 29
Brown, S. 51, 52
Bultmann, R. 31, 131, 132
Byrne, B. 51, 53, 54, 56
Byrskog, S. 24

Cadbury, H. J. 29
Callahan, A. D. 28
Carter, W. 3, 112, 141
Chilton, B. and Evans, C. A. 107
Clark, K. W. 1, 52, 66
Collins, J. J. 39
Collins, R. F. 20
Connolly, R. H. 124

Conzelmann, H. 59
Corwin, V. 152
Cousland, J. R. C. 159
Cullmann, O. 28

Davies, W. D. 68, 69, 70
Davies, W. D. and Allison, D. C. 1, 4, 37, 40, 50, 68, 69, 70, 78, 96, 99, 130, 131, 132, 135, 140, 141, 158
Deines, R. 145
Dibelius, M. 113
Dodd, C. H. 5, 81
Donahue, J. R. and Harrington, D. J. 31, 148
Donahue, P. J. 150, 152
Draper, J. A. 124, 133
Drews, P. 124
Dunn, J. D. G. 11, 38, 162, 168, 171

Edwards, M. J. 142
Enslin, M. S. 61
Ewherido, A. O. 2, 141, 147

Fitzmyer, J. A. 29, 58, 61
Flusser, D. 128, 131
Forster, E. M. 42
Foster, P. 2, 52, 111, 145, 147, 149
Frankemölle, H. 105, 106
Franklin, E. 65

Gale, A. M. 140, 141
Garland, D. E. 32
Garrow, A. J. P. 7, 124
Goulder, M. D. 5
Grant, R. M. 149
Grässer, E. 87, 99

Guelich, R. A. 126, 130, 135
Gundry, R. H. 76, 108, 131, 139, 141, 158

Haenchen, E. 165
Hagner, D. A. 2, 51, 55, 70, 111, 147, 158
Hare, D. R. A. 2, 147
Hare, D. R. A. and Harrington, D. J. 18, 51
Harrington, D. J. 12, 13, 25, 51, 159
Hartin, P. J. 6, 116
Heinemann, I. 136
Hengel, M. 106, 109, 113, 117, 119, 168
Hübner, R. M. 142
Hurtado, L. W. 13

Iverson, K. R. 156, 157

Jefford, C. N. 142, 148
Jeremias, J. 162
Jervell, J. 57, 60, 62, 63
Johnson, L. T. 105, 106, 107, 118
Johnson, M. D. 54

Keener, C. S. 156
Klijn, A. F. J. 176
Klijn, A. F. J. and Reinink, G. J. 176
Kloppenborg, J. 116, 123, 133
Konradt, M. 106, 117, 118, 119
Kugelman, R. 35, 36

Lambrecht, J. 131
Lechner, T. 142